# Pauline's

*by* Pauline Tabor

*illustrated by* David Stone Martin

TOUCHSTONE PUBLISHING COMPANY
*Louisville, Kentucky*

First Printing—December 1971
Second Printing—December 1971
Third Printing—January 1972
Fourth Printing—February 1972
Fifth Printing—February 1972


International Standard Book Number 0-87963-008-6

Copyright © 1971 by Pauline Tabor
Library of Congress Catalog Number 70-172511

Manufactured in the United States of America

*for*
**Kathryn**
*whose enthusiasm never failed*

*and for*
**Barbara**
*whose faith in me I treasure*

## Foreword

What happens when a young and respectable woman—a Sunday-school teacher struggling to support two small sons—suddenly thumbs her nose at convention and embarks on a career as the madam of a whorehouse in her own home town?

For Pauline Tabor, the world didn't come to an end, as some of her horrified relatives and friends gloomily predicted. But the small-town tranquillity of Bowling Green, Kentucky, was severely shattered back in the depression days of 1933 when Pauline—after a hectic, hilarious two-day training course in "madamship" at a notorious Tennessee bordello—opened her own sporting house with a rollicking house-warming party.

Never in the long, lurid history of the world's oldest profession was there a less qualified candidate for the rough, tough, bawdy life of a brothel-keeper. However, Pauline was a determined woman who managed to survive and prosper despite her blunders and the hostility of the town's proper folks from whom she was quickly exiled.

For the next four decades, Pauline and her girls continued to shock the righteous citizens of Bowling Green. As the years passed—and after two brief excursions into the shadowed world of vice in Indiana and Louisville—Pauline finally managed to build her dream house, an elegant emporium of sin whose fame soon spread far beyond the borders of Kentucky. In the process, she became one of the nation's most colorful and most successful madams, a legend in her own lifetime.

After her famous house on Clay Street was closed and razed two years ago to make way for an urban renewal project, Pauline retired with her memories and the secrets she had shared over the years with a multitude of pleasure-seeking males from all walks of life.

It is said that "the walls of a whorehouse never talk." This, however, does not necessarily apply to the madam of the house. In her retirement, Pauline has written her memoirs, vividly recounting the struggles, the successes and failures, the heartaches and laughter, the human frailties and follies she encountered during nearly forty years of merchandising sex.

Pauline Tabor makes no attempt to apologize for her career on the back streets of society, nor does she sugar-coat it with false glamour. She tells it like it was, providing a frankly revealing, lusty insight into the secrets of her house and her profession, and a compassionate yet frequently humorous study of the lives and hangups of her girls and the "tricks" of their trade—the customers of the house.

*October 1971*                                                    John McDowell

## *Author's note*

Writing a book of this kind presents its own peculiar problems. The writing must be factual, but the people written about must be protected by anonymity. Generally speaking, slight alterations of time and place along with the use of pseudonyms far removed from actual names will satisfy this requirement. There are times, though, when even the occupation of a given character must be disguised and the character must go unnamed.

Now, since all of the episodes recounted in this book are true—they *did* happen—the names and occupations of characters are altered or eliminated and times and places are disguised, not so much to protect the innocent as to protect the guilty.

## Acknowledgments

I owe thanks to so many people who have helped and encouraged me in the writing of *Pauline's* that I am not sure just where to begin.

I'll start with David Stone Martin, whose delightful drawings enliven these pages; and Peggy Fox Fraser, who designed the dust jacket.

Then there are Jim Wilkins, Ronnie Summers, and Richard Fiss. These are the enterprising young men who bought the building at 627 Clay Street, tore it down, and sold it a brick at a time as souvenirs of my best-known cathouse. They even made bookends and candlesticks and other things from the timbers!. They have earned my thanks even though I'm jealous because it was they, instead of me, who thought up that moneymaking scheme.

Donnie Firkins, who did the acryllic painting of the house that is reproduced as the frontispiece in this book, has earned my thanks.

Kathryn Rogers and John McDowell deserve special thanks, for without them this book would not have been written.

Now, if Harold Hall hadn't introduced me to Donald E. Ragsdale, president of Touchstone Publishing Company, I might still have a manuscript instead of a book. Special thanks to them, too.

Other people from Touchstone have also earned my gratitude: Mary Kay Judd, secretary to the president, for being a tower of strength when I was ready to give it all up; Robert Brown, production manager, and Jeanne Weaver, his secretary, for keeping things going smoothly; P. Dale Breeden, mechanical superintendent, and all his crew for turning manuscript into type; Andrée Coers, executive editor, for soothing my ruffled feathers; Earle Miller, art director, and his people for their hours of painstaking work; Connie Wilson, quality control, for an excellent job of coordinating the hundred and one things that go into overseeing the printing and binding of a book.

For Virginia Cook, my friend and helper, my deep appreciation and thanks. Without her, I could not have gone through all of the conferences that were held in my home. It was she who saw to it that they came off in fine style.

I have the uncomfortable feeling that I have failed to name others to whom thanks should be paid. There are many, many people who helped make this book possible. To all of them, my heartfelt gratitude.

*Pauline Tabor*

# Contents

*from acryllic painting by* Donnie Firkins

The house on Clay Street

*What's a nice girl like you
doing in a place like this?*

## *What's a nice girl like you doing in a place like this?*

It's been nearly forty years, but I remember Armistice Day of 1933—or, to be more accurate, the night of that patriotic holiday— like it was only yesterday. After all, how often is a whorehouse opened with an old-fashioned, neighborly housewarming?

The house on Smallhouse Road—a two-story, five-bedroom relic which I had rented from an unsuspecting preacher who had been called to tend a new flock in another town—was really jumping. But despite the festivities there wasn't a customer in the place that night. The merrymakers were my friends, men and women, who had come calling with soda pop, liquor, beer, sandwiches, and all the other ingredients for a "bon voyage" party for one of the good girls of Bowling Green who was embarking on a life of sin.

Now, by some folks' moral codes, I suppose I wasn't exactly a "good girl." I was a divorced woman, twenty-eight years old, faced with the problem of trying to support two small sons and a newly widowed, ailing mother in the midst of the worst depression in the nation's history. I had been a mistress—a "kept woman"—for a year. I had even served a brief, disillusioning apprenticeship as a call girl. However, on that long-ago November evening with the first frosting of late autumn snow blowing in across the hills of Western Kentucky, I didn't feel like a scarlet woman. I may have been laughing on the outside, but inside I was as scared as a sniveling six-year-old being dragged off to her first day at school.

As I remember it, the big jukebox in the middle parlor was blaring —a record with some vocalist crooning about a shanty in ol' shanty town—and several couples were dancing. Ice was clinking in glasses, people were laughing and chattering, and one of the town's merchants, a man I'd known for years, was sitting beside me on a sofa, holding my hand and trying to talk me out of my determination to become the madam of a sporting house.

"Pauline Tabor," he said, "what's a nice girl like you doing in a place like this?"

During the years that followed, I've been asked that question, with minor variations, more times than I care to remember. And I've developed a routine answer which may shock some persons even though there's a lot of truth in it: "After you've screwed one man, it gets easier and easier to screw more."

But back on the evening of that party in 1933, I didn't have any fast, flip reply to my friend's question. In fact, my "good girl" conscience had been nagging me with the same sort of questions. Suddenly, despite all my brave intentions to defy traditions and convention, I was overwhelmed with the realization that not only was I sitting in a whorehouse but it was my own whorehouse, right smack in my home town. "Pauline," my conscience scolded, "how can a small-town Sunday school teacher like you expect to become a successful madam? What's going to happen now, after the party's over, after your friends are gone, and customers start ringing the bell?"

The answer to that question, of course, is history now. The logic of my conscience that night failed to sway me from my newly adopted profession. The house on Smallhouse Road opened for business the next day. And for nearly four decades I continued to operate as a madam, a successful businesswoman dealing in one of mankind's most basic commodities: sex.

Now that I'm retired, I have no regrets. I'm much too busy enjoying life—my children and grandchildren, my friends, a lovely country home, a healthy bank account, and priceless memories of a happy marriage. Yet from the vantage point of hindsight, I guess there is one thing I'd do differently if I were able to reshape the course of my life. If there were a second time around, I'd start business in a distant city where my private life could remain a secret and my family could be spared a lot of unnecessary grief and notoriety.

Back in 1933, however, the wisdom of such action was not so evident. Bowling Green was the town of my birth, the only place I'd ever lived, except for a few months as a working girl in Louisville after the breakup of my first marriage in 1930. So, when I decided to start merchandising sex instead of giving it away, it seemed logical to open a house in my home town where I would be operating in familiar surroundings and dealing with people I knew.

To understand the full impact of that decision, it's necessary to know something about my background at the time I opened my first house. If I had been just another street girl from the wrong side of the tracks who decided to go into business for herself, the citizens of Bowling Green wouldn't have cared one way or the other. But I was the daughter of a respected middle-class family with deep roots in Western Kentucky. For seven years, I had been the wife of the son of a town merchant. I had belonged to the right clubs, attended church and taught in Sunday school, indulged in all the proper pastimes favored by the circle of respectable young couples in which we moved. In brief, I was as unlikely a candidate as could be imagined for a career as a madam.

Much has been written about the Roaring Twenties—a decade of bootleg booze, easy morals and cigarette-puffing flappers with bobbed hair, painted lips, rouged cheeks, and scandalously short skirts that exposed heaven knows what. Well, life in the big cities during those years may have been wild, loose, and lawless. But out along the backroads of America a lot of folks still were hard-working, God-fearing people who never saw the inside of a speakeasy, people whose lives were never touched by such exotic trappings of a wayward decade as gangsters, stock market gambling, "free love," and the frantic gyrations of the Charleston.

The Bowling Green in which I grew up, married, and became a mother was one of those towns in which old standards of morality, old concepts of right and wrong still endured during the Twenties and Thirties. This is not to say that the Bowling Green of that era was free of mortal sins. Many of its citizens—good and bad alike—practiced in one form or another all of mankind's vices, lusts, and perversions. But for the most part they kept their hangups carefully hidden behind a wall of self-righteousness. Sex was an indelicate subject, seldom discussed in mixed company. Thus, when Pauline Tabor, a member of the town's respectable establishment, suddenly became a lady of easy virtue, openly flaunting commercialized sex, the pillars of the community not only were scandalized; they were as full of phony indignation as the husband who returned home from an evening at the local whorehouse to discover his wife bedded down with his best friend.

At the time, I was deeply grieved by the town's reaction. The housewarming party given by my friends had bolstered me with a false sense of security. But I later realized they were more worldly, sophisticated people who, though not completely agreeing with my choice of profession, admired my spunk in thumbing my nose at the accepted ethics of my elders who so often failed to practice the morality they preached.

Most of the townspeople, and even some members of my family, were not so understanding. They did not look upon me as a financially desperate woman, with heavy responsibilities as a breadwinner, who had set out alone in a tough world to make a living by doing what comes naturally to any female past the age of puberty. Instead, I quickly discovered that I had become a social outcast among people I had known all my life. And although I shouldn't have been surprised, I was still naive enough to be hurt by their attitude.

Fortunately the human spirit is not easily destroyed. It instinctively builds defenses against attack. In my case, I soon developed a protective armor of cynicism about my fellow man. The once-naive Pauline Tabor, like an old soldier, just faded away. She was replaced by a hard-nosed, cash-on-the-line madam who operated on the philosophy that all God's children have feet of clay. That philosophy, I might add, was firmly founded on the knowledge that many of the gentlemen who snubbed me in public were patrons of my house; that many of the public officials who cried out the loudest against vice were the first in line to accept supposedly "soiled money" in return for closing their eyes to the vice against which they crusaded; that many of the respectable ladies who scorned me and my profession were failures as wives, frigid females whose sex-starved husbands turned up at my door to buy an illusion of the love and human warmth they couldn't find in their own homes. So in time I learned to ignore the barbs of a disapproving society, and I was able to laugh all the way to the bank.

I know that persons unfamiliar with the shadow world of vice will wonder how a woman with a strict middle-class upbringing—a woman with absolutely no previous contact with a house of ill repute—managed to stray into the unconventional life of a madam. Well, I can tell you one thing: there's no training school for madams except the school of hard knocks. After looking back across the years of my life, I guess the answer (and you must pardon the expression) is that madams are made, not born.

Certainly there was nothing in my childhood and teens—no miseries of poverty, no rebellion against parents, no overwhelming adolescent sex urges—that could possibly have shaped my future as an entrepreneur on the back streets of society. I was born in Bowling Green on April 11, 1905, less than two years after Wilbur and Orville Wright launched the Air Age by making man's first flight in a motor-driven plane. But there was no high-flying life for me or my brothers and sisters, for our parents were of the straitlaced, no-nonsense school when it came to the upbringing of their children.

My father started out as a paperhanger, but by the time I arrived on the scene he had become one of Western Kentucky's top tobacco auctioneers. Later he went into business as a farm and household auctioneer. During this period, we lived on several farms which my father bought, improved, and sold. I guess it was during these years of farm life that I developed my lifelong love for the land, for working with plants and animals—a factor which in later years led to my leading a double life as a madam and as a farmer.

Both my father and mother—a beautiful, devout woman—were warm, friendly people who loved to entertain. It seemed as if we always had company for dinner, and our home echoed with laughter and conversation. But as I grew up, attending parochial school and high school, I learned that the pleasures of family life also were tempered with certain rigid parental rules. Children were seen, not heard, and we did as we were told with no back-talk or questioning of authority.

It wasn't just in my family that this stern code of child behavior was applied. Practically all the boys and girls I grew up with lived under similar parental controls, but I can't recall that we did much complaining about such restrictions. It was the only way of life we knew, and we generally accepted it as part of growing up. A few youngsters, of course, rebelled. But they were known as "fast" boys and girls, and we were forbidden to have anything to do with them.

In those days, parental supervision of girls was especially strict. I remember that I was sixteen when I was permitted to attend my first dance, and then my father insisted that his youngest brother be my date. I felt real sophisticated, being squired by a grownup man, even though he was my uncle. We had—or at least I had—a wonderful time, round-dancing until ten o'clock that night. Boy, oh boy, I thought, the world has just begun to come alive for me!

After the ball was over, though, I returned to my pig-tailed, cloistered adolescence. It wasn't until about a year later that I was allowed to start dating boys. And then there were new rules. My date, after being approved by my parents, had to come to the house where he'd sit squirming in the parlor under a barrage of questions about where we were going and what we planned to do. Finally, after getting firm instructions about what time to come home, we'd leave on our date, accompanied by a chaperon. Even then, if the boy of my choice should fall from grace in the eyes of my parents, our dating was promptly halted. I remember that one of the youths I dated decided he was madly in love with me and started talking about marriage. However, my father discovered one day that my suitor, who had dared nothing more than a few fumbling embraces and feverish kisses, was over twenty-one. My father was shocked at the idea of his young daughter "dating a man old enough to vote," and he ordered an immediate and absolute end to our budding romance—an edict which I meekly and tearfully obeyed.

Not only was the virtue of the good girls of Bowling Green guarded as closely as the gold at Fort Knox but, likewise, our supposedly delicate sensibilities were carefully shielded from all of the basic details concerning human procreation. Our knowledge of even the elementary mechanics of carnal pleasures generally was limited to dire but vague warnings voiced with considerable embarrassment by our parents ("Don't let boys fondle you here," my mother advised me one time, nervously pointing out with her hands the vital parts of the female anatomy to which she was referring. "Keep yourself pure for your husband!") and to whatever lurid rumors or misinformation about sex we girls managed to acquire and pass along with self-conscious giggles whenever the parental vigil was relaxed.

As a result, not only was I a 100-proof physical virgin when I was married at the age of eighteen; I was an unblemished virgin mentally, with only the haziest ideas of what sex was all about. And my husband, also eighteen and ready, willing, and able, actually wasn't much wiser or more experienced in ways of the flesh.

In the early Twenties, young marriages were looked upon as a healthy, safe way to avoid the sinful pitfalls that tempted those giddy youths who sought to avoid the responsibilities of wedlock. Certainly neither my parents nor his opposed the marriage. We had grown up together, gone to school together, came from good, socially responsible, hard-working families. There was no reason, our elders decided, why we shouldn't be married and get down to the serious business of making a living and raising a family.

We were married in Mitchellville, Tennessee, on June 3, 1923, and —after dinner at a restaurant—returned to the home of my husband's parents for our wedding night. During the drive back to Bowling Green, I wasn't fretting about not having a honeymoon. Such things were considered an extravagant luxury, especially since my brand-new husband was expected back on the job at his father's store the next morning. But I was nervous, wondering just what I was going to discover about sex in the hours ahead.

Well, let me tell you, I was shocked when the connubial ritual began once we closed the door of our bedroom in his folks' home. I had modestly undressed and put on a new, frilly nightgown in an upstairs bathroom. When I hurriedly slipped under the covers on the big, four-poster bed, my young husband began to undress—a masculine process which I never before had witnessed. Within seconds, he was stripped for action, standing beside the bed. I stared at him with dismay. I had seen sketches of the male sex organ in the medical guide my mother kept hidden in her closet. And those sketches showed this vital part of a man's anatomy as a limp, drooping thing. But my husband's sex apparatus didn't remotely resemble those sketches. It jutted forth menacingly, stiff and huge.

"My God," I said to myself as I cowered under the blankets, unable to take my eyes off the suddenly exposed monstrosity. "What in the world is the matter with him? I bet I've married a deformed man!"

Despite his eagerness to get on with his deflowering chores, my husband evidently saw the stricken, frightened look in my eyes.

"What's the matter with you, honey?" he asked.

"Nothing's the matter with me," I replied shakily, clutching the blankets under my chin. "But what's wrong with you?" And I pointed to his erect, swollen organ.

He looked down, puzzled at first. Then, realizing that I indeed was an innocent maiden, he laughed and laughed. "Pauline, there's nothing wrong—that's just a hard-on," he finally managed to explain with understandable pride. "And it's a jim-dandy!"

My young groom that night was not a polished lover, but he had admirable stamina that permitted several demonstrations of the natural talents of his "jim-dandy." When I awoke in the morning, sore but proud of the fact that at last I was a woman, I could hardly believe that I had lived for eighteen years and hadn't even suspected what sex really was. After the first discomforts and the embarrassed realization that everyone now knew I no longer was a virgin, I decided that my husband's "deformed" equipment was a mighty comforting thing to have around the house.

Several years and two babies later, I still was an enthusiastic participant in the delights of sex. Unhappily, though, such pleasures began to be clouded by an awareness that there was a lot more than sex involved in marriage. If we had been lucky in our youthful marriage, my husband and I would have discovered as we grew into full adulthood that we shared a variety of common interests and ambitions in addition to sex. If such had been the case, I'm sure I would have lived my life as a typical respectable small-city matron, deeply involved in the everyday affairs of my home, my family, my church, and my community. But we weren't lucky. As the years passed, it became increasingly evident that we had nothing in common outside the bedroom, and even in that department my husband's interest began to stray to other, newer pastures.

However, I'd be a hypocrite if I claimed that the ultimate breakup of our marriage was entirely the fault of my husband. If there was any blame beyond the fact we had married too young, we both shared it, for I now realize that neither of us had any awareness of, or compassion for, the needs of each other as human beings.

As is so often the case with girls, I matured much more rapidly than my husband. I was interested in homemaking, in our two sons, in club, church, and social activities, in planning and working for the future. My husband, on the other hand, became an over-age adolescent, reluctant to give up the boisterous, carefree pursuits of his youth. His idea of really living was an endless roller derby of fun and excitement. The responsibilities of home life, parenthood, and business seemed to frighten or repulse him. He liked to wander and frolic, and if I didn't want to tag along he could always find other footloose and fancy-free companions.

I suppose if I had been a wiser young woman—if I had then been blessed with the knowledge of human nature I later acquired as the custodian of a bawdy house—I might have saved our marriage by helping my husband grow up without his realizing it. Instead, I made the common female mistake of nagging, arguing, and complaining, and I only succeeded in driving him farther and farther away from the nest.

Ironically, the final disintegration of our marriage began in the autumn of 1929, right at the time when the big crash on Wall Street was putting an abrupt end to the free-wheeling prosperity of the Twenties and plunging the nation into a long and dreadful depression. A year later, by the time my divorce was granted in 1930, hard times were really setting in.

After separating from my husband and disposing of our home, I moved in—bags, baggage, and two small, lively sons—with my parents. It was not an ideal arrangement. With all of their children grown, my mother and father were set in their ways, and I was a strong-willed young woman accustomed to doing things my own way. Putting an added strain on our crowded, two-family household, my father's once-prosperous business, like so many others after the crash of '29, was failing. The court had ordered my former husband to pay $45 a month support for our children, but after receiving one $40 payment I never got another cent from him to help out with the costs of food, housing, doctor bills, clothes, school, and all the other financial responsibilities of raising children. As a result, with my parents' savings steadily dwindling, I had no choice but to get out in the world and help make a living for all of us.

Today, with so many job opportunities available for women, this would not be any great challenge. In that era, however, even during good times women had a limited choice of jobs, especially in the nation's smaller cities. And in 1930 when, as a woman with no training or experience beyond that of a housewife and mother, I went out looking for work the results were soul-shattering. With business worsening day by day, the local merchants and businesses were cutting back on their staffs in a desperate effort to survive. The once-thriving tobacco market, for years the mainstay of Bowling Green's economy, was only a shadow of its former prosperity. Even the more unskilled jobs were hard to find. College-trained men and women were pleading for the most menial kind of work, and nobody—but nobody—had a job for Pauline Tabor.

Finally I spotted an advertisement in the town newspaper's brief help-wanted column, announcing that applicants for the job of door-to-door saleslady, "with unlimited earning possibilities," would be interviewed the following day. I showed up at a downtown office early the next morning only to find at least twenty-five other women ahead of me. Nevertheless, when I finally was interviewed by a hard-bitten, cynical-eyed pitchman, I did some fast talking, voicing a confidence in my untested sales ability that I really didn't feel inside. I guess I did a good job of selling myself though, because I was one of five women hired, on a strictly commission basis, to ring doorbells and sell cosmetics and silk hosiery.

Door-to-door selling during the Great Depression was an experience that one never forgets. Money was scarce and sales were few and far between. The so-called opportunity for "unlimited earnings" turned out to be $10 to $15 a week in commissions if you were lucky, worked hard, and talked fast. I soon learned that the job had hazards beyond that of sore feet, a battered morale, and the frustration of sweating out overdue commission checks from the home office. In addition to the routine harassments of unfriendly dogs, doors slammed in my face, and sly housewives trying to quietly filch a few goodies from my sample case, I encountered almost daily propositions from amorous males. Unfortunately for my budget, these propositions rarely involved offers of cash payment. Even the big-time spenders talked only in terms of $1 or $2—a cut-rate price which I had no qualms in rejecting. Times were tough, but not that tough. And most of the domesticated Romeos I encountered in my door-to-door venturing were easier to turn down. They seemed to think that I would welcome a chance to rest for a spell on their mattresses and enjoy the recuperative blessings of their stud services. Retaining one's virtue in the face of such preposterous proposals was no problem. But it did teach me the fact that the average male feels he has a unique sexual prowess which no woman in her right mind can possibly turn down.

My first fall from grace as a door-to-door saleslady started out innocently enough. My commission check—some $40 for three weeks of toil along the streets of Bowling Green—was overdue and cash was getting dangerously low in our household. In desperation, I decided to take time out in my selling to see if one of the local merchants, a long-time friend of my family, could stake me to a temporary loan until my commission check arrived.

It was a hot summer day, and I had been walking the streets and knocking on doors for hours with only a couple of small sales to compensate for my labors. As I approached the store, I noticed a well-dressed, gray-haired man standing near the entrance. Although I pretended not to see him, I was aware of his "once-over" stare as I entered the store. Later, as I sat sipping a soft drink and talking with the store owner, I glanced out the window and noticed that the distinguished stranger was still standing outside staring at me. However, I didn't pay much attention to him. I was too busy discussing the need for a loan with my merchant friend—a request which he regretfully turned down "because money is awfully tight right now." But my friend did tell me he would see if he could raise some cash to help me out and suggested that I stop at the store the next day.

The stranger was still outside as I left, but I quickly forgot him as I renewed my wearisome doorbell-ringing rounds. The following day, though, when I returned to the store, my friend quickly revived my memory of the stranger who had eyed me so curiously.

"Pauline," my friend said, "did you happen to see the tall gentleman who was standing out in front of the store yesterday when you came in?"

I allowed as how I had seen him. "In fact," I said, "he gave me goose pimples, the way he kept staring at me. He was just about the most prosperous-looking person I've seen in a long time."

My friend laughed and explained that the stranger was indeed prosperous—an honorary colonel and well-to-do Northern Kentucky businessman whose dealings frequently brought him to Bowling Green.

"After you left," my friend confided, "the Colonel came in and asked me who you were. I told him you have just been divorced, that you have two small children and are having a tough time making a go of it financially." My friend then hemmed and hawed self-consciously and finally admitted he told the Colonel that I had been in the store to ask for a loan.

"You told him what?" I exclaimed indignantly.

"Well," my friend stammered, "I told you yesterday I'd see what I could do about raising some money. I know the Colonel, and he's a fine gentleman. In fact, he said he'd be happy to help you out, and he asked me to please tell you that he was anxious to meet you."

My friend handed me a slip of paper. "Here's the Colonel's address and telephone number," he said. "If you're interested in meeting him, call him at seven tonight."

I reluctantly put the paper in my purse and thanked my friend. "I'll have to think it over," I said. "I don't make a practice of meeting strange men, even if they're rich, handsome gentlemen. I don't know why any man would want to help me, with no strings attached."

My friend shrugged as I turned to leave. "Do as you think best, Pauline," he said. "But I don't see any harm in at least talking to the Colonel. He's no sex maniac, if that's what you're worried about."

I was still simmering with anger and suspicion when I left the store. But the longer I pushed doorbells and parroted unsuccessful sales pitches that afternoon, my friend's advice seemed to make more and more sense. Surely, I told myself, there could be no harm in at least meeting and talking with the Colonel.

By the time I'd made my last futile call of the day, my sales kit seemed to weigh a ton, my feet and my ego ached, and I guess I was ready to date the devil himself to break the penny-pinching despair of my life and times in the Big Depression. So it was not surprising that, upon returning home, I announced I was going out that evening. For awhile it was just like old times in our household. My father, glumly reading the melancholy news in the daily paper, didn't pay much attention at first, but my mother was instantly on the alert. Faced with her suspicious cross-examination, I felt as guilty as a jittery teen-ager returning home after violating a dating curfew. Finally I indulged in a bit of fibbing, saying I was going to have dinner with the Colonel, a gentleman whom I had met through our friend at the store.

Dropping the paper, my father—obviously acquainted with the Colonel through past business dealings—hurriedly barged into the family dispute. "Pauline," he roared, sounding like the stern parent of my youth, "you've lost your mind! That man is married, with grown children."

"That's right," mother added somewhat maliciously. "He's as old as your father!"

Father glowered indignantly at this uncalled-for reminder of his unwelcomed approach to a sideline role as a senior citizen. More and more, age had become a touchy subject with him. But this time he apparently decided to put his daughter's honor ahead of any rebuttal to mother's tactless insinuation of senility. Instead, he summarily ordered me to "have nothing to do with that old goat."

By this time, my temper was rising. The question of my going out with the Colonel rapidly disintegrated into a parent-daughter donnybrook, climaxed by my heated pronouncement that "I'm a grown woman and I know what I'm doing."

I kept the date that evening, arriving a few minutes before seven without even having eaten because I had foolishly—and without any foundation in fact—told my parents I was having dinner with the Colonel. This white lie, of course, was voiced to convince my folks that it was to be an innocent get-together, but that fact did not appease my burgeoning appetite, sharpened by a hard day's work. So it was a mighty hungry young lady who rang the Colonel's doorbell, a working girl who was practically ready to surrender everything in return for one hearty meal. The Colonel was as handsome as I remembered him. And he assured me he was delighted to see me, claiming he had been as nervous as a schoolboy, fearing that he had insulted me with his overtures through a second party.

"Well," I admitted, "it is just about the strangest date I've ever had. But my friend told me you were a wonderful gentleman, and I was curious. I guess I wanted to see for myself if there really was one real gentleman left in Kentucky."

The Colonel chuckled and assured me that he hoped he was a gentleman. However, after he invited me for a ride in his new car—a sporty maroon Packard coupe—I began to have my doubts again, asking myself if this impulsive escapade was going to end up merely as a high-class version of the same old propositions that plagued me almost every working day.

As it turned out, though, the evening was a pleasant surprise. The Colonel quickly staked a claim on my heart by stopping at the town's finest restaurant for a seemingly extravagant dinner, followed by a leisurely drive through the countryside during which the subject of sex never once was mentioned. Instead, the Colonel emerged in my eyes as a lonely man who desperately needed a friend he could talk with. He was, I learned, a college-educated man in his late fifties—not quite as old as my father—and he did indeed have a wife in another town, and grown children. His marriage, he said, had for years been a loveless, meaningless arrangement which he and his wife were reluctant to end because of the children and the family's social reputation. I guess we chatted for an hour or so, discovering each other, before the Colonel mentioned, after parking outside my parents' home, the question of a loan.

"Pauline," he said, "your friend told me you needed a loan to tide you over some rough times. I wish you'd take this as a friend, and pay me back whenever times get better." Saying this, he handed me four $10 bills, a sum that seemed at the time like a veritable fortune. And silencing my attempt to thank him, he added, "I want you to know there are no strings attached. I value your friendship, and I hope it can continue."

Indeed, our friendship continued and within a few weeks deepened quite naturally into an emotional relationship—my first sexual involvement since the breakup of my marriage. Subconsciously, perhaps, the Colonel was a "father image," but I didn't see him as a man some thirty years my senior. To me he was not only a skilled, considerate lover but also a highly sophisticated man with a wide range of knowledge and interests, a man who stirred my first awareness in the world of books and the meaning of life. He also was a generous benefactor. Although—to keep up appearances and to retain a feeling of independence—I continued to work, my economic pressures were suddenly eased. The Colonel continued to help me out with cash "loans," gifts which, I told myself, he could afford and which I earned through services rendered faithfully and enthusiastically.

However, as this extra income began to be reflected in new clothes for myself and my children and an increasing amount of money for our two-family budget, my parents' suspicions solidified into a stricken realization that I had become a kept woman. Recriminations and quarrels became a daily nightmare, putting serious new stresses and strains on a household already beset by the problems normally involved in two families living under the same roof. At last, to help ease the tensions, the Colonel gave me a hand in renting and furnishing a small apartment for myself and my sons. With this move, I gained a renewed sense of adult independence, clouded only by the knowledge that I now was an authentic, full-fledged mistress.

My liaison with the Colonel continued in this comfortable pattern for a year. Gradually, though, I became bored and restless. Although I admired and liked the Colonel as a friend, I began to look upon him as a generous but over-age man of another generation whose demands upon my time were becoming a bit wearying. After much soul-searching, I decided that a woman in my precarious financial position could not afford to cling to a starry-eyed, romantic outlook on life. It was a tough world outside my apartment, a world in which a person, to get ahead, had to be hard-headed and realistic. Slowly and painfully, I faced the unpleasant fact that, no matter how hard I might try, I had no special skills or training that would enable me to accomplish a great deal in life through my own efforts. It dawned on me that everything I wanted in life would have to depend on my ability to use other people to my own advantage. Once I evolved this practical philosophy, I saw my relationship with the Colonel as a one-way, dead-end street. There were, I told myself with a growing sense of confidence, bound to be many other men who would be just as generous, and perhaps even younger, than my present sugar daddy.

One evening, after building up my courage, I told the Colonel what was on my mind. He was distressed and sought to change my mind. But when he realized that I was determined to make a break, he proved to be a perfect gentleman to the bitter end. He even used his influence to get me a job as a clerk in the office of a tobacco company in Louisville so I could start out in new surroundings with a more secure position than door-to-door selling.

It was a relief to get away from Bowling Green—a relief which I'm sure was shared by my family. Although my involvement with the Colonel was not generally known because we had been discreet, it had shocked members of my family, who had lived in fear that this dreadful skeleton ultimately would be exposed. In making the move, though, there was one problem. Until I could get settled in Louisville and firmly adjusted to my new job, my two sons would have to remain in Bowling Green. My father's health was failing rapidly, so it was out of the question for my parents to take over as full-time baby-sitters. But the problem was solved when my former mother-in-law, a fine, compassionate woman with whom I had remained on friendly terms, volunteered to take care of the children.

My new life in Louisville as an apprentice career woman with my own small apartment was an exhilarating experience. Unhappily, it didn't last long. After working for six months, making new friends, and developing new interests, I was stricken with typhoid fever. For several weeks, I was desperately ill, and as I slowly recovered, with my income shut off and even the future of my job in doubt, my bills piled up to a critical level. Finally I had to call upon my parents for help. After a family conference, it was decided that the only solution would be for me to move back in with them in Bowling Green.

Thus, late in 1932 I found myself back where I started—no money, a mountain of unpaid bills, and once more imposing on my hard-pressed parents. In addition, I no longer was the slender, vivacious Pauline of the past. My illness had affected certain glandular functions. By the time I was fully recovered I had gained more than a hundred pounds, which no amount of dieting could melt off. Suddenly, my five-foot, six-inch frame had expanded into solid but hefty matronly proportions. I wasn't sloppily fat, just an imposing hunk of female flesh which I gradually learned to live with.

When my strength had returned, I went back to my old job selling hosiery and cosmetics from door to door. This time, however, I didn't have the Colonel's generosity to bolster my income. After helping me get settled in Louisville, he had removed himself permanently from my life. And this, as I quickly learned when I returned to ringing doorbells, was a severe financial loss. Times had been tough before I gave up selling and moved to Louisville. But they were a lot tougher now. President Hoover's promises about prosperity being just around the corner had failed to materialize, and though some folks said things would get better when newly elected Franklin Delano Roosevelt moved into the White House, such hopes seemed like whistling in the dark.

Jobs were few and far between in late 1932, more businesses were going broke, relief roles and breadlines were growing. Few people had money to spend on such luxuries as silk stockings and cosmetics. The important question in those days of gloom and doom was not whether the lady of the house was stylish and beautiful; it was a far more basic question of whether or not she and her family had enough to eat.

Nevertheless, as 1932 limped forlornly off into the darker pages of history and was succeeded by 1933 with its equally depressing prospects, I managed somehow to eke out a living of sorts. But it wasn't easy, working endless hours for meager commissions. Complicating matters, my father's health worsened, and by summer he was dead. Under this barrage of struggle, worries, and sorrow, my next steps from the so-called path of righteousness seemed to me of little significance. Sinning, as preached from the pulpit of the church I faithfully attended every Sunday, had little meaning in a world in which mere survival seemed constantly in doubt.

Like the long interlude with the Colonel, my next misadventure came about accidentally. I had gone to a downtown hotel to have lunch with a friend. As I was leaving, a Negro bellhop whom I had known for years approached me with understandable nervousness, for men of color in those days rarely conferred with white ladies on delicate subjects, especially down south in Kentucky.

"Miss Pauline," the bellhop stammered, "a gentleman done give me this note for you." He thrust a piece of hotel stationery in my hand and scurried away.

I stopped at the hotel entrance and—after making sure no one in the lobby was watching me—I read the note hurriedly, then reread it more carefully.

"I couldn't help admiring you when you came into the hotel," the note said. "I would be highly honored to meet you. I'm in Room 322." The note was signed: "An Ardent Admirer."

Even to a semi-innocent such as myself at that time, the meaning of the note was clear. The "mystery guest" obviously had visions of a quickie romance. I snorted scornfully, crumpled the note, and quickly left the hotel. Outside, though, I stopped suddenly to review the situation.

"What the hell," I told myself. "You're a big girl now and you need the money real bad. As long as you've got the commodity he wants, why not see what this character has in mind?" I turned, walked back into the hotel, and darted into the nearest elevator.

Up on the third floor, I knocked on the door of Room 322. It swung open and I found myself staring at a tall, attractive man clad in a good-quality satin lounging robe and, judging by the bare, hairy legs that jutted from below the hem, not much else.

"Baby, you're a sight for sore eyes," he exclaimed in a bit of overworked dialogue that immediately pinpointed him as one of the breezy, back-slapping traveling salesmen who frequented the hotel. "Come on in and have a drink!"

I entered the room, wondering just how a girl goes about arranging a commercial transaction of this type, and perched gingerly on the edge of the nearest chair while my "Ardent Admirer" got out a silver flask and prepared a couple of hefty highballs. Looking about nervously, I saw a bed looming obscenely in the middle of the room. "My God! What kind of a fix have you got yourself into now?" I asked myself, realizing that it was too late to weasel out of my predicament.

My new "friend" interrupted my despairing thoughts, handing me a highball and lifting his own glass for a toast that must have wowed the girls at Pumpkin Center once upon a time. "Here's to a girl with plenty of class," he proclaimed grandly, diplomatically leaving unvoiced the second line of that time-worn dirty jingle.

Although I had never cared for the taste of liquor, I took a big gulp, thinking it would help prop up my fading courage. Lord, I still remember that drink! It must have been 200-proof panther piss. I coughed and sputtered and gagged. Finally I managed to regain my breath and deposit the highball glass on a table.

"What's the matter?" the hotel room Lothario inquired with a grin. "Is that white lightnin' too strong?"

"It's too powerful for me," I managed to wheeze. Then, struggling to regain a semblance of composure, I decided to get down to the nitty-gritty details of the transaction. "I didn't come here to drink," I said in what I hoped was a professional approach. "Just what did you have in mind?"

My "roommate" grinned again, winking lewdly. "You know," he said. "I thought we could have us a nice party if the price is right."

The price? I hadn't even thought about price. "How about ten dollars?" I suggested hopefully.

"Ten dollars!" he snorted. "Honey, I don't want to buy you. I just want to rent you for awhile. Five bucks and nothing more!"

"Well," I thought with weary resignation, "that's five more than I've earned today, so why not?" I accepted his offer, pocketed his money, and got down to business. A half hour later, I was walking out of the hotel again, five dollars richer and, oddly enough, not feeling a bit unclean or guilty. "Hell's bells," I told myself, "that was a quick and easy way to earn money. Maybe I've been overlooking a gold mine right in my own backyard!"

The question was, how does a girl get customers—the well-heeled visitors in town, not the local yokels with big, gossipy mouths and skinny bankrolls? I put this question to a colored girl I knew and trusted, and she informed me that the bellhop who steered me to Room 322 had a brisk side-business arranging "dates" for certain ones of the available-at-a-price women in town with lonely guests at the hotel. In return, of course, he expected to get at least a dollar cut out of the deal.

Taking the hint, I dispatched my friend with a one-dollar token of appreciation for the flesh-peddling bellhop. She made the necessary arrrangements, and I soon found myself working as a part-time call girl in addition to the daily peddling of hosiery and cosmetics.

No doubt about it, sex for sale was a fast-buck business. But for me it proved to be a disillusioning and not very rewarding experience. There seemed to be an endless haggling over price, and, sometimes, when I'd arrive as scheduled at a customer's room, he'd turn me away because I was "too big." After two wretched months, I informed the bellhop that I was no longer interested in his brand of dating. Once again, I found myself depending entirely on making an honest living as a doorbell pusher. But as I made my rounds with my kit of samples, I couldn't help but think there had to be some smart way to capitalize on sex. Experience had taught me to view the "grand passion" with a strictly commercial attitude. I also knew from experience that this could be a business in which there never was a shortage of customers. The question was: how does a girl get into the business I had in mind—the operation of a whorehouse where other girls handle the strenuous labor of servicing the male animal?

Oddly enough, I discovered the answer to that question during an evening bridge party at the home of a friend. There were several tables of card enthusiasts. One of the players at my table was a visitor from Tennessee—a worldly sort of fellow who seemed to delight in regaling us with stories of his wicked, wicked ways. One of his tales dealt with a famous madam named May who ran a notorious bordello in Clarksville, Tennessee.

"That's not a very big town," I observed, sensing that maybe I was on the right track at last. "How can a madam of such a place make a living in a town like that?"

Madam May, the gentleman from Tennessee assured me, had made a fortune in Clarksville because she operated a high-class house that drew customers from all nearby states, including Kentucky. "She's a really remarkable woman—one of my very favorite people," he said quite seriously.

Conversation at the table drifted on to other subjects, but my interest was aroused. As the evening ended, I cornered the Tennessee storyteller and told him I would like to meet and talk with May. He looked at me quizzically, as if he feared he was either being quietly kidded or was faced with some kind of a female nut. Finally he seemed to decide that I was joking.

"Why do you want to meet May?" he asked, his eyebrows raised in mock alarm. "Have you decided that you want to go to work in her house?"

"Of course not," I replied with a frankness that even startled me. "But if May can be so successful running a brothel in a town like Clarksville, I see no reason why I can't do the same thing here in Bowling Green. And if I could meet her, maybe she'd give me some advice."

My bluntly spoken ambition seemed to delight the fun-loving Tennessean. "Pauline," he said, "you're a real trouper. Of course I'll help you." And he not only gave me May's address and unlisted telephone number, but he advised me to mention his name when I called her. "If you ever open a house here, let me know and I'll be your first customer," he said.

The next day I stopped at a telephone booth and invested some money in a long-distance call to Clarksville. It proved to be the wisest investment I ever made. The phone at the other end of the line rang a few times, and then a soft, cultured woman's voice answered: "Miss May speaking. May I help you?"

Hurriedly, I identified myself and told her how I had gotten her private phone number from one of her friends. Before I could go any further, May exclaimed happily about what a great guy the Tennessee gentleman was. "Any friend of his is a friend of mine," she said. "What's the problem—do you want to turn some tricks down here at my house?"

At that time I had no idea what a "trick" was, but instinctively I realized that May was offering me a job. "I don't want to work in your house," I explained with as much tact as I could muster. "But I heard so many wonderful stories about you that I'd like to open a house just like yours here in Bowling Green. The trouble is, I don't have the faintest idea how to get started, and I thought you might be kind enough to give me some advice. Sort of teach me the business, I guess."

May's laughter tinkled like silver bells across the miles between Clarksville and Bowling Green. "I've had some funny requests in my time, but this beats everything," she said gleefully. "I never thought I'd be asked to teach a course in running a whorehouse." Suddenly, her laughter erupted again.

"Well," I said when May's mirth had subsided, "can I impose on you and come down to Clarksville for a visit?"

"Honey-child," May said, "any girl with your gumption is bound to succeed. You come on down any time you please. The welcome mat will always be out for you at my house."

*The making of a madam*

# The making of a madam

My impulsive quest for basic training as a madam was a real shoe-string operation. Telling my mother I was going to spend the week-end with friends, I set out for Miss May's house in Clarksville with a battered suitcase containing a few delicate undies, cosmetics, and my best black silk evening dress, $3.50 in my purse, and an optimistic hope that the famous Tennessee brothel-keeper would somehow help me solve my seemingly insoluble financial problems.

After investing $2 of my bankroll for a round-trip ticket to Clarksville—and selling a new pair of silk hosiery and a bottle of perfume (items I'd stuffed into my purse as a hedge against total bankruptcy) to a kindly gentleman on the train—I arrived in Tennessee with the princely sum of $4. Leaving the depot, I realized that, beyond an address, I had no idea where Miss May's house was located. Reluctant to brazenly inquire about the location of such an establishment, I decided I had no choice but to take a taxi and risk the chance that I'd have enough to pay the fare. For all I knew, my destination could be miles out in the country.

Recklessly, I climbed into the only cab in front of the train station and directed the driver to take me to 1116 College Street. I was positive that the address by itself would not reveal the kind of place I was visiting. But I was mistaken.

Upon hearing the address, the taxi driver, who had displayed little or no interest in me when I entered his cab, turned quickly and submitted both me and my suitcase to a long, disconcerting stare. Then apparently deciding that his ears had deceived him, he asked, "You mean Miss May's house?"

"That's right," I said, hoping—once my dark secret had been discovered—that I sounded like a self-confident woman of the world.

The driver turned silently, started the motor, and off we went with a clashing of gears. But as the blocks flashed by I could sense that the cabbie was staring at me in the rear-view mirror with puzzled disbelief. Finally he could contain his curiosity no longer.

"Pardon me, mam," he blurted. "But you sure don't look like one of Miss May's girls!"

Still self-conscious about my oversized proportions, I didn't know whether to view this as an insult or to feel flattered that I didn't look like a lady of easy virtue. Deciding it would be foolish to take offense at this bit of snooping, I brushed aside his remark by coolly replying, "Oh, I'm not one of the girls. I'm just a friend of Miss May."

"Well, she's a mighty fine woman," the driver observed, seeming to be satisfied with my explanation.

A few minutes later we turned off a quiet street into a winding driveway that meandered through dense clumps of shrubbery and trees to a large, stately house atop a hill. "Good Lord," I thought as we stopped in front of the two-story house set like a precious gem in the midst of a broad, green lawn, terraced gardens, and a large lily-bedecked pool, "this must be the wrong place. Surely this isn't a whorehouse."

"Quite a place, isn't it," the driver remarked as he accepted the fare, plus tip, and helped me out of the taxi—a courtesy which, I noted, he had not shown when, as an unknown female toting a big suitcase, I had struggled into his cab a few minutes earlier. Evidently any friend of Miss May automatically earned respect in his eyes.

For a few moments I stood surveying the big house and its luxurious setting with awe. "Wow!" I silently exclaimed. "If the wages of sin are death, this is a mighty fine way to go!" Slowly I picked up my shabby suitcase and climbed the broad steps leading to the front door for my first visit to a house of ill repute.

A colored maid in a stylish black and white uniform answered the doorbell. Briefly, in the face of such splendor, I felt faint. My knees were as weak as water and my mouth and lips were as parched as an old spinster's kiss. What, I wondered desperately, was I going to say to the lady of such a grand house?

"I'm—I'm Pauline Tabor," I at last managed to blurt breathlessly. "I've come to see Miss May."

The maid didn't seem to notice my bumbling, self-conscious introduction. She smiled gently, took my suitcase, and said, "Oh, yes, Miss May has been expecting you. She's waiting in the library." She turned, and I followed her along a broad, red-carpeted hallway leading to a vast, winding walnut stairway extending majestically up to the second floor. I was so absorbed in studying my surroundings— a beautifully carved grandfather's clock at the foot of the stairway, a long, dark table with a blue Chinese vase filled with freshly cut flowers, and several tall, red-upholstered chairs along the hallway's walls—that I at first didn't notice the slender, gray-haired woman standing in a doorway with her hands outstretched in greeting.

"Hello, honey," she said in a soft, warm voice as cultured as her surroundings. "You must be Pauline."

I could only nod dazedly, desperately trying to regain my wits. Miss May seemed to sense my discomfort. She took me by the hand,

led me into the library, and seated me on an antique love seat upholstered with blue and gold tapestry. "Honey, I've been simply dying to meet you," she exclaimed, seeking to make me feel at home. "Ever since that fantastic phone call, I've been trying to picture just what you're really like."

"Well," I said ruefully, finally regaining my tongue, "there's quite a bit of me, as you can see, and right now every pound of me is scared to death."

"For heaven's sake, why?" she asked. "I'm not a witch, and not even a bitch very often any more. I'm just a little old lady running a cathouse in a small Tennessee town."

Somehow, such blunt language from the lips of a kindly, elderly, and obviously wealthy lady stirred me back to life.

"That's the problem," I admitted. "You're a very successful, very famous madam. And here I am, a Miss Nobody who's never even been inside a house like this before, thinking that I can make a success out of the same kind of business. The minute I got here and saw this beautiful house, I knew how foolish and simple minded I must seem to you—and probably am, really."

"Pauline Tabor, you listen to me," Miss May snapped peevishly. "If I thought you were foolish and simple minded, I never would have invited you to come calling. But listening to you on the phone, I knew it took a lot of old-fashioned guts for you to make a call like that, and guts is something a woman needs in big supply to make a go of it in this business. So if you're truly, sincerely interested, I'll do my best to teach you what I know."

"Believe me, Miss May," I said, "I was never more serious in my life. But—it's just that I'm overwhelmed. How could I hope to even come close to this?"

"Don't think for a minute I started out with a house like this!" Miss May snorted indelicately. "Only a millionaire could afford to start out in this high-toned style, and if you've got a million you don't need to run a whorehouse."

"But you're surely wealthy, and you're running a whorehouse," I pointed out undiplomatically.

"Sure I am," she replied. "I've been in this business longer than I care to remember, and I'd feel lost now if I retired. But when I started out, I was nearly broke. Had a small rented house, and I pitched in and helped three girls handle the customers. Money? Nobody had much in those days. Sometimes we'd take eggs, chickens, and produce as pay because we needed food on the table."

Miss May sighed as she called a halt to her memories. "Enough of that prattling about the old days," she said, rising from her chair. "It's time for dinner, and you must be starved after your trip. Come along and meet my girls, and we'll have a long, long talk later."

Miss May must have been approaching sixty then, but as she led me to the dining room that evening she bounced along as sprightly as a schoolgirl, chattering zestfully about her house and its furnishings. Like any successful merchant, it was plain to see she was mighty proud of her establishment.

The chandeliered dining room was decorated and furnished in excellent taste. But its regal atmosphere was overshadowed by the beauty of the eight girls who already were seated at a long, formally set dining table. Blond, brunette, and redhead; tall, petite, and medium height; slender and pleasingly plump—Miss May's high-class line of merchandise obviously had been carefully selected to offer a variety of choices to even the most discriminating customers. Seeing this array of female talent, it was immediately evident why my brief venture as a professional had been a flop. A woman of my dimensions certainly couldn't compete in the sex market with beauties like these. My instincts had been right, I thought. My only chance for success in the oldest profession was a career as a madam, merchandising younger, more exotic female flesh.

Having never had, to my knowledge, any previous contact with a professional prostitute, I didn't know what to expect when I met Miss May's girls. All were properly and tastefully dressed, all had good manners, and their conversation at the table was typical female chitchat, as free of vulgarities and profanity as a get-together of proper young matrons at a country club luncheon. In brief, my preconceived mental picture of a prostitute as a coarse, sin-hardened woman, with the marks of her trade clearly visible in her face and her manners, quickly faded. Out in public, in even the finest of society, there wasn't a girl at the table who would be recognized as a fallen woman.

Later I mentioned my sense of shocked amazement to Miss May, telling her of my discovery that not a single one of her girls "looked like a whore." Miss May immediately set my thinking straight.

"A whore and a prostitute are two completely different breeds of pussycat," she said. "A whore is a cheap chippie with a big itch who'll spread her legs for anything in pants without thinking about what she'll get in return. But a prostitute is a professional. She knows what she's doing and why she's doing it. She has pride in herself and pride in her abilities, and she expects to be paid, and paid well, for her services. If you get into this business, get rid of any whores that end up in your house. They're nothing but trouble, and they lower the class of your operation."

As the years went by I learned through some mighty unpleasant experiences to appreciate and even expand upon the wisdom of Miss May's sharp distinction between a prostitute and a whore. A prostitute, I found, is a woman who has learned to look upon sex as a business, and who—to improve her business—works a lot harder than most wives to learn the art of pleasing a man in the boudoir. A whore, on the other hand, is a woman whose life is dominated and distorted by the sex urge, and who, in a frantic, futile grasping for fulfillment, gives to the sex act about as much beauty and human warmth as the coupling of two alley cats. However, on that long-ago visit to Clarksville, I learned a lot more than the basic definitions of—to use Miss May's expression—two different breeds of pussycat.

Lesson No. 1 came shortly after dinner. I had gone to my upstairs room to change into my one good evening gown, preparatory to spending some time in the big parlor observing the intricacies of the night's trade, when Miss May came knocking at my door.

"Honey," she said, "there's a special friend of mine downstairs—a man who's been a tremendous help to me in my business. He'd be most honored to meet you."

Downstairs in the library—a room which I later learned Miss May reserved as her own hideaway in a sometimes hectic house—I was confronted by a mountain of a man dressed in a uniform and sporting a badge. Any doubt about his profession was removed by Miss May, who introduced him as the chief of police and then left to get the house and girls ready for a long, busy Saturday night.

The Chief beamed happily down at me from a height of at least 6-foot-4, settled his 300-plus pounds in a big leather-upholstered chair, patted the broad plateau of his knees, and beckoned to me with a hamlike hand.

"Come on over and sit on my lap, Little Lady, so we can talk a spell," he boomed.

Little Lady? Hell, for nearly two years, since my illness, I'd been pushing 215 pounds around with all the grace of a 10-ton tank. Now, suddenly, I felt dwarfed as I cautiously perched on the Chief's king-sized lap like a moppet awaiting the reading of a bedtime story.

"So you're the Little Lady who wants to learn how to run a whorehouse," the Chief said, caressing my cheek with an affectionate pawing that nearly jolted loose a couple of molars.

I admitted that I was, but my mind really wasn't on the conversation. I was nervously wondering if this refugee from the age of dinosaurs might be harboring some sort of primeval romantic ideas. "Really," I said, "I'm afraid I'm much too heavy to be sitting here on your lap."

"Nonsense," he thundered. "You're light as a feather." And he jiggled me up and down on his lap, like some giant hobbyhorse, to prove his point. Then he got down to the business at hand—namely, the education of Pauline Tabor. Miss May, it seems, had asked him to brief me on the business from a lawman's point of view.

"The first thing you've got to remember," he said, "is that you're going to be operating an illegal business. So you're going to be faced with a constant threat of being closed down by the law, and maybe even going to jail."

"Well, I sort of figured on keeping my business a secret, except to customers and friends," I said.

The Chief snorted derisively. "Little Lady, the whole town is going to know about it in twenty-four hours after you open. There's no such thing as a secret whorehouse, believe me."

"If that's the case," I asked, "how come Miss May has been able to stay open so long?"

"Don't kid yourself," the Chief said. "Miss May has had more than her share of tangles with the law through the years. Even now, when the Holy Joes around town start putting on the heat about vice, I have to keep them happy by making a raid, arresting some of her girls, and closing the place down."

"What happens then?"

The Chief shrugged his thick shoulders. "Oh, Miss May comes down and pays the girls' fines. Then she and the girls take a vacation. When the heat's off, they return to town and the house opens again. Miss May and the girls have lost a few bucks, and the customers have had to drive to Nashville or other places to get their jollies. But nobody has really been hurt."

"It all sounds pretty silly to me," I said. "I'd think you'd either let the place operate, or close it down for good."

The Chief patiently explained that life in any town is not that simple. "There's a lot of folks here, including myself and some mighty important people, who figure that Miss May's house is a real asset to the town," he said. "The way we look at it, she runs a high-class place that gives Clarksville a decent outlet for all kinds of sex urges. Her girls are clean—get medical checkups every week—and Miss May and the girls mind their own business and stay out of trouble. Why, there's more hell raised at some homes around town on a Saturday night than there is at Miss May's in a year."

"Why bother to raid the house then if it's good for the town?" I wanted to know.

"Little Lady," the Chief replied, "you're going to find out that every town has got more than its share of Holy Joes—men and women who have nothing better to do than stew about the morals of other folks. Every once in a while some crusader comes along, starts preaching about sin. Before you know it, all the Holy Joes are screaming about the cancer of vice destroying the town. They preach sermons, make speeches, write fiery letters to the editor, sign petitions, telephone the mayor, threatening to have his scalp at the next election. Pretty soon the politicians are scared, and I get a phone call suggesting that I close down Miss May's house until the heat's off. So, I raid the house, keep it closed for a few weeks, and the Holy Joes are happy again until the next time some crusader crawls out of the woodwork."

It was a long speech, but—coming from the chief of police—I was impressed. In fact, I was stricken with memories of sitting in church, nodding virtuously as the preacher cried out against sin, alerting his congregation to the spreading threat of vice in our town. My, how goody-good I felt then, being a part of a war against immorality even though, for the life of me, I couldn't think of a single "palace of vice" in Bowling Green except, perhaps, a couple of seedy joints frequented by the town's fast set.

In later years as I fought my own wars against the Holy Joe crusaders, I would vividly remember the Chief's accurate analysis of the conflicting forces within a community—part condoning and part condemning—that plague the life of a madam and her girls. On that evening, however, I was more concerned with any advice the Chief might have on how I could go about winning friends and influencing people in the right places. That, it appeared to me, would have to be my first step in setting up business in Bowling Green or anywhere else. Again, the Chief laid the cards on the table.

"As Miss May tells it, you want to open a house in Bowling Green —in your home town," he said. "Well, that's got its drawbacks and its advantages. You're going to shock a lot of people. They're going to feel that you've betrayed everything they stand for, and they're going to be howling for your head on a platter. But, on the other hand, you must know at least some people in important jobs—businessmen, politicians, lawyers, and police. Maybe you can get some of them on your side. At least they'll know it's a local girl of good reputation setting up a house, and not a stranger, or maybe some big-city underworld syndicate."

Then the Chief got down to specifics. Confirming my own grasp of the situation, he advised me to first talk with some important people I trusted and tell them of my plans so they wouldn't feel later that I had tried to sneak over something behind their backs.

"Assure them it's going to be a high-class house, with medical checkups for the girls," he said. "Assure them that you'll not let your girls gad about town when they're not working, and that you'll keep your place as free from trouble as possible. If you do this, the powers that be might let you alone, waiting to see how the town accepts your house."

However, the Chief cautioned me not to expect easy sailing. Aside from the Holy Joes, he said, there are always some law-enforcement officials who operate strictly by the book, who say that if a place is illegal it should be closed even if it isn't hurting the community. And, he warned, there isn't a madam in business who doesn't have to live with the problem of making payoffs.

"One thing you've got to remember," he said. "Never offer a payoff or a bribe. That either sets you up as a sucker asking to be milked or insults some honest official who'll really try to nail your hide to the wall."

"But what if somebody demands a payoff?" I asked.

"When that happens," the Chief said, "make damned sure your money is buying something of value. Make sure that the guy who's got his hand out really can produce what he claims he can. And never pay or do special favors for a cop on the beat or a vice squad detective who claims he can provide you with protection. That's a lot of crap! Cops at that level don't make policy."

The Chief had just finished his advice on payoffs when Miss May hurried into the room.

"I hate to interrupt you two," she said. "But things are getting lively in the big parlor, and I thought Pauline might want to sit in on the fun."

I scrambled hastily off the Chief's lap and thanked him kindly for his "bedtime story." He caught the sly fun-poking in my remark immediately. "So it was a bedtime story, was it?" He chuckled. "Little

Lady, you've got a real sense of humor. And, God knows, you're going to need it."

On that somewhat pessimistic note, the Chief departed, and Miss May led me out into the hallway en route to the parlor which, even from a distance, was echoing the blare of a jukebox and the sound of voices and laughter. We had just started down the hall when the doorbell rang. Miss May halted me with a firm hand. "Let's wait here until someone answers the door," she said. "Some of our customers get jittery if there are many people around when they first come in."

Seconds later, a lovely young brunette, dressed in an expensive low-cut red gown that daringly accentuated her charms, hurried into the hall from the parlor and opened the door. She murmured a greeting, and two well-dressed men entered the house. I gasped with horror. My mouth flew open and my eyes bulged. I turned and ran for the stairway, almost knocking Miss May down in my panic-stricken flight. Miss May, after recovering her equilibrium, must have come rushing up the stairs directly behind me because I was still gasping from the exertion of my mad dash when she burst breathlessly into my room.

"Pauline, what in the world happened?" she asked, wide-eyed and pale. "You almost knocked me down flat on my back when you took off. Are you sick?"

"My God, no, I'm not sick!" I exclaimed. "I wish I were, though. I wish I were sick a thousand miles from here."

"What in tarnation are you gibbering about, girl?" Miss May said. "Talk some sense!"

"It's those men who came in—they're from Bowling Green," I said. "I'll simply die if they find me here."

"Nonsense!" Miss May retorted sharply. "You're imagining things. Those gentlemen are two of my best customers. They've been coming here for years, and they're from Guthrie, Kentucky."

"Guthrie, hell!" I replied heatedly. "If that's what they told you, they're a couple of champion liars. I've known them for years in Bowling Green. The short man is a prominent lawyer, and his buddy owns one of the richest farms in Warren County. They're both leading citizens in my home town, and my name's mud if they catch me here."

Miss May erupted into a storm of laughter—no refined tittering, but real belly-deep guffaws. When she finally recovered, she managed to gasp, "Why those old reprobates! It's getting so you can't believe anybody any more."

Then Miss May abruptly became serious. "Pauline, you've just had another lesson," she said.

"Another lesson—what on earth do you mean?"

"In the first place," Miss May replied, "there's no need for you to be worried about what would happen if they saw you in this house. Believe me, honey, they would be a sight more upset than you if they realized that you had seen them here. And in the second place, if they say they're from Guthrie, Kentucky, when they come to my house, then they're from Guthrie, Kentucky. The customer is always right, no questions asked, as long as he pays the bill and behaves."

Having delivered this lecture in defense of the fibbing gentlemen from Bowling Green, Miss May got down to the basic facts involved in the ethics of a whorehouse operation. A madam can be successful, she said, only if her customers know they can absolutely trust her to respect their privacy and to keep their secrets.

"A lot of important men come through these doors," Miss May said. "Just their being here is an admission that they've got problems at home, that they're lonely or that they've got some kind of hangup that they can't gratify easily anywhere else. Some of these customers talk freely and honestly while they're here. Others, like your friends from Bowling Green, try to cover their tracks with phony names and phony stories. But whatever the case may be, these men pay a good price for the service they get. And in return, they know that the walls of this whorehouse, or any good whorehouse, never talk."

Despite Miss May's assurances that I had nothing to worry about, I at first resisted her efforts to talk me into venturing out of my room for a visit to the parlor. It was only after she convinced me that the "boys from Bowling Green" always spent the night there with their two favorite girls—that there was no chance of seeing them downstairs again—that I reluctantly agreed to join in the festivities going on below.

I discovered there actually were four parlors, two large and two small. And on this night they all were crowded with at least twenty customers—"tricks," as they were called behind their backs. Only three or four of the girls were there, mingling gaily with the throng while they waited to be picked by some eager trick. The other girls evidently were busy upstairs. The smaller parlors each contained only a large jukebox with all of the top hits of the day available for a quarter a record. The floors of these two rooms were slick and worn from years of dancing. The two large parlors were carpeted and far more luxurious. These rooms were furnished with sofas and lounge chairs, and a variety of paintings decorated the walls. Adding to the creature comforts were several large soft-drink machines—providing choices of soda pop at a quarter per bottle—and small bars, complete with ice, where customers who brought their own bottles could mix their highballs.

The traffic between downstairs and upstairs that night was brisk. Evidently, except for the two big-time spenders from Bowling Green, there were no all-night tricks. Girls would leave the parlors quietly with customers in tow and be quickly replaced by girls who had seen their latest tricks to the door, a polite custom which I learned Miss May insisted upon. Her motto was spend your money or get out. But as long as a man was willing to put money in the jukeboxes and soft-drink machines (a lucrative sideline income) and ultimately invest in female entertainment, he was to be treated royally, as a welcome guest of the house. Thus, Miss May tolerated no hurried "wham, bam, thank you, sir" assembly-line servicing by her girls. Each trick was treated like a very special person, receiving full value for his investment.

Miss May's fees, when times were tough and money scarce, were $2 for a "straight" party and $5 for the specialty of the house, a "trip around the world" in which the girl livened up the action with a bit of tongue-tickling love play. There was a time limit of twenty minutes per customer, and any extra time in the saddle cost more. Also, there were special fees for customers with more exotic tastes in sex, ranging as high as $50 or more for some brands of off-beat hangups. Actually, a smart girl, by skillfully manipulating the sex urges of a trick and artfully catering to the male ego, could frequently parlay the basic fee into a sizable payment, including at times a generous tip which Miss May, as operator of the house, shared on her customary 50-50 split of all money received.

"But don't you have a problem of girls trying to hold back on this extra money, without giving you a share?" I asked after Miss May briefed me on the financial facts of life in a whorehouse while we sat in one of the parlors watching the goings-on.

Miss May's blue eyes sparkled frostily behind her steel-rimmed glasses. She may have looked like a gentle, gracious grandmother, but behind that mild façade dwelled a hard-headed businesswoman with a heart of pure dollar signs. She could be generous, friendly, and helpful —as she was with me—but not when her bank account was involved.

"Sure," she said, "once in awhile I get stuck with a bad apple who tries to double-cross me. But she doesn't last long. Any madam who's on the ball knows her customers, their hangups, and their spending habits. Also, the girls talk and the tricks talk, and pretty soon you know something's dead wrong with a girl's arithmetic. So you give her a quick heave-ho and get another girl. Before long the word gets around that cheating doesn't pay. A high-class house like this can be a gold mine for a girl. If they have any sense they won't risk their jobs for a few quick bucks."

Another time during the lengthening night when Miss May took time out from mixing with the tricks to brief me on her operations, I pointed out that several of the customers seemed content to just sit around and talk without making a trip upstairs with one of the girls.

"Talk is cheap," I said. "Isn't it a losing proposition, having these guys sit around gabbing?"

"Indeed not," Miss May explained. "A lot of my good customers are lonely men. Most times they pick out their favorite girl, but sometimes they just come here to be with people, to talk and laugh and joke. They play records and buy drinks and lots of times they give me a nice tip when they leave. But I never charge them for just visiting. I want them to feel welcome, and it pays off in the long run."

However, Miss May quickly added, this hospitality applied only to good customers, not to Johnny-come-lately characters who tried to loaf around the parlors, dance with the girls, and get their kicks by "copping a few free feels."

"That kind of cheapskate gets a quick rush," she said. "I tell him to invest in the merchandise or get out."

It was nearly three in the morning when I decided to cut short my apprentice training in the parlor and get some sleep. Several more of the girls had vanished upstairs, apparently bedded down with all-nighters. But even at this late hour, customers were still arriving and departing in a steady flow that added up to a big Saturday night gate for Miss May and her girls. For the first hour or two I had tried to keep count of the traffic, but I soon gave up attempting to add up the take. Nevertheless, I knew that Miss May's receipts for the night were fantastic, and visions of a similar untapped bonanza waiting for me in Bowling Green danced through my head as I giddily snuggled down in bed.

Except for the all-night tricks who generally depart discreetly in dawn's early light, there are no early risers in a whorehouse. It was almost noon when the first signs of life began stirring in Miss May's sex emporium on that bright summer's Sunday so long ago. I had been awake for some time, spinning wild fantasies about my approaching madamhood, when a maid knocked on my door and announced cheerfully that breakfast would be served in the kitchen in a half hour.

Unlike dinner the previous evening at which Miss May's dining room had an unreal atmosphere of a finishing school for proper young ladies, breakfast was an informal, hilarious affair. The girls, hair rumpled and without makeup, straggled sleepy-eyed into the big kitchen, clad in a variety of robes and kimonos which did nothing for their now-dormant sexpot images. However—although the exotic sirens of the night now looked like an ordinary gaggle of females trying to collect their energy for another day's vicissitudes—their conversation was earthy and liberally spiced with gossip and bawdy recollections of the previous evening's business. Startled by this transformation, I couldn't help think, as I listened to the breakfast table chatter, that Miss May's skilled courtesans were no different than a group of schoolgirls giggling over the latest wicked tidbits about teenage misadventures.

"It's lucky for a lot of men that this kind of talk doesn't get beyond these walls," I told myself as the girls merrily exchanged fascinating information about the tricks they had serviced. With devastating frankness, they discussed the sexual capabilities—and shortcomings—of the various customers. So-and-so was "hung like a horse, absolutely enormous, darling." Young Sammy W., the son of a town attorney, had set a new track record by "ringing the gong" in fifteen seconds flat. Old Mr. C., once the town's No. 1 stud, had labored valiantly but futilely for two hours, trying to generate new life in his obsolete equipment, and had left dejectedly after self-consciously doling out $40 as a tip to compensate for his date's "disappointment."

"Believe me, I earned that tip," the plump little blonde who had serviced Mr. C. exclaimed. "I worked and worked over that old goat —tried everything I knew—but there wasn't a sign of life."

"I'm sure sorry to hear that." Miss May sighed. "He used to be one of our big spenders. Lots of times he'd take on three or four girls a night. But now I guess we won't be seeing much of him any more."

However, the prize breakfast table anecdote was supplied by Judy, a tall, sensuous redhead with remarkable chest dimensions. "Maybe some of you missed it, but the poodle man paid us another visit last night," she said during a lull in the conversation.

That bit of news touched off a flurry of giggling around the big kitchen table.

"Did he go for the same routine?" Miss May inquired.

"He sure did! That's the damnedest dog I've ever seen."

"It sure is," another girl, who evidently had memories of servicing the poodle man on other occasions, observed. "Maybe you ought to hire that dog, Miss May. It could make you a fortune!"

"Well, now, that's an idea," Miss May said, half joking and half serious. "I never heard of a house with such a talented dog."

"Hey," a slender brunette named Clara exclaimed in mock alarm. "I don't want to compete with a dog!"

The table rocked with a new outburst of mirth. Miss May, apparently seeing the puzzled look on my face, put a stop to the tittering. "Pauline doesn't know what in the world we're talking about," she said. "You'd better tell her about your poodle man."

The redhead told her story with gusto. The customer in question, a well-to-do businessman from Nashville, had been showing up at Miss May's house regular as clockwork every other Saturday night for at least three years. And, without fail, he was accompanied by a thoroughbred poodle named Fifi, with the traditional dainty fur collar and —as subsequent action disclosed—a lusty, amorous appetite.

"The poodle always comes upstairs with us," the redhead explained. "When we get in the room, the mutt sits by the bed, panting and leering like a nasty old man, while we get ready for our party. And when the action starts, that damned dog begins barking, whining, scratching at the bed, and pacing the floor like some kind of sex maniac."

Evidently visions of the poodle man's strange hangup were vividly clear and excruciatingly funny, for the redhead's tale was interrupted by a new outburst of laughter. Finally she managed to regain her composure and continue her story. "You've never *really* lived until you've had a party with the poodle man. With that excited mutt yapping and scratching and jumping around the room, it's like trying to screw in the middle of a dog pound. And the fun really starts after the poodle man shoots his wad."

Assuring me that it was true even though I probably would find it hard to believe, the redhead described in language that left little to the imagination how this particular trick got his real kicks. After performing proficiently and normally in the bed, the customer quickly prepared for his odd encore. Climbing off the bed, he sat on a nearby stool with his legs spraddled to provide easy access to his now-deflated manhood. At this point, Fifi eagerly leaped into action.

"So help me," the redhead giggled, "that mutt's got a real educated tongue. It licks and nuzzles and sucks until the trick has a brand-new erection and gets his jollies all over again. It's the funniest sight I've ever seen. That damned dog has a genuine talent for frenching!"

It was early afternoon by the time the story of the poodle man was finished. The girls returned to their rooms to rest and begin leisurely preparations for the generally light Sunday afternoon and evening trade. With the train for Bowling Green due to depart in a few hours, Miss May took me back to the library for a final briefing on the problems of starting and running a brothel.

During this heart-to-heart session, I leveled completely with Miss May, telling her all about my background as a nice girl, a respectable matron, and a divorced mother of two young sons. I told her about my struggles to earn a living and even confessed that, to help finance my trip to Clarksville, I had peddled a pair of stockings and a bottle of perfume to a fellow passenger by convincing him they would make a nice returning-home gift for his wife.

At this mention of finances, or the lack thereof, Miss May's dollar instincts were alerted. "Honey," she said suspiciously, "I sure enough hope you aren't planning to hit me for a loan. I don't mind helping you with all the advice I can give. Advice doesn't cost anything. But if you've got any ideas about me bankrolling a house for you, forget it!"

I was indignant, for such an idea had never entered my head. "I had no intention of asking you for a red cent," I fumed. "If I need money, I've got friends in Bowling Green. I just came here to learn something about this business because I didn't know where else to turn."

Mollified by my heated assurance that I had no designs on her bankroll, Miss May quickly reverted to her friendly, helpful grandmother role. "Don't get on your high horse, honey," she said. "I just wanted to make sure. Now, let's get down to business."

First she reassured me that it didn't take a fortune to start a house on a modest scale, recalling that when she went into business she had to prop bed springs and mattresses on empty Coca-Cola cases because she couldn't afford the cost of regular beds. Then she bluntly told me of the drawbacks, beyond a shortage of cash, that I faced as an aspiring madam.

"I can't recall ever hearing of a woman with your kind of background getting into the business of running a whorehouse," she said. "Make no mistake, it's a rough and tough business. Mostly, madams are women who are set up in a house by a racketeering boyfriend or their pimp or, like me, prostitutes who are smart enough to get off the mattress and start their own operations with a stable of girls to do the work."

Also echoing the police chief's earlier warning, Miss May questioned the wisdom of opening a house in my hometown.

"You're going to be hurt, and hurt bad, by your family and friends," she said. "If you can develop a thick skin, though, you'll eventually realize that money and the security it brings can make up for a lot of the heartache."

With that little sermon off her chest, Miss May devoted the next hour to discussing a lot of the basic details involved in operating a house—how to find first-class prostitutes, how to quietly but effectively publicize your house, how to set up a profitable schedule of fees, how to arrange a fair cut of the receipts, how to keep peace among a collection of temperamental girls and among the customers, and how to cope with a number of other problems which regularly confront a madam. Indeed, Miss May—more than any other person in my life—taught me how to make money. Unhappily, though, she neglected to teach me how to save it!

At last, with my head bulging with new and enlightening information, I said my good-bys and, heartened by the well wishes of Miss May and her girls, headed back to Bowling Green. As the train started out that Sunday afternoon, I leaned back in my seat and let my dreams run wild. I was sure that I was heading for an instant fortune—sure that with Miss May's formula for success I now knew just about everything one needed to know about becoming a madam. What an innocent, lost lamb I was at that point! Before long I was going to find out just how wrong I was.

*A madam builds a dream house*

# A madam builds a dream house

It was midsummer of 1933 when I returned to Bowling Green with all sorts of grandiose plans generated by my crash course in madamship at Miss May's school of sexual technology. But despite my eagerness to get the show on the road, late October found my career as a madam still stalled on one critical front.

Soon after my visit to Clarksville, I had confided in a few influential friends, striving to "sell" them on my plan for a bordello. The immediate reaction of even the most worldly of these men was one of shocked disbelief. They tried to convince me that I had temporarily lost my senses; that I had no conception of the difficulties I'd have to face; that a respectable woman just doesn't get into *that kind* of business, especially in her home town.

Their logic may have been valid, but with my rough-and-ready experience in door-to-door selling, I was not a person who wilted easily in the face of sales resistance. After seeing that I was determined to go ahead with my project despite all opposition, my friends apparently decided to humor me in my headstrong rush toward disaster. They began to view my unconventional ambitions with amused tolerance. In the end most of them agreed to help clear my path with whatever influence they could quietly exert in the community.

Partly as an instinctive bit of female strategy and partly in a spirit of reckless cussedness, I included among the friends I recruited to my cause one of the Bowling Green gentlemen I had spotted in Miss May's house of pleasure. Like the others I had contacted, he indignantly lectured me on the impropriety of a woman in my position—a mother of two young sons—even considering such scandalous *illegal* ideas.

"You'll end up a social outcast," he warned.

"Perhaps so, but at least I'll be making a good living for my family," I snapped. "I don't notice the folks in Bowling Green rushing to buy my hosiery and cosmetics. Maybe I just need to handle a sexier kind of merchandise."

My friend promptly jumped on that kind of reasoning. "How can you delude yourself about making money running a brothel? Even if, by some miracle, the police let you stay open, you don't know the first thing about *that kind* of business."

"I most certainly do," I quickly retorted.

"Baloney! Where would you ever learn how to operate a . . . a whorehouse?"

"At Miss May's house down in Clarksville," I replied sweetly. "Ever hear about Miss May?"

My friend was thunderstruck. He eyed me suspiciously as he groped for words. "At Miss May's house!" he finally sputtered, not even bothering to claim he knew nothing about the notorious Tennessee madam. "Are you telling me you worked for Miss May?"

I couldn't help giggling. "Don't be silly. I'm hardly the type. But I do know Miss May, and I spent a weekend with her recently. She was kind enough to give me all kinds of pointers about starting and running a house."

It was plain to see during the ensuing pause in the conversation that my friend was doing some rapid recollecting, and that a horrible possibility was beginning to take shape on the horizons of his mind. If I really had spent a recent weekend at Miss May's house, there was a chance I had seen him. Perhaps he even recalled the frantic flight of some unknown female at the far end of the long hallway. In any event, his resistance to my plans began to crumble.

"Well," he muttered at last, "it must have been an interesting weekend."

"It certainly was," I replied. And I casually recounted a few memories of the house and Miss May and her girls.

By the time I'd finished, my friend had no doubts, I'm sure, about my having visited Miss May. His only doubt was—had I or hadn't I seen him on one of his tomcatting expeditions? From that point on he was on my side, and later wielded considerable influence on my behalf. But he never did discover the answer to the big question.

After mustering my secret little band of supporters, the next problem was locating and furnishing a suitable house at a price in line with my anemic budget. By September I had found my house—a huge, ancient barn of a place on Smallhouse Road which I leased for a year for $30 a month, a rather substantial rent in those days of depression.

I guess the preacher who owned the place was in a hurry to move his family on to his new pastorate and delighted to find a tenant who agreed so quickly to his asking price because he never once questioned my story of planning to open a roominghouse. In fact, even after the true purpose of the house was known and irate citizens began writing indignant letters to the good padre at his home in another state, I never received a single protest from my ordained landlord. He may have stood foursquare against sin, but as long as he got his rent checks promptly he seemed willing to bend his conscience a bit. Or perhaps I'm too harsh in my judgment. Maybe he simply was too busy battling sin in his new town to be bothered by the devil's doings back in Bowling Green.

Furnishing the big house was my next task, and that empty monster, with four bedrooms upstairs and one downstairs, looked like a bottomless pit. Surprisingly, though, furnishing the house wasn't as tough or as costly a problem as I had feared. I still had considerable furniture, linens, and other essential housewares from my years of marriage. This stockpile went into the house along with what furnishings and bric-a-brac my mother could spare. To complete the task, I found several bargains in used furniture stores, scrounged a few pieces from relatives, and even resorted to buying some items on the "dollar-down-dollar-when-you-catch-me" installment plan. Also, one of my friends made discreet arrangements to have a large jukebox and three soda-pop vending machines moved in on a rental-percentage deal.

By mid-October my house was furnished. Surveying the results, I knew it could not hold a candle to Miss May's elegant establishment, but it was comfortable, with a secondhand sort of charm. At least, I told myself, the house from top to bottom was decked out in as good a taste as I could afford. Now, except for three still-unsolved problems, I was ready to make my debut as a madam.

First, I tackled two unpleasant personal dilemmas. The moment I had been dreading came when I brought my mother to see the house on Smallhouse Road for the first time. I had told her the same story I had handed the preacher—that I was going to open a roominghouse. It took my mother about two minutes to discover just what kind of a roominghouse I had in mind. She walked through the small parlor and large adjoining living room, her eyebrows arching at the sight of two vending machines looming suggestively amid a profusion of chairs and sofas of all sizes, shapes, and vintage.

"Must be expecting an awful lot of thirsty guests," she observed pointedly.

From the living room, she proceeded on into the dining room—a room I had converted into a dancing area. There wasn't a stick of furniture in the room; just the big, garish jukebox and another soda-pop dispenser squatting along one inside wall.

Mother stopped and surveyed the room and its accessories. "I see . . . I see," she murmured. She turned slowly, staring at me sadly. "I do hope and pray you know what you're doing, Pauline," she said. Without another word, she marched out of the house. Years later she confessed to me that she hadn't been surprised that day on Smallhouse Road. She recalled that shortly before his death my father had warned her that, in hard times, I had become a willful, determined woman who could be expected to do unconventional things if there seemed to be no other solution to life's problems. And he had asked her never to turn her back on me, no matter what I might do. She never did, nor did she ever utter a single word of reproach about the path I chose to follow. It simply was a subject that we never discussed.

The other personal problem was what to do with my two sons. No matter how high class it may be, a brothel just isn't designed for the care and rearing of children. In my case, I couldn't ask my mother for help with two rough-and-tumble boys because she was in frail health. So once more I turned to my former husband's mother. I visited her and frankly told her what I was going to do and why I was doing it. Like others in whom I had confided, she was shocked and certain that I was making a terrible mistake. But at the same time she understood my grave financial problems and sympathized with my desperate searching for a way to make a better living for myself and my family. Without hesitation, she agreed to again take on the job of helping raise her grandsons. From that time on she kept the boys and I paid the bills.

My third pre-opening problem was not so painful, but it was considerably more difficult. The operation of a house requires one basic commodity—girls. And despite the rudimentary knowledge I had acquired during my visit to Clarksville, I discovered to my dismay that I didn't have the foggiest notion of how to go about recruiting high-quality prostitutes. You don't fill that kind of position by advertising in the help-wanted columns, and you don't walk up to some strange female and say, "Pardon me, dear, but could I interest you in a good-paying job screwing in my new cathouse?"

Miss May had told me to pass the word around about my plans to open a house, and she had assured me that before long I'd have plenty of applicants. Well, I had passed the word along, but my friends, although willing and able to assist in other critical areas, scarcely qualified as recruiters of female flesh. Most of them, I knew or suspected, patronized prostitutes from time to time. But they looked upon these ladies of pleasure as something that was always available, giving no thought to where they came from or how they were hired.

One of my friends, a bachelor with a naughty reputation as a tireless, devoted skirt-chaser, provided me with the names of several of his easier conquests—girls whose reputations as loose women were widely known and talked about in Bowling Green and several adjoining counties.

"Good lord," I said, "those dames have bedded down with half the male population. I'm not looking for amateur whores. I'm looking for a couple of young, attractive professionals who'll be fresh and new in Bowling Green."

My friend shook his head. "Except for the local talent, I'm afraid I can't be of much help." Then recalling my stories of the weekend at Clarksville, he suggested, "Why don't you call Miss May? Maybe she can help you."

I hated the thought of imposing upon Miss May again, but I could think of no alternatives. So for a second time I found myself telephoning the Tennessee madam for a helping hand.

"Miss May," I admitted after indulging in the customary formalities of telephone etiquette, "I've got a terrible problem. I've rented and furnished a big, five-bedroom house. I've talked with the right people, and I'm ready to open. But the trouble is, I haven't been able to find any girls. I just don't know what to do."

Miss May was sympathetic. "I don't have a single contact in Bowling Green," she said. "But I'll talk with the girls. Perhaps they'll have some ideas."

The following day, I received a phone call from Miss May. One of her girls had a friend who had recently moved to Bowling Green after being busted by police while working as a call girl in Louisville.

"The judge let her go when she promised to get out of town," Miss May explained. "So she moved to Bowling Green and took a job waiting tables at a restaurant until the heat's off up in Louisville."

Miss May said the girl's name was Joyce. She advised me to contact her at the restaurant where she worked and quietly sound her out about coming to work in my house. My Clarksville friend, after providing me with this lead, suggested that she might have an additional solution for my woman-power problems.

"Even if Joyce goes to work for you, it will take more than one girl to support your big house," Miss May said. "Eventually, if your place is successful, the word will get around and you'll be able to get all the girls you want. But right now it seems to me you'd be smart to run a house of assignation."

"A house of what?" I asked, fumbling through my vocabulary for a clue to what Miss May was talking about.

Miss May's explanation was explicit. "A house of assignation is a place that rents out rooms by the hour to itchy couples who want and need some privacy for their loving. With only one girl to handle the 'stags,' you can rent out your other four bedrooms to the 'hot-pillow' trade. Once the word gets around, you ought to be able to rent each bedroom three or four times a night."

Excited by the moneymaking potential of Miss May's suggestion, I hurriedly sought out my bachelor friend. I was certain he, as one of the town's busiest studs, could offer expert advice on the feasibility of opening a house of assignation in Bowling Green. To say that he was delighted with the plan would be an understatement. He was ecstatic. No doubt recalling uncomfortable, acrobatic couplings in the back seats of cars, furtive trystings in hotel rooms, and nerve-wracking, risky embraces in the bedrooms of absent husbands, he immediately endorsed the idea.

"Why didn't I think of it!" he exclaimed. "That's what this town has needed for a long time—a place where a guy and a gal can make out in style without worrying about being seen or being shot by the Old Man. Pauline, you've got a gold mine in those empty bedrooms!"

Heartened by my friend's enthusiasm, I could scarcely wait until midafternoon, when I knew the restaurant trade would be light, to look up Joyce, the refugee call girl from Louisville. Back in those days, when it was a town of about 18,000 population, Bowling Green didn't have too many restaurants. But Joyce worked as a waitress in one of the town's better beaneries, an establishment that catered to downtown businessmen and their employees during the day and to the traveling salesman type of transient clientele in the evenings.

Except for a cashier and four or five waitresses sitting at a rear table sipping coffee and idly gossiping, the big dining room was empty when I hurried into the restaurant in my search for professional talent. When I settled down at a table in a remote corner of the room, one of the waitresses—a middle-aged, sway-backed veteran of many, many weary moons of hashslinging—shuffled over and handed me a menu. I ordered a coke and a sandwich I really didn't want, figuring that for the sake of appearances I'd better be a paying customer. When my order arrived, I asked if Joyce was working.

"Yeh, she's here," the waitress replied, jerking her head in the direction of the table where her companions-in-labor were resting during the break in their daily chores.

"Please tell her I'd like to chat with her. Tell her a friend down in Clarksville asked me to drop in and say hello."

Seconds later a slender, dark-haired girl sat down at my table and eyed me suspiciously. Despite her unstylish, work-stained white uniform, it was immediately apparent that Joyce was an extremely attractive girl in her early twenties with a shape that was being wasted in such drab surroundings.

"M-m-m-mary s-s-said you w-w-wanted to t-t-talk with m-m-me," the girl stammered, her speech impediment doubtlessly worsened by frantic wondering if something from her past had caught up with her.

I smiled and asked her to have a cup of coffee or a coke. She declined with an impatient shake of her head, still staring at me with big, questioning brown eyes. "W-w-what's this a-a-about a f-f-friend in C-c-clarksville?"

"Really, it's nothing serious," I assured her. "It's just that I happened to telephone Miss May the other day, and she mentioned that Ruth wanted me to look you up and give you her regards."

Joyce was really wide-eyed with disbelief now. Obviously, she couldn't picture me as even remotely involved with the strange world in which she and Miss May and Ruth operated.

"H-h-how c-c-come you know M-m-miss M-m-may and Ruth?" she demanded.

"Miss May is a friend of mine, and I met Ruth during a visit to the house on College Street last summer," I said, adding just enough recollections to convince Joyce I knew what I was talking about.

At last Joyce relaxed. She sighed with relief and lighted a cigarette. "H-h-honey," she said through a cloud of smoke, "you s-s-sure had m-m-me fooled. I'd n-n-never take you for a h-h-hooker."

Again, as I had been forced to do on several occasions since making the acquaintance of Miss May, I found myself explaining self-consciously that unfortunately I had neither the beauty nor form for a career as a sexpot. But, I quickly added, I was starting out as a madam. In fact, I said, I was just about ready to open a house in Bowling Green.

Joyce looked at me long and hard. "I g-g-guess you know s-s-something about m-my b-b-background."

I admitted that I did. "Miss May told me you got a rough deal in Louisville."

"I s-s-suppose you want m-me to c-c-come to work for y-you?"

It was ironic. During our conversation, I had been trying desperately to figure out how to diplomatically ask Joyce if she wanted to work in my house. And now she was the one who popped the vital question. Speechless at this unexpected turn of events, I could only nod in agreement.

"W-w-well," Joyce said thoughtfully, "it would s-s-sure beat t-t-this d-d-damned job. S-s-suppose I take a l-l-look at your p-p-place, and then g-g-give you an answer."

I agreed, gave Joyce my address, and, after getting her promise to visit me after work that evening, I departed. A few hours later she showed up at my place on Smallhouse Road. I scarcely recognized her as she took off her coat and hat. Her shoulder-length black hair was carefully groomed. Her makeup was in the best of taste. And a smartly styled blue silk gown really accentuated the positive. Joyce, the somewhat bedraggled scullery maid, had blossomed magically into an enchantingly lovely butterfly. Even her stammering seemed to add a heart-wrenching quality to her charm.

After a studious tour of the house, during which Joyce inspected every nook and cranny with the practiced air of a woman who knows what she's doing, we settled down in the parlor for a long, business-like talk. I told Joyce of my plans to run a house of assignation—at least until I could recruit three or four more top-quality girls—and we discussed and agreed upon a schedule of fees and on my cut of the proceeds. In turn, Joyce told me of her background. She, too, had come from a respectable middle-class family in a town in Eastern Kentucky. Her life had been uneventful until, after graduating from high school and going to work in an office, she fell in love with her boss. They had an affair, and Joyce became pregnant. Her outraged parents threw her out, and she went to work for another, more under-standing family in town until she had her baby. When the baby died shortly after birth, she left town in disgrace and settled in Louisville. There, she worked in an office during the day and made a good living as a call girl at night until the law caught up with her and she came to work in the Bowling Green restaurant.

It was nearly midnight when Joyce finished her recollections—a story which, in the years ahead, I would hear in one form or another hundreds of times. But hearing it for the first time, I was deeply touched. I also was elated, for Joyce had agreed to come to work for me after giving the restaurant a week's notice—a courtesy which I insisted upon because I didn't want to unnecessarily attract the ire of any of the town's businessmen. At last, I gloated after Joyce left, I had the beginning of my stable of girls. In one more week I'd be ready for business.

Actually it was nearly two weeks before the house opened. There were all sorts of last-minute details to tend to, not the least of which was the task of quietly spreading the word that Pauline's house would be open for business right after Armistice Day. For the most part, my friends took care of this word-of-mouth publicity, reporting the news to bellhops and desk clerks, taxi drivers, barbers and waiters, and other key people in such strategic places as the big tobacco market. In addition, my bachelor friend joyously passed on the welcome word that Pauline would be renting out rooms to passion-bent couples, and I visited a carnival, in town for a one-week stay, to inform the owners of the rides and concessions of the grand opening of Bowling Green's new whorehouse. They not only promised to show up the first night, but vowed they'd spread the word along the countryside as the carnival continued its travels.

The rollicking Armistice Day housewarming, of course, produced still more interest in my Smallhouse Road enterprise. By the following evening, when I first opened for business, the existence of the new whorehouse in the staid environs of Bowling Green was the worst-kept secret in Kentucky. My well-intentioned friends had succeeded in overpublicizing my house. News of the opening night might just as well have been printed in big headlines on page one of the town's newspaper. Even before my first customers arrived, the whole town was buzzing, and much of the talk was anything but friendly.

Nevertheless, opening night passed without incident. With the tobacco market in full swing, drawing well-heeled buyers and growers from a wide area, my house was packed with eager customers—lonely "stags" shopping for a date and amorous couples seeking a room for their romantic rendezvous. Succeeding nights were equally hectic. My bedrooms should have had revolving doors to handle the couples trade. It was a slow night when I failed to rent each of the rooms at least four or five times. And Joyce, as the only girl-in-residence, had customers lined up night after night, impatiently waiting their turn in the saddle. In fact, business was so good that I had to pitch in from time to time, servicing the tricks who were in too big a hurry to wait for Joyce's more delectable brand of goodies.

With the house on Smallhouse Road erupting into a nightly chaos reminiscent of dollar day in Macy's basement, my guardian angel must have stepped in to ease the strain. I had been open about a week when the doorbell rang one afternoon. Deciding with exasperation that some early-bird trick was trying to beat the evening's rush traffic, I threw open the door. Standing there, suitcase in hand, was Ruth, the girl from Miss May's house who had put me in touch with Joyce.

"I've come to work for you," Ruth announced as she followed me into the parlor. "I got a note from Joyce the other day, saying you were swamped, so I decided maybe I could help out."

"You're a gift from heaven," I exclaimed. "But I don't want Miss May to think I'm stealing one of her girls."

Ruth quickly assured me that she had discussed the move with the Clarksville madam, and Miss May was pleased to have her offer to help me.

"I've been with Miss May about a year, and I'm kind of old hat down there," she explained. "Miss May likes to keep her customers happy with new faces, so I guess it was time for me to move on."

Ruth may have been "old hat" in Clarksville, but, I realized, in Bowling Green she'd be just about the biggest sex discovery since Adam and Eve nibbled at that pesky old apple. A divorcee with long, platinum-blond hair, Ruth at twenty-five was a talented prostitute who knew all the arts of her profession. In addition she was blessed with a sensational figure and a warm, friendly manner that seemed to win the hearts of all her tricks. Her main hangup was a nagging fear that someday she'd be discovered in a bawdy house by her brother, a prudish man who worked as a reporter for a Northern Kentucky newspaper.

"Every time the bell rings I get jittery, figuring he might walk in," she said. "If he found me working as a prostitute, he'd kill me."

During the months she worked for me, Ruth's brother never made an appearance. But she never took any chances. She never entered the parlor or living room without first peeking cautiously around a corner to make sure he wasn't mingling with the other customers. Actually, I guess Ruth's bogeyman brother never did discover her dark secret. After leaving my house she worked for awhile as a call girl in Louisville and then fell in love with one of her customers. They were married and had several children. The last time I heard from her, Ruth was a respectable matron in a western city. At the time I had a good laugh, thinking how the onetime star attraction of my stable could tell some tales that would shock the girdles off the stodgy old hens at the weekly women's club luncheon.

With Ruth adding a glamorous new piece of merchandise to the house, our "dating" trade was busier than ever. However, it couldn't compare as a moneymaker with my flourishing room-renting business. Never before had I realized just how many of the good citizens of Bowling Green were indulging in affairs on the sly. When I began my house of assignation, I was certain that most of my room-renting trade would be among the unmarried set—unattached men and women seeking privacy for their romantic grapplings. How wrong I was! Most of the couples featured a married woman with either one of the town's bachelors or another woman's husband. Before long I had quite an extensive dossier on who was screwing whom, and, to put it mildly, it was an impressive who's who that included some of the county's pillars of respectability.

When I began the hourly room-renting business, I established my rates—$2 per hour per room or $10 for the entire night—on the theory that the average male seldom lets such mundane matters as the pocketbook interfere with his pursuit of promising pieces of tail. The rates were high for those times, but I reasoned that it would only be the more affluent gentry who could afford to play around. It was, as my bachelor friend predicted, a gold mine—a bonanza which I didn't have to split with the girls because their talents were in no way involved in this side of the business.

Primarily because of this lucrative catering to dallying couples, my once-depleted savings account had mushroomed at the end of my first five weeks as a madam. Even the president of the bank—an austere man who always had been icily aloof during my years of genteel, good-girl poverty—began to nod and smile politely at me when I entered his establishment to deposit my nightly whorehouse receipts.

However, storm clouds were beginning to gather over my prospering domain. Some of the women who indulged in rented-room romancing made no attempt to hide the fact they were jealous of my girls, making catty remarks that infuriated Joyce and Ruth. Sometimes my house echoed with the outcries of lovers' quarrels. And, far more serious, the gallivanting couples frequently would recognize other customers of the house. Before long all manner of juicy gossip was spreading through town.

After six weeks of hot-pillow traffic, one of my friends in the sheriff's department paid a visit to the house on Smallhouse Road. He warned me that the gossip was stirring up considerable ill feeling in town against my house.

"You don't have to rely on these cheating husbands and wives to make a good living," he said. "Most of those dames are nothing but married whores. They've got big, gossipy mouths, and that spells big trouble for you. Put a stop to this couples trade. All you need for a good business is one or two more clean, sexy prostitutes like Joyce and Ruth."

Deep down I knew that my lawman friend was right, but I was reluctant to kill the goose that was laying all those beautiful golden dollar bills.

A few nights later the first of two near-disasters changed my mind in a hurry.

It started out as a routine busy night, with the jukebox grinding out the hit songs of the day at a quarter per tune and the upstairs traffic keeping up a steady, moneymaking pace that added up to a lot prettier music in my ears. Indeed, all was right with the private world of Pauline Tabor until one of our local businessmen entered the scene with his young, nubile secretary on his arm.

The businessman and his lady love were frequent customers, a fact which had puzzled me because the old boy only a year or so earlier had married a much younger woman who seemed admirably equipped to cope with her husband's over-age appetites. However, questioning the motivations of philandering husbands was not my business. I showed them to a room, made sure everything was in order, and left them to their fun and games.

I had scarcely settled down in my favorite parlor rocking chair when the doorbell rang again. Answering the summons, I ushered another couple into the house. It wasn't until we reached the parlor that I recognized, with a sense of helpless panic, who the newly arrived guests were. The man was a well-known farmer—a vigorous, thickset gent with a triggerlike temper and a reputation for straying from his browbeaten wife's bed. And this time his female companion was the young, discontented wife of the businessman who at that very moment was romping on the mattress with his secretary.

"Dear God, what do I do now?" I asked myself, desperately wishing I could be inspired by some divine wisdom. The best I could come up with was to hopefully advise them that all my rooms were in use at the time. Perhaps, I thought, they'll decide to leave. It was a futile hope.

The wayward businessman's errant wife glanced at her watch and, quite possibly determined to enjoy a moment of revenge for her mate's neglect, announced quite firmly that she and her companion in sin would wait until a room was available.

What does a madam do in such a crisis? Well, I'll tell you one thing—you don't tell the promiscuous wife and her boyfriend that they'll have to leave because her husband and his girlfriend are having a party upstairs. As for me, I just prayed that never the twain would meet. My prayers were answered. Minutes later one of the bedrooms was vacated by a couple who apparently had just dropped in for a quickie. I hurriedly changed the linen, did a fast bit of straightening up, and rushed my problem couple into the privacy of a room only two doors distant from the other half of this weird domestic quadrangle. I returned downstairs to pace the floor, thinking of all the horrible happenings that could occur if the Mr. should chance upon his Mrs., or vice versa. I almost burst into tears with relief when, about an hour later, the businessman and his secretary came into the parlor, settled their bill, and quietly departed, leaving the unsuspecting wife blissfully frolicking in her upstairs loveland.

*A madam builds a dream house*    83

I was still shaken by this harrowing experience when the second near-disaster occurred the very next night. One of the town's thirtyish matrons—a pleasingly plump wife of a professor at Bowling Green's Western Kentucky University—came calling in the company of a handsome, well-known tobacco auctioneer. Judging by their giggling, playful mauling of each other as they followed me to their bedroom, both had been partaking of the grape before ending up on my doorstep. But as long as they weren't obnoxious, I had no cause to turn them away.

Everything was in good order in the house for an hour or more. Then the serenity was shattered by a woman's scream and a terrible thump-thump-thumping on the stairs. I ran into the hall to discover the professor's wife sprawled in a heap at the bottom of the stairs. She was unconscious. Her dress was ripped and crumpled up above her waist, disclosing to one and all that the campus matron had neglected to replace a vital part of her wardrobe. Looking down at the frightful scene from the top of the stairway was the auctioneer, his face ashen, his eyes bulging with fright.

"My God," he croaked hoarsely. "Is she all right? She started downstairs and tripped or lost her balance and fell. I tried to catch her but I couldn't."

"Don't stand there blabbing like an idiot," I shouted, thinking of the scandal that would erupt if the woman was badly injured or dead. "Get your ass down here and help me carry her into my room."

By that time the uproar had aroused the entire house. Joyce and Ruth, clad hastily in robes, rushed to the scene to help the auctioneer and me carry the still-unconscious woman to the big bed in my downstairs bedroom. They were joined by a cluster of curious customers in various stages of undress. Luckily, one of the customers was a doctor. He soon revived the woman and, after as thorough an examination as possible under such conditions, he announced that, except for a few bumps, scrapes, and bruises, she apparently had miraculously escaped injury.

"But you'd better check with your own physician," he advised the now-sober matron. "That was a nasty fall."

"God forbid," the woman muttered, shaken by the thought of even a hint of her mishap passing beyond the walls of my house. Then turning to the object of her recent affections, she said, "Let's get out of here. I've got to get home and pull myself together before the Old Man gets back."

Thus, a second potential disaster faded into the night. But, I told myself after things settled down, the third time might not be so lucky. I decided to put an end to my couples trade, no matter how profitable it was. From then on I never operated a house of assignation.

Fortunately for the income of the house on Smallhouse Road, Joyce and Ruth were able to recruit two more young, attractive prostitutes with whom they once had worked—a redhead from Nashville and an auburn-haired girl from Louisville. Later I added a fifth girl to the stable, a Bowling Green divorcee who sold me on the idea of hiring her as a part-time prostitute to work in the house on our busy Friday and Saturday nights.

With this staff of competent professionals, my house continued to prosper. In fact, business was so good that I paid little attention to a rising tide of antivice sentiment in the town. Ministers began thundering about vice. Newspaper editorials and letters to the editor waxed indignant about the spread of vice in Bowling Green. I even received threatening phone calls vowing dire consequences if I continued to operate my house. I just shrugged off such harbingers of doom, forgetting the warning about the Holy Joes voiced to me by the Clarksville police chief months before.

I had been operating on Smallhouse Road almost a year when the blow fell. A law-enforcement friend called on me one day with the bad news that the county attorney, a real rough cob of a man, was determined to put me out of business. He was, in fact, getting ready to haul me in front of the next session of the grand jury as the main target in a probe of organized vice in Bowling Green.

"What should I do?" I asked, fearful of the prospect.

"There's only one thing to do," my friend replied. "Close down and get out of town—at least until the trouble blows over."

"How long will that be?"

My friend shrugged. "Who knows? A year or two maybe. Certainly not until we get another county attorney."

I was stunned. It was bad enough to be an outcast. But the thought of being forced to flee from my home town seemed almost as intolerable as the idea of closing down my now firmly established, moneymaking house. I had no choice, however. Reluctantly, I said good-by to my girls, moved my furnishings into storage, and locked the doors of the empty house on Smallhouse Road. My first venture as a madam had come to a sudden end. It was the first of several painful ordeals that I still had to face over a period of years before finally achieving my "dream house."

With no house and no girls and the law breathing down my neck, I had to make a quick decision about my future. Of one thing I was sure. Somewhere, somehow, I was going to open another house. I had a few thousand dollars in the bank—not as much as I should have saved because I had spent money recklessly, certain that my gold mine on Smallhouse Road would never fail me. Now it was too late to fret about past extravagances. I had to get back in business before my small nest egg vanished.

I went to a trusted friend for advice. He thought it would be wise for me to get out of Kentucky. "I've got several good friends—very influential men—in Indiana up around Columbus," he said. "Why don't you go up and talk with them. Perhaps you can develop something there."

A trip to Indiana and visits with my newly established Hoosier contacts convinced me that Columbus could be a lucrative location for a high-class house. I went house-hunting, finally locating a large unfurnished place for rent on a lonely country road. It seemed ideal for what I had in mind—four bedrooms and plenty of privacy—so I quickly closed the deal with the owners, a middle-aged couple who lived in Columbus. It wasn't until later that I learned that my nearest neighbor was a boys' club camp, about a half-mile on down the road. It was this camp which ultimately proved to be my downfall.

This time, after having my furniture moved from Bowling Green to my Indiana house, I had no problems recruiting girls. My year on

Smallhouse Road had made me a considerably wiser, tougher female in dealing with such problems. I had heard that Indianapolis was a wide-open city with an abundance of top-quality professionals. No longer caring about what other people might think, I drove up to Indiana's capital city, contacted cab drivers and bellhops in the better hotels, bluntly told them I was a madam looking for some high-class prostitutes. I tipped my carefully selected band of recruiters, gave them my address and phone number, and asked them to have any worthwhile prospects get in touch with me. Within a week, I had a stable of five lovely girls—three full-timers and two part-timers who came down from Indianapolis for the weekend trade.

Business in Columbus proved to be just as good as in Bowling Green. And even though Indianapolis was some fifty miles away, the trade during the big 500-mile Memorial Day Race festivities was beyond belief. I guess we had customers from just about every state during race week, and the girls practically worked around the clock to handle the traffic in our house.

Unhappily, as I later learned, our booming day-and-night race week business proved to be our Waterloo. A county judge, driving out to the boys' camp one day late in May, noticed a number of cars— many from out of the state—parked in the large yard around my farmhouse. Puzzled by evidence of such heavy traffic on an isolated country road, he made some inquiries and soon discovered that a whorehouse was flourishing right next to the boys' club camp, his favorite community project.

Early in June the outraged judge went into action, calling upon state police for help because he evidently mistrusted the local law-enforcement agencies. I happened to be in town that day, buying supplies for the approaching weekend, when five customers came knocking at the door. My girls suspected nothing. The men acted like any group of tricks looking for a good time. They bought drinks at my small bar, played the jukebox, danced, and kidded with the girls. Then after a frank discussion of prices and what they could expect for their money, one of the "tricks" flashed a state police badge, told the girls they were under arrest, and demanded to "see the madam."

"She's gone to town to do some shopping," one of my girls replied.

"Well," the state trooper in charge of the raid said, "we'll just wait here until she gets back, and then we'll all take a ride."

I returned an hour or so later, my car packed with groceries and my head filled with plans for a busy weekend. I noticed two cars parked in the yard, but nothing seemed amiss. It wasn't until I walked into the living room and saw my three girls huddled on a sofa with five strange men hovering about the room that I realized I had trouble on my hands. At first I thought it was a holdup, because we'd had no problems with police during six months of operation.

One of the strangers quickly straightened me out on that score. He showed me his badge and asked, "Are you Pauline Tabor, the operator of this establishment?" I admitted that I was. "You're under arrest," the stranger snapped. Without any further conversation, the men herded us into their cars and I found myself headed for jail for the first time.

At the courthouse, they booked us, took our fingerprints and "mug shots," relieved us of all possessions including our purses, and locked us in small, gloomy cells equipped only with hard, narrow bunks and stained, odiferous porcelain commodes.

It was late afternoon when they led us from our cells into a courtroom. An elderly black-robed judge—the same one, I was told, who had spotted my busy house—glowered down at us from the bench. The girls, he announced, were charged with vagrancy and soliciting. The penalty, a $100 fine or 30 days in jail. He cleared his throat and turned his cold stare on me. I was charged with operating a house of prostitution and selling liquor without a license. The penalty, a $500 fine or six months in jail.

If this had happened a year earlier, I would have been both terrified and shamed. Quite possibly, after such a degrading experience, I would have abandoned my new profession. Now, though, I was able to accept the raid and my arrest and jailing as one of the hazards of the business. I had no time for such finer sensibilities as humiliation. I was too occupied trying to figure how I could get my girls and myself out of this predicament.

Fortunately, I was carrying a fair-sized bankroll when I went shopping. I asked the judge for my purse, and it was brought to me from wherever it had been placed by police for safekeeping. I counted my cash. I had $337 and some small change, enough to pay the fines for my three girls. They, however, had only a few dollars in their purses. Like most prostitutes, they kept their earnings carefully hidden in their rooms until they had a chance to bank it or get it safely to whatever outside source they used to handle their finances.

With their fines paid, the police agreed to drive the girls out to the house so they could pack their possessions and get out of town. They left, promising to return quickly with money to repay my $300, and maybe even enough for my entire $500 fine. An hour later, they were back at the jail to hysterically report that someone had looted the house during our absence.

"It's terrible," one girl cried. "The whole place has been ripped apart. All our money is gone."

That left me sitting in a jail cell in Columbus with less than $40 in available cash. My savings were stashed away in Bowling Green, where I had continued to send most of my earnings each week. Wearily, I asked for permission to use a telephone. I made a collect call to a friend down home, explained my dilemma, and asked for a loan until I could get to my savings. My friend agreed to wire the money as soon as the bank opened the next day.

It was a long, sleepless, miserable night in the jail cell. By the following noon when the money finally arrived, I was pacing back and forth like a caged animal. I quickly paid my fine and hitched a ride with a sheriff's deputy out to the house. My car was still there, but all the groceries had been stolen. And the girls had told a true story. The house was a shambles. Everything had been turned upside down and ripped apart in a frantic search for money.

For the first time in several years, I was ready to give up. Somehow, after losing a second prospering house, the struggle to survive seemed to be too painful. But after a few hours of wallowing in self-pity amid the ruins, I pulled myself together and got busy. Within a week I had disposed of my robbery-scarred furnishings at a considerable loss. I locked up the house and headed my car back toward Kentucky. I'd had enough of the famous Hoosier hospitality to last me a lifetime!

By midsummer of 1935 I was back in business again, this time as the madam of a call house in Louisville. Originally I had planned to open another brothel, but after talking with several prominent Louisville madams including Mary Hanson and Hannah Ames, I decided a high-class call house would be a better, safer deal in a large city.

A call house operation and a whorehouse, I soon discovered, have little in common except for the basic commodity—sex. In a whorehouse, the customers come to you. The madam is able to personally supervise the entire operation, from screening customers to setting fees and handling the money. In a call house, however, the madam rarely has any contact with customers except the telephone. She has a stable of girls and, just as in a brothel, provides their living quarters and food. But the tricks never come to the house.

Through her contacts the madam places her phone number with strategic sources throughout the city. The prospective customers telephone, disclose the kind of service they want, agree to a price, and set up their own rendezvous site. With the preliminary business completed, the madam dispatches one of her girls on the date. From that point on, the girl is on her own. She has to collect the money and, if special or additional services are requested, haggle over a new fee. Equally important, the girl has the serious responsibility, after meeting her date, to size him up quickly and decide whether he is safe and not some dangerous freak or a vice squad detective out to bust an unsuspecting prostitute. In brief, except for recruiting her girls, establishing an efficient network of contacts, and handling the telephone business dealings, a madam has little personal control over call house operations.

Today, I know, the call system is far more efficiently organized and operated. If I were to go into business again, I'm sure it would be a call house. But back in those days in Louisville, I found many irksome drawbacks in the operation. I had a pleasant, ground-floor, three-bedroom apartment on Brook Street. I had a stable of three attractive, capable girls, and I had established a reliable system of contacts. But I wasn't satisfied, even though there were far fewer dangers of entanglement with the law.

The main problem, I guess, is that I was accustomed to bossing my operations with a tight rein. In a call house this was impossible. Also, the business was unpredictable. Frequently the girls ended up on wild goose chases after a telephone call. Sometimes there would be no one at the agreed-upon rendezvous, and occasionally a customer, after seeing his date, would reject her. This resulted in wasted money on cab fares and lost time that might have been devoted to a paying customer.

There were other financial shortcomings. I learned that men are much more generous and spend much more money on extra services when they go to a whorehouse. Perhaps it is the male ego that generates a desire to show off when surrounded by other men and women —a desire to impress the madam of the house as a big-time spender. Somehow, though, most men lose this freewheeling attitude when they make an impersonal telephone date and eventually have a strange girl knocking at their door. Then the whole affair shapes up as a business deal. The customer gets the merchandise, pays for it, uses it, and sends it on its way back to wherever it came from. No sentimental encores, no grateful gratuities. In fact, my girls sometimes would return in tears, reporting that customers had refused to pay the agreed-upon price, and they had accepted the cut rate rather than end up with nothing.

However, the biggest danger in those days—and today, too, I'm sure—was faced by the call girl. In a brothel, a madam instinctively develops a sense of suspicion which helps weed out the weird, sexually psychotic male. As I learned to my regret in later years, some mentally disturbed men slip by despite all of a madam's precautions. Several times during my years in Bowling Green, my girls barely escaped death because I failed to spot danger signals or respond to hunches.

Among the call girls, however, they had no madam to personally screen the customers beyond whatever questions she could ask over the telephone. Thus, it was up to the call girl, when she first met the customer at the prearranged trysting place, to rely on her judgment as to whether a trick was safe or not. And frequently the girl's desire for money overcame any doubts she may have had about the man's motives or mental stability.

On two occasions my Louisville call girls were badly beaten, not by sadists or other perverts but by sexual psychopaths driven by an insane hatred of women. Only the screams of these girls, which roused other guests in the hotels where the trysts were being held, saved their lives. After these incidents, I never accepted a customer via telephone unless he could identify a contact whom I trusted. Even then I would double-check with my contact to verify the identity and reputation of a customer.

The sex psychotic, of course, is a menace not just to prostitutes but to all society. Some are driven by an insane religious fanaticism to "cleanse" the world by punishing, or slaying, so-called women of loose morals. Certainly the annals of violent crime are filled with such cases, and this particular type of psycho is the secret dread of almost every woman involved in the sex-peddling business.

The question, of course, arises: just how can a madam or a call girl —or, for that matter, even a psychiatric expert—spot such sex psychos in advance? Well, there are such warning signs as a wild, fanatical look; nervous, peculiar actions; or a man's reputation as an oddball. But the answer, as far as I am concerned, is that there is no foolproof way to detect a sex psycho in advance. My decision, and I'm sure that many times it was unfair, was based on a hunch or an inner feeling I'd sometimes get that there was something dangerously off-beat about a customer. Whenever I would have such a hunch or feeling, I would turn the customer away even though the trick may have been perfectly normal. Nevertheless, I learned to always follow my hunch, and very few times did I have cause to regret it.

However, my hunches could not be of much help during my years as a call house operator in Louisville. Even with my precautionary double-checking, I was always fearful for a girl's safety when I dispatched her on a date in Louisville. This, I'm sure, is another reason why I disliked and distrusted the call girl system in those days. However, despite such hazards, there is no denying that my basic disenchantment with the call girl business back in those years was financial, as well as the fact that it was an operation I couldn't personally control at all times.

Beset with such uncertainties and operating as a relatively small fish in a big-city pond, my Louisville business was far from prosperous. But it limped along and even enjoyed brief boom periods, especially at Derby time. Looking back at that period of my life, I suppose I might have remained in Louisville and eventually expanded and prospered if it hadn't been for the Big Flood.

The rains came in late January and early February of 1937. Lord, how it rained—nearly thirteen inches in just one twenty-four-hour period, as I recall. The Ohio River rose steadily and, as the deluge continued, it began to overflow its banks. Quickly the water spread through the low river-front section of Louisville where my apartment was situated. Before I realized the extent of the danger, the area was flooded, with swirling, muddy water rising up to the level of my front door. By nightfall I found myself marooned in the apartment with two of my girls and a gambler friend who had dropped in for a visit earlier in the day.

Resigned to whatever fate was in store for us, we decided not to worry about the water which already was beginning to seep into the apartment. We had just settled down for a game of pinochle when we heard a loud hallooing echoing from the flooded street in front of the apartment. I looked out a front window. At my steps in a small motorboat, holding a lantern, was a lawyer friend of my family.

"Are you okay, Pauline?" he shouted.

"Hell, yes, I'm okay, if you can call sitting in the middle of a river okay," I replied through the open window. "But what the hell are you doing here?"

My lawyer friend explained that he had been in Louisville on business and had received a frantic phone call from my mother wanting to know if I was safe, for the radio was reporting terrible floods along the Ohio.

"Your phone is out, so I had to rent a boat to get down here and check on you," he said.

"Well, tell Mother I'm safe, along with three other people in the apartment."

My friend waved encouragement. "I'll send back some help to get you folks out," he shouted as his small boat disappeared into the night.

Our rescuer arrived a few hours later—a man poling a large raft up to my doorstep. With nothing but the clothes on our backs, we climbed aboard for a lurching ride along flooded streets to an apartment building on a high ground at Second and Oak Streets, where one of my friends lived. We spent nine uncomfortable days and nights in this friend's apartment before the floodwaters receded and the city began struggling back to normalcy.

I returned to my apartment with a dark sense of foreboding. Sure enough, the apartment was a soggy mess. Getting it back in shape would be a hard and costly task. Complicating this problem, the newspapers were headlining dire warnings that health officials feared the outbreak of a typhoid epidemic as a grim aftermath of the flood. The headlines stirred chilling memories of my nearly fatal encounter with typhoid fever. I looked at the chaos of my apartment, remembered the terrors of typhoid, and decided impulsively that the time had come for Pauline Tabor to return home.

There were no traces left of the once starry-eyed matron filled with vague ambitions and prone to foolish blunderings when I returned to Bowling Green in the spring of 1937. I had served a long, tough apprenticeship in the school of hard knocks. I had encountered heartbreaking setbacks, but I had survived, becoming an experienced, professional madam wise in the ways of the flesh and the devil.

Despite my past failures, I had no intention of retiring and trying to live down with a lifetime of repentance my reputation in Bowling Green as a fallen woman. With my hated adversary, the crusading county attorney, no longer in office, I renewed old contacts and made some new ones, and—using my modest savings—I opened a three-bedroom house at 1st and Center streets with a stable of three girls.

This was the beginning for me of nearly thirty-three years of successful operations as a madam in Bowling Green. Unlike my first bungling venture in sin in my home town, my latter-day houses prospered with only occasional harassment from the law and a few bitter blows at the hands of Dame Fortune.

My return to business was blessed with instant success. Within a year the place at 1st and Center was too small to handle my burgeoning trade. I went shopping in the spring of 1939 and purchased a lovely eight-bedroom colonial house on five acres of land outside Bowling Green. This, I was sure, was my "dream house."

During the next several booming, exciting years my colonial country house became a palace of pleasure with widespread fame. My bank account grew steadily, and it seemed I was set for life. But once more Fate stepped in with a knockout punch. My beautiful house was destroyed in a fire touched off by a household accident. Again I was a madam without a house.

Finally, after months of gadding aimlessly about the country, I returned to business in April of 1944, opening my last house in Bowling Green. It was this establishment at 627 Clay Street that became my true "dream house." It was here during the next quarter-century that I finally was to realize the full potential of being a madam, a potential I had only dreamed about when I returned from my visit with Miss May so many years before.

*Girls, girls, girls!*

# Girls, girls, girls!

If there is such a thing as a public image of a madam, I'm certain it must be a wholly unpleasant caricature of a tough, grasping, cold-hearted woman with about as much human warmth and sentimentality as a statistics-incubating computer at the Census Bureau.

I'll plead guilty of partially conforming to such an image. By the time I returned to Bowling Green after my ill-fated ventures in Indiana and Louisville, I had learned that a madam has to be tough to survive. I didn't smoke and I rarely took a drink, but I could, and did, cuss like a dock worker when the occasion arose. I'd had my "baptism" as a jailbird. I was thoroughly indoctrinated in the hard-boiled ins and outs of brothel-keeping. And with my girth expanded to the 240-pound proportions of a professional football tackle, I also was quite capable of taking over the job of bouncer when a customer became obnoxiously unruly.

To compound such felonies against society's code of ladylike behavior, I was mercenary. I was a sex merchant for the same basic reason that motivates other people to peddle pills, groceries, clothing, toys, cars, and all manner of other wares—to make money and acquire the better things of life. I believe this materialistic instinct is deeply ingrained in most women. In fact, I've often suspected that a lot of a married female's animosity toward prostitution is generated by jealousy. She simply can't stand the thought that some women are profiting on a commodity she gives away. In any event, I was as commercial as the devil himself when it came to sex. From my cynical viewpoint, rooted in a constantly growing disillusionment with mankind's furtive sexual attitudes, love was just a four-letter word, and it definitely wasn't spelled with an "L."

Yes, I'll cop a plea on all of these alleged shortcomings. But there's one thing, with all my faults, that I wasn't. I wasn't cold-hearted, and I wasn't devoid of warmth and sentimentality. Try as I might to keep these human qualities in check when the practical objective of making a buck was concerned, I was never completely successful in having my head rule over my heart.

After a long lifetime as a madam, I'm convinced that compassion and sentimentality are frequently found in overabundance in a whorehouse. The reason for this strange mixture of hardheaded commercialism and softhearted emotionalism is simple. Beyond the moneymaking process, there is no glamour in the merchandising of sex. A madam and her girls are cut off from the normal society in which they once moved, exiles in a lonely little world bounded by the walls of their house. As a result, they tend to "adopt" each other as a family. Although they indulge in gossip, petty jealousies, and quarrels, they develop a sense of loyalty and concern for one another's problems—a tolerant acceptance of human faults which sometimes even extends to the customers they serve.

Today, in my retirement, I am linked with the past by a host of sentimental memories of my girls. Some of these memories are sad. Others—like classic fairy tales—have happily-ever-after endings. And many still sparkle with bawdy humor. I recall, for example, one frantic night in my colonial country house when Rosie, an "apprentice" in the business, really earned her status as a professional lady of the evening.

It was during the early days of World War II. Across the land, military installations were jammed with young men in uniform—newly converted civilians, far from home and loved ones, with a singular devotion to the pursuit of carnal companionship before they went marching off to war. Kentucky's Camp Campbell was one of these wartime posts, and it provided me with a never-slackening flow of G.I.s eager to sample the pleasures of my house. At times, particularly right after the army's payday, this military traffic, when added to my usually busy civilian trade, was almost more than my stable of six girls could handle.

On one of these hectic weekend nights after payday, when the tricks had passed steadily through the house hour after hour like an endless, impatient chow line, I found myself without enough girls to go around. It was after two in the morning and all but one of my girls had bedded down with all-night customers when three soldiers arrived. With their amorous ambitions magnified by an evening of beer guzzling and their bankrolls still in a healthy state, they were horny and raring to go and determined to enjoy the luxury of $25 all-night dates.

"Well, fellows," I said, "it's awfully late. Most of my girls are tied up for the rest of the night, but I'll see what I can do." Slowly, I climbed the stairs to assess the situation. I hated the thought of turning away a three-man $75 deal. Hopefully, I thought that perhaps the energies of a couple of the earlier all-nighters would have faded, and I'd find two or three of the girls relaxing in a small, private upstairs sitting room where they sometimes retreated for a cigarette when their overnight tricks were sleeping after an especially arduous session of love-making. Unfortunately, this night's tricks were of a hardier breed. Rosie was the only girl in the room—the only one of my stable who didn't have an all-nighter.

Rosie was a newcomer to the business. She had come to my house in search of a job about a month earlier, an attractive twenty-one-year-old brunette from a small town south of Bowling Green. She told me that after completing two years of college, she had run out of money. However, she was determined to finish her education and get a teaching degree, and she decided that a temporary career as a prostitute was the most practical, quickest solution for her financial difficulties. When I protested that she had no experience in our tough trade, she overcame my objections by cooly pointing out: "I've been giving it away for pleasure since I was in high school, so I might as well get paid for it for awhile."

As is so often the case with girls who become prostitutes with a definite, worthwhile ambition in mind, Rosie was a quick and willing learner. Thus, when I hurried into the room that night, she instantly realized that an emergency had arisen.

"What's the problem?" she asked. "Have we got a late customer panting in the parlor?"

"One customer!" I exclaimed. "We've got three beer-soaked G.I.s down there, and they don't just want their ashes hauled. They want all-night parties."

Rosie grinned impishly. "I'll take them on."

"Honey, those boys aren't looking for a gang bang. Each wants a girl for his very own."

"Leave it to me," Rosie said. "When I get through with them, they won't know the difference. Just tell them there's only one girl available right now, so two of them will have to wait until two more girls are free. Then, turn the lights in the parlor down low, give 'em a couple more beers, and I'll handle the rest of the details."

I couldn't see how Rosie planned to turn herself into three girls. But with a $75 stud fee involved, I was willing to try anything. So I followed her instructions. The soldiers accepted my explanation that two of them would have to wait until more girls were available. They flipped a coin, and a big, brawny sergeant won the "first girl."

Minutes later, Rosie entered the room, wearing a pale yellow evening gown, with her long, dark hair freshly brushed. The sergeant claimed his date and went lurching upstairs for his all-nighter. His buddies whistled in appreciation.

"Hot damn!" one of the soldiers said. "If the other two gals are as good as that one, we're in luck."

"Believe me, fellows," I said as I fetched beers for the eager pair. "The other two girls will be *exactly* as good!"

The two remaining Romeos in Khaki were working on their third bottles of beer when Rosie returned to the parlor about forty minutes later. This time she was wearing a sexy, lacy blue negligee, and her hair had been redone in an elegant upsweep style. The G.I.s ogled her hungrily and repeated the coin toss. The victor and his "new girl" hurried upstairs, leaving one soldier still at the starting gate.

To keep him busy, I told him that no more upstairs bedrooms were available, and I asked him to help me prepare a convertible sofa in a first-floor back parlor. By the time we were finished with the bed-making preparations for his party and I had supplied him with another beer, Rosie was back downstairs. This time she was dressed in a low-cut red gown, and her hair was braided and pinned smartly across the top of her head.

"Baby, it was a long wait, but it was worth it," the third musketeer sighed as he tottered off to the back parlor with *his* date for the night.

Fearing complications in Rosie's game of "musical beds," I didn't get any sleep that night. However, there wasn't a single outcry by an indignant soldier. I was still in the parlor at nine o'clock that morning when the G.I. trio began to assemble for their departure. They showed up in the parlor at about twenty-minute intervals, in the same order in which they had claimed their "dates" the previous night.

"What a woman I had," the sergeant chortled to his companions. "Four times, I had it—four fucking times!"

"Me, too!" each of his buddies exclaimed, marveling at the coincidental proof of their virility. And they left the house arguing about who had the best girl for the night.

As soon as I saw the soldiers out the door, I rushed to the upstairs sitting room. Rosie was sprawled in a lounge chair, wearily puffing on a cigarette.

"My God, Rosie, I still don't believe it," I said. "Those soldiers left here happy as jaybirds. And each one was sure he had his own date for the night. How in the hell did you do it?"

In the first place, Rosie explained, she was sure that—after a night of bar-hopping—the three G.I. tricks wouldn't have too much endurance. She took the sergeant to bed, gave him a brisk workout, and he dozed off to sleep. She slipped out of bed, put on a negligee, fixed her hair in a different style, and went down to claim her second date. She repeated the performance, and after No. 2 quickly fell asleep following his manly exertions, she donned still another costume, changed her hair-do again and showed up for her third date, who followed the same bang-bang, beddie-bye pattern as his buddies.

That was the start of a busy night for Rosie. With No. 3 safely asleep, she hurried back upstairs to the bed of No. 1. She awakened him and said she was "lonely." Being a gentleman, he rose to the challenge, took care of her loneliness and promptly dozed off again. She repeated the performance with No. 2 and No. 3, with the same results, then began her rounds through the house once more.

On the third time around, the three soldiers responded groggily but valiantly to Rosie's call to arms, although No. 2 fell asleep in the midst of the action. She tenderly tucked him in bed and proceeded on to the now-rumpled couch of No. 3 who, apparently having regained his wind, frolicked through a long party before resuming his interrupted napping.

It was well past daylight that Sunday morning when Rosie started her last—and most critical—tour of duty. To convince each of her tricks that he had truly had an all-night date, it was vital that she be in his bed when he awoke. To accomplish this, she had to rely on the probability that the combination of many beers and three lusty sex sessions in a few hours would finally put her dates into a deep sleep.

She hurried to the bed of soldier No. 1. He was snoring contentedly, but she shook him awake. "Darling," she whispered sexily, caressing him gently, "it's getting late, and I have to get ready for church. But you've been so sweet, you deserve one for the road before you leave."

Rosie made sure the last one was a quickie. Then while the first soldier was showering and getting dressed, she scurried to the bedroom of No. 2, woke him up, repeated the performance, and scampered on downstairs to her last encore with No. 3. An amazing performance? It was magnificent—so magnificent, in fact, that she got a generous tip from each of her grateful all-night dates in addition to the $25 per man fee.

Obviously great things can be expected of a girl with that kind of determination and talent. And Rosie didn't disappoint my high expectations. Although she never again equaled that night's triple-threat endurance record, she worked in my colonial house for more than a year. At last, with a hefty bank account, she "retired," returned to college, and graduated with honors—a graduation which I attended at her invitation. After getting her diploma, she went to work as a teacher in a southern city. In a few years she married and raised a family of four children. Her husband never suspected her onetime career, but—like the three tricks she handled so deftly that frantic night—I'm certain he fully enjoyed her remarkable, satisfying talents.

Rosie, however, was just one of a number of my girls—and I guess that several hundred worked for me at one time or another over the years—who used prostitution as a steppingstone to a better, more prosperous life in a society from which they had once retreated.

Like Rosie, these smart girls retired as soon as they had accumulated enough money to realize their hopes for the future. Generally these ambitions were centered on plans to acquire a profitable, respectable business of their own—a dress shop, a beauty salon, a restaurant, or varied other enterprises. Quite often these plans for a return to respectability also included dreams of romance, marriage, and children.

Fay was one of my smart girls, a truly unique human being. She came unannounced to my house on Clay Street one day, asking if I had an opening for a girl. I could scarcely believe my eyes. My house was famous for its good-looking girls, but a woman like this just wasn't the type you expect to find in a small Kentucky town. Everything about Fay—her poise and bearing, her vocabulary, her chic, expensive clothing—was eloquent testimony to a well-bred, cosmopolitan upbringing. Fay, indeed, was a lovely young woman, and she possessed a rare exotic quality beyond her beauty of face and form. Tall and willowy, with raven hair that cascaded below her shoulders, dark, snapping eyes, and a flawless olive complexion, Fay had an old-world sort of charm and an elusive air of mystery that could drive men out of their minds. She was, in brief, a man-devastating package of pure sex.

Seated in my parlor, I quickly sized up Fay's bountiful physical endowments as well as her obviously costly, custom-made beige suit and her handsome leather handbag. This, certainly, was no girl from the back country. "I don't mean to be nosey, honey," I said, "but you don't look like a girl who'd want to work in a house in Bowling Green, Kentucky. You look more like Park Avenue to me."

Fay smiled enigmatically, as if she were enjoying a personal kind of joke on herself. "You're close," she replied in a soft, cultured voice. "I'm from New York, but I became bored with big city life and decided it was time for a change."

"But how did you learn about me? I'm sure my house isn't exactly a household word in the Big City."

Fay explained that she had been driving across country, looking for a town that suited her fancy. "Bowling Green appealed to me. So I stopped at a hotel and asked a bellboy if there was a high-class house in the area. He recommended that I talk with you."

During our conversation, Fay had been glancing appreciatively about the parlor and a portion of my large living room visible through an archway connecting the two rooms. I could see that she was quietly evaluating the quality of the decor, including the authentic antiques I had extravagantly collected over a period of years.

"Judging by what I see," Fay added, "the bellboy knew what he was talking about. This is certainly no ordinary house. It's beautiful!"

Fay couldn't have chosen a better compliment to win my heart. I was inordinately proud of the job I had done in transforming the big brick house from a state of shabby disrepair into a luxurious establishment. As far as exterior elegance and setting were concerned, my house on Clay Street couldn't compare with the beauty and charm of my colonial country place before it was destroyed by fire. The Clay Street house was surrounded by a large yard which I had lovingly landscaped. But even the well-kept lawn, shrubbery, and flower gardens couldn't disguise the fact that the house was situated across from the railroad tracks, near the town's stockyards. It was an ideal location for privacy, but it certainly was a far-from-perfect environment for a "dream house."

However, after the loss of my colonial house, I had decided that the operator of a bordello can't expect to have everything. My country place had an abundance of charming atmosphere, but its remoteness was an inconvenience for customers. The alternative was to buy a place in town. To get the in-city privacy my business required, I had to locate in a nonresidential area safely removed from the prying eyes and easily aroused indignation of respectable neighbors. Thus, to make up for its seedy locale, I had spared no expense in converting the interior of the house on Clay Street into another world. Here I catered lavishly to my expensive tastes in interior decorating and antiques, filling the house with beauty. Once inside the door, my house was indeed a posh place for gentlemen who had a cultivated appetite for gracious loving—an establishment truly worthy of a regal courtesan like Fay.

Despite the satisfaction of having my house praised by a discerning woman, I found it impossible to believe Fay's story that day. Sophisticated, well-educated young ladies like her just don't wander impulsively along the nation's highways and byways looking for a job as a prostitute. But I wasn't about to question the veracity of her explanation for she was the kind of girl a madam dreams about but rarely finds. Although she provided me with no information about her past experience, it was obvious from her knowledge of house operations and fees, which she frankly discussed on a sharp, businesslike basis, that Fay was no amateur. I welcomed her to my stable with open arms.

I never had cause to regret my action. Fay became an overnight sensation and continued to be the star attraction of my house during the three years she worked for me. As I had realized at our first meeting, she was a highly skilled professional. She could get more money out of a man than any girl I've ever met, and still satisfy the customer so thoroughly that he'd come back for more time after time. I've seen many a trick, after a date with Fay, hurriedly leave the house to replenish his bankroll and return an hour or so later for another party with her.

There was only one thing that bothered me. Fay was a loner. Her past, her problems, her ambitions, and her true identity remained a mystery. With the customers she was an outgoing, vivacious person, full of laughter and human warmth. But in her free time she withdrew into her own private world, rarely mixing with the other girls during off-duty hours.

Fearing that her withdrawals might be an indication that Fay, behind her shell of seemingly calm reserve, was waging a lonely inner battle with some desperate problem, I asked her one day if something was troubling her.

She appeared to be surprised by the question. "Of course not," she replied. "Whatever gave you that idea?"

"Well," I said, "the other girls are puzzled because you keep to yourself so much. They think you're either stuck up and feel you're too good for them, or terribly unhappy about something. They just can't figure you out."

Fay expressed immediate concern, saying she hadn't realized she was creating a morale problem among the girls. "I certainly don't feel that I'm better than the others," she said. "It's simply that after a long night's work, trying to please all sorts of men, I enjoy relaxing in my room, reading books and magazines, writing letters, working on embroidery, and just plain daydreaming. I didn't realize it might look snobbish. From now on, though, I'll try to spend more time with the other girls."

Fay kept her word. From then on she did more socializing with the girls. She didn't have much to say, but she'd laugh at their jokes, listen to their gossip, and occasionally join in their lusty recollections of the more fascinating hangups of their customers. However, she never discussed her past—a generally popular pastime among prostitutes.

Fay worked tirelessly for more than four months without a break even though I frequently urged her to follow the schedule I recommended for all my girls—three weeks on the job, followed by a week or two of relaxation away from the house. Then one day she asked for time off.

"I have to go home on business," she said without adding any details. "I'm not sure how long I'll be gone. Perhaps three or four weeks."

I regretfully said good-by to Fay, telling her to have a fine vacation. In my heart, though, I was convinced that she had tired of Bowling Green and would never return. She left most of her clothing and other personal possessions in her room, but I figured she planned to send for these later after she was safely removed from any painful parting-of-the-ways scenes.

I was wrong, however. About a month later Fay returned to the house on Clay Street as casually as if she had just been on a brief errand at the corner grocery. She revealed nothing of where she had been or what she had done; she merely returned to the job of delighting her customers.

After that month's absence Fay continued to work for me for more than two years, interrupting her labors of love periodically for her mysterious business trips. It wasn't until she announced abruptly one day that she was retiring from the business that Fay finally lifted the curtain of secrecy with which she had shrouded her past life. As might be expected, it was an extraordinary story from an extraordinary woman, and I listened spellbound as she told it to me.

Fay had, as a child and young girl, enjoyed the luxury of being one of two children of a wealthy Connecticut couple. During the depression, however, her father's business failed. By the time she graduated from college, the last traces of her family's fortune had faded and her distressed father had killed himself rather than live out his years in unaccustomed poverty. Fay's younger brother at that time had just started the long and costly study for the priesthood, and she was determined to help him financially.

"I settled in New York and got a job as a model," she said. "In that job, I made a lot of important contacts. Before long I was offered a profitable sideline job as a high-priced call girl. I accepted the offer with no qualms because making money had become my biggest goal in life."

Between modeling and servicing well-to-do gentlemen, Fay's annual income flourished in the comfortable five-figure brackets. She was able to pay her brother's education costs, help support her widowed mother who was living with a sister in New England, and still accumulate a sizable savings account. By the time her brother was ordained as a priest, she had invested a large portion of her savings as a down payment on a long-established summer-and-winter vacation resort in Vermont.

"Then the roof fell in," Fay said. "After my brother was ordained, he was assigned to a parish in New York City. I realized immediately that I would have to leave New York, for if I were ever caught in a vice raid or involved in a scandal, it would ruin my brother's life. There's not enough room, even in New York, for a brother who's a priest and his sister who's a prostitute."

Fay, however, decided that she would continue in the profession in some distant, off-the-beaten-track town until she had earned enough to pay off the balance due on her resort investment. That's how she ended up working in my house in Bowling Green. And her periodic business trips were devoted to overseeing the operations of her resort and visiting her mother and brother, both of whom thought she was employed as the manager of a women's apparel shop in Kentucky.

"When I left New York, I vowed that I'd quit the business the day I mailed the last payment on my resort," Fay said. "Today I put that last check in the mail. Now I'm going back to run *my* resort full-time."

A week or so later, I received a telephone call from the post office, informing me they had just received a large, heavily insured package protected by a sturdy wooden crate. The cumbersome package was addressed to me, the postal clerk said, and would I please come down and take the blasted thing off their hands.

Burning with curiosity, I rushed to the post office, wondering who could be sending me something in such an elaborate wood-protected package. I made no attempt to get the heavy crate in the trunk of my car. Instead, two postal workers and I tackled the crate carefully. We pried off the wooden cocoon and found a package bundled in heavy wrapping paper. At last we came to the gift. It was a large gilded and inlaid antique mirror—an exquisite piece of hand craftsmanship. Attached to the mirror was a brief note: "My dear Pauline: I want you to have something nice to *always* remember me by. Love, Fay." It was the last time I ever heard from Fay. But I still see her lovely face every time I stop in the foyer of my home and look in that mirror!

I guess that Fay and Rosie are two of the main reasons why I fume and snort and fly into a rage when I read the opinions of some so-called experts who claim they have made exhaustive studies of the compulsions that motivate prostitutes. These textbook geniuses maintain that a woman turns to prostitution for one of three basic reasons —(a) she is a nymphomaniac driven by an endless, tortured seeking for sexual fulfillment; or (b) she is too lazy to hold down a legitimate eight-hour-per-day job; or (c) she is a feebleminded female whose only talent for making a living is conveniently situated between her legs. Such purportedly scholarly reasoning is ridiculous. It's just another example of supposedly profound opinions which, in the cold light of reality, turn out to be plain old barnyard manure.

Undoubtedly these pitiful types are found in the business. But it is idiotic to lump all prostitutes under these three classifications. In fact, I discovered during my years as a madam that "nymphs" and dim-witted females rarely last more than a few days in a high-class house. They may end up in cheap "cribs" or join the legions of street-walking, bar-infesting whores, but they lack the class required for a career as a successful prostitute. And as for a lazy woman seeking the "easy life" of a prostitute, all I can say is that these experts ought to try working a ten- to twelve-hour shift in a busy house sometime.

I've never known a girl who turned to prostitution for pleasure or because it was an easy way to make a living. When a girl goes to work in a brothel she is, in effect, cutting herself off from the rest of the world. While she's in the house, generally for a two- or three-week stretch without a break, there's no outside dating, no gallivanting around town during off-hours, no movies or dinners by candlelight, no shopping or beauty shop appointments unless she's chaperoned by the madam. In brief, she's a prisoner of her profession, isolated for the single purpose of servicing sex-hungry males. A glamorous, easy business? What a laugh! Any woman who works in a whorehouse has a critical problem or she wouldn't be there in the first place. And almost always that problem is closely linked to money.

As a matter of fact, I've found that it's the young women who need money desperately—and not those who merely want money for the luxuries of life—who make the best prostitutes. Often this need for money involves children. One of my hardest working girls was a young mother with five small children to support. She was another example of the potential tragedies involved in young marriages. Married at fifteen, her husband walked out on her when she was twenty-three, leaving her stranded with no money, no family to turn to, five youngsters, and no training for a decent-paying job. Luckily, her looks and figure had survived the rigors of mass reproduction. She turned to prostitution as the most practical solution to her critical economic problems. The last I heard, she was working as a call girl in Chicago, still grinding out money to support her brood and a full-time housekeeper.

My memory is cluttered with similar examples of girls who labored in my house as breadwinners for their fatherless children. One young divorcee had a crippled son. She spent most of her earnings on medical and hospital bills, trying desperately to cure, or ease, the boy's physical handicap. Another of my girls, imbued with the determination to make a better life for her two sons, used her hard-earned money to send them to an expensive military academy. I could go on and on, and all of my stories would involve women who accepted a life as prostitutes only because no other kind of work for which they were qualified provided such reliable moneymaking opportunities.

Josie was such a woman. Like so many tiny, Dresden-doll sort of females, she had a will of iron and the stamina of an elephant. Unhappily she also was one of those ill-starred humans who seem doomed from birth to failure and tragedy. No matter how hard she worked and saved, success and happiness always managed to elude her just when she thought they at last were safely in her grasp and she could begin to enjoy life.

Unlike most girls, Josie didn't get into the business by chance nor was it a career she deliberately chose to follow. Her mother kicked Josie out of her home when she was twenty-one, ordering her to go to work in a brothel and learn to be a prostitute.

Although her action doubtlessly was extremely drastic, Josie's widowed mother had reason to be disillusioned with her only child. She had provided her with a good home and a sound education, but Josie was a headstrong, impulsive daughter. She left college and married when she was nineteen. By the time she reached twenty-one, she was divorced with a baby to support. She returned home to mother, got a job clerking in a store, and promptly fell in love with a worthless exconvict. Soon she was giving every cent she could earn to her jobless boyfriend. It was at this point that Josie was confronted by her angry mother.

"Look here, Josie," the distraught mother raged, "there's going to be no more of this promiscuous laying around every two-bit motel in town with some lazy bum. If you're determined to screw around, by God, you're going to do it for money. You're going to be a prostitute, not a damned cheap chippie." And having delivered that ultimatum, the mother gave Josie the name and address of the madam of a large house in another part of the state.

"I've already talked with this woman," she said. "She's agreed to take you in and teach you the business."

Josie obeyed her mother. She dutifully set out to learn the skills of prostitution. By the time she came to work in my Clay Street house, she was a top-quality professional, a pretty little doll, warm and cuddly. The men really flipped over her. In addition to her abilities in bed, Josie turned out to be a sharp businesswoman. She was investing her earnings in a farm and a large house in Louisville which she was personally converting into apartments during her "off" weeks. Often she would return to my house exhausted, with her dainty hands scarred from her manual labors.

"Josie," I told her after she returned from one of her house-remodeling trips, "you've got to slow down. If you're going to work in my house, I can't have you looking like a scrubwoman, with rough hands and bags under your eyes."

"I've got to have security for myself and my child," Josie protested. "It's a tough job, working here and trying to build up my farm and my apartment house. But I'm big enough to handle it."

"Honey," I replied, "you're making good money here. Hire some people to take care of your outside projects."

Josie, however, solved her problem in another way. A month or so later she phoned me during her week off. She was bubbling with joy. Several months previously she had met a young truck driver. They had dated whenever she was in Louisville, and they had just been married. They were going to sell the Louisville house and settle on Josie's farm in Illinois. I gave Josie my blessing and figured that another of my girls had realized her ambition.

I was mistaken, however. A few years later, Josie showed up at my house one day. She was careworn and obviously deeply distressed. Seated in my parlor, she told me her tragic tale. Her marriage to the truck driver had started out with great promise. They had invested the money from the sale of the Louisville house in stocking their farm with a dairy herd. To bolster their income, her husband continued driving a truck, a job that took him away from home for several days at a time.

"Fred was worried that the job of taking care of the farm was too much for me," Josie said. "Finally, he persuaded his younger brother to live on the farm and help run it."

That's when Josie's troubles began anew. With her husband away so much of the time, Josie soon found herself involved in a romance with his brother. Ultimately Fred learned about the affair, but he didn't play the part of an outraged, cuckolded husband. Instead, he blamed himself for neglecting his wife. He quit his cross-country driving job and went to work as a gasoline truck driver in a nearby city so he could be home every evening and help Josie with the farm.

"Everything seemed to be going fine," Josie said tensely. "Then a few months later Fred's gasoline truck was involved in an accident. He was burned to death." The girl began sobbing. "It was my fault, Pauline. I killed him. I did wrong, and Fred had to pay the price for my sinning!"

When she finally recovered her composure, Josie asked if she could return to work in my house.

"I don't know what else to do, Pauline," she said. "I can't stand the thought of living on the farm. There are too many bad memories there. But I can't let it go. It's all I have left, and I've got to make money to keep it."

Josie was like so many girls. She couldn't let loose of the idea that she could always rely on prostitution for a good living. However, I didn't have the heart to tell the grief-stricken girl that I thought she was "over the hill" as far as the sex game was concerned. She returned to work in my house. But as I feared, she had lost her vital, youthful spark. She met with only indifferent success and finally drifted on to newer pastures. The last I heard she was working as a call girl, still trying desperately to grab the golden rings from a merry-go-round that suddenly was whirling too fast for her. Youth was gone. All Josie had left was the fading hope that somehow she'd once more find her way to the magical money tree.

If prostitution happened to be a low-paying proposition, there would be damned few women willing to work in the business. But all of the preaching and crusading in the world will never succeed in making sex unpopular with the masses. Like food, clothing, housing, medicine, and—to be grimly factual—funeral parlors, sex is a mighty important commodity that will always command a good price. And the sale of that commodity will always attract women like Josie who are desperate for money.

Before they're very old, girls come to realize that they're equipped with an exceedingly popular, highly marketable set of accessories. Most young females strive to use these sexual assets to gain and hold a man and thus enjoy the security of a family and a home. Even after attaining this objective some married women still are acutely aware of the commercial value of their charms. During the years a number of wives have approached me, wanting to supplement their family's income by working in my house part-time. I always rejected them because I was convinced that their presence would be as dangerous as a live bomb in the house. But I do know that it is not a rare occurrence for wives to earn extra money for life's luxuries by working as part-time prostitutes. In fact, many of the present-day call girls in the larger cities are young wives who accept paying dates when their unsuspecting husbands are busy at their jobs.

In view of this willingness among married females to bend the moral code occasionally when a quick and easy profit can be gained, it is not surprising that unattached women often turn to prostitution to solve their money problems. In doing this some girls find themselves wrestling with deep-seated spiritual or emotional conflicts which even money cannot ease. They generally quit after a few months, or end up as physical and emotional wrecks.

Other girls, however, learn to accept their lives as prostitutes philosophically. They adopt the attitude that they're working in a house for one reason—to earn enough money to solve their specific problems or to attain a definite objective. Not all of them succeed, of course. Some hang on too long, squander their earnings, and end up as frowzy barroom floaters, wondering dimly in their alcoholic haze what happened to them on the quick road to fortune. Others, seeking new kicks, get hooked on drugs or mess up their lives completely in emotional entanglements with pimps, hoodlums, and other male misfits. And some, jaded by constant exposure to all sorts of masculine appetites, turn to the dubious delights of lesbian relationships in their off-duty hours.

Every house has occasional problems with lesbians. Girls with a yen for other girls are not readily detectable unless they're true masculinelike dikes, and that mannish breed just doesn't come looking for a job in a whorehouse.

My first problem with lesbians arose about a year after I'd opened my house at 1st and Center streets following my return to Bowling Green in 1937.

With the nation gradually pulling out of its long, dreary economic tailspin, business at my house was improving steadily. It was time, I decided, to expand my modest three-girl stable. As if in answer to my expansion plans, two girls came to my door one day looking for jobs, saying they had decided to shop around for a better deal after working in a house in Covington, Kentucky. They seemed to be exactly what I was looking for—young, pretty professionals with pleasant personalities. Wanda was a tall blonde with a classic hourglass figure. Her friend, Julie, was a seemingly gentle, petite girl with auburn hair and a pert, elfinlike face. Both appeared to be completely feminine. I soon learned that appearances can be deceiving.

One afternoon about a week after Wanda and Julie joined my stable, I was relaxing in the parlor when Betty, another of my girls, came storming downstairs. Her hair was disheveled, her lounging robe was ripped, her bra was partially torn off, and her female sensibilities were shattered.

"What in the hell happened to you?" I asked, frantically thinking that some rape-minded male freak had managed to sneak into the house.

"It's that goddam Wanda," the outraged girl screeched. "She came in my room while I was taking a nap. And the first thing I knew she was trying to rip off my clothes. She's a goddam, filthy, son-of-a-bitchin' butch!"

I was horrified, for the possibility of a lesbian working in a whorehouse had never occurred to me. But before I could calm down Betty and decide on a course of action, bedlam erupted upstairs. Rushing to the new scene of disorder, I found Wanda and Julie wrestling furiously on a bedroom floor.

Julie, despite her tiny proportions, was assailing Wanda with teeth, fingernails, fists, and feet like an enraged wildcat. Her larger friend, with most of her clothes ripped off, was desperately trying to protect various tender parts of her anatomy.

"Goddam you—you two-timin' bitch—I'll teach you not to make a pass at another girl," the once-gentle Julie was screaming as I raced into the room.

Wanda spotted me as she struggled to break away from the hellcat who at that moment was busily clawing the big blonde's writhing legs, inching ever closer to a far more vital region. "Help me, Pauline," she pleaded. "Get me out of here."

"Stop this dammed nonsense right away!" I shouted. But Julie was too busy and too angry to heed my orders.

"I'm gonna kill this goddam cheatin' dike," she panted. "She's two-timed me for the last time. I'm gonna pull her pussy out by the roots!"

Wanda howled with fear and pain as Julie's bloodied fingers clawed closer to target. Realizing something had to be done quickly, I stepped up close, braced myself, and landed a haymaker punch on the side of Julie's dainty chin. She toppled across her two-timing girlfriend's body like a felled ox. The fight was over, with Wanda's treasure box still intact.

It was at least an hour before order was restored. The other girls revived Julie and straightened up the wreckage of the room while I patched Wanda's wounds. When the first-aid job was completed, I ordered the two lesbians to pack up and get out before nightfall.

After that experience, I was always suspicious when two buddy-buddy girls arrived together looking for jobs. I never again hired a twosome without checking with the madam of the house they had worked in previously. As a result, I was able to keep my house clear of lesbian couples. Despite precautions, however, unattached butches occasionally would fool me and infiltrate the house. They never lasted long. Invariably they'd make a pass at one of my girls within a few days, and I'd send them packing. It wasn't that I was prudish about such antics. If loving another girl was their cup of tea, that was their business. But I wouldn't tolerate it in my house, for lesbians are bad news. They not only resent the object of their affections paying attention to other girls, but become violently jealous of the paying male customers. There are enough problems keeping order in the boy-girl business without worrying about the insane emotional flareups that can explode at any time when a couple of lesbians start playing games in the house.

Actually, plain old-fashioned female jealousy—not the more violent, perverted lesbian variety—is always a problem in the behind-the-scenes operation of a whorehouse. Girls will be girls, and that means that deep down below their civilized shell they instinctively resent, and are suspicious of, one another. Typically this female jealousy comes churning to the surface over all manner of silly, inconsequential things. One girl resents a co-worker's ability to entertain the tricks with an endless repertoire of bawdy jokes. Another is miffed because so-and-so has a sexier wardrobe, or has earned more money during the last week than she has. Still another is madly jealous because she thinks her favorite customer is making eyes at other girls in the house. And so it goes, an endless chain of niggling spats, angry accusations, and bruised feelings which the madam must handle quickly and diplomatically if she hopes to maintain at least an armed truce among the temperamental female population of her house.

The most exasperating, and in some ways the funniest, epidemic of jealousy in my house was caused by an "ugly duckling." For three years Fay had reigned as the star attraction of the house on Clay Street without stirring a single spark of jealousy among the other girls. At times they resented her aloofness, but they respected her beauty and were somewhat awed by the strange allure she so effortlessly employed in taming the male animal. She was the champ, a model of the professionalism they hoped to attain some day. Fay's replacement, however, was not so fortunate.

Louise was the most unlikely prospect imaginable to follow in the footsteps of fabulous Fay. She came to my house highly recommended by one of my madam friends in Louisville. But when she reported for duty, my first despairing thought was that I'd really bought a pig in a poke.

There was no other way to describe Louise but to say that she was a plain Jane, an ugly duckling in a business in which beauty is a girl's best friend. She was only five feet tall and underdeveloped. She had mousy brown hair, a freckled face, a pug nose, small buds of breasts, and slender, boyish hips. Her big, brown eyes—glowing with a lively friendliness—and a merry smile and an easygoing personality seemed to be her only assets. She was twenty-five years old, a divorced mother supporting three children, but she looked like a teen-aged tomboy—an impish Wendy right out of the pages of Peter Pan.

In sending Louise to me, the Louisville madam had assured me she was an experienced trouper, a "really different sort of girl." To say she was different was a monumental understatement. After meeting her for the first time, I couldn't believe she was for real.

"Honey," I said, almost overwhelmed by one of my rare maternal moods, "are you absolutely sure you want to work in a house? You'll have to pardon my blunt talk, but you look like a child who's just starting to mature."

Louise wasn't ruffled by my gruff reference to her adolescent appearance. Quite the contrary, she giggled delightedly. It was apparent that she was enjoying my shocked discomfort. "I've worked in three houses in the last three years, and every madam said exactly the same thing when they first saw me," she said.

"Well," I managed to stammer in the face of such frankness, "I know you've got experience. But I just don't know if my customers will cotton up to a girl so . . . so young looking . . ."

"And so homely, with freckles and skinny legs and almost no boobs at all," Louise interrupted, candidly voicing the thoughts I couldn't bring myself to express.

I shrugged. "You've got to admit, honey, that you're not exactly a Cleopatra. It's hard to imagine you making out in a house filled with sexpots."

Louise sighed in agreement. "I know what you mean. I look in the mirror and tell myself I'm a mess, that no man could possibly be interested in me. But somehow I always do okay. I can't imagine why, though."

I quietly surrendered. You can't argue with someone who agrees with you on every point you bring up. I reluctantly agreed to give Louise a tryout, confident that a couple weeks of cold shoulders from the customers would convince her that she was out of her league in my stable of sexy sirens.

My girls were equally flabbergasted when they met Louise. They looked her over with amazement, then began teasing her. "Hey, little girl," one of them jested, "you don't have to come to a whorehouse to get your cherry busted. Just ask one of the horny boys at school to do the job."

The other girls roared at this coarse witticism, and Louise joined heartily in the laughter. That put a damper on the teasing because there's no point poking fun at a girl who seems to be able to laugh at her own shortcomings.

However, the girls resumed their giggling that evening when Louise showed up in the parlor. She was about the strangest sight I'd ever seen walk into a brothel parlor to mingle with the tricks. Instead of a tight, slinky gown—the customary uniform of the evening for my girls—Louise wore a modest, high-necked, lace-trimmed gingham dress. Instead of costly high-heeled slippers, she wore a simple pair of maroon loafers. Instead of artfully applied makeup, her freckled face was fresh-scrubbed, without even a hint of lipstick or mascara. Instead of an elaborate hairdo, her brown locks were braided and tied with ribbons.

The impact of Louise's carefully created illusion of schoolgirl innocence was fantastic. At first the tricks eyed her with disbelief. Gradually, though, they began to cluster about her to find out what manner of precocious child I had imported to Clay Street. In a few minutes she was the center of attention, listening avidly to the customers' stories and telling a few tall tales of her own, her strangely childish laughter filling the room. Within a half hour she was leading her first trick upstairs, looking for all the world like a wholesome Miss Teen-age America innocently heading for her first sexual misadventure. Somehow it seemed obscene, and I had to remind myself that the "child" climbing the stairs was a twenty-five-year-old veteran prostitute.

From that point on Louise was a hit attraction. Perhaps some of her appeal was her eager-to-please personality, her ability to make a man feel that everything he said was vitally important to her. But, I quickly decided, Louise's biggest asset was her unique talent for projecting an eternal image of an innocent, virginal maiden. In any event, she soon had succeeded Fay as the big moneymaker of the house.

I was astounded, but pleased, to find myself blessed with such an unsuspected winner. But at the same time I was concerned, for the other girls were viewing Louise's overnight success with considerable angry resentment. It wasn't only the money she was making that infuriated my girls, but the horrible fact that so many customers were ignoring their charms and seeking the company of a scrawny ugly duckling. My temperamental beauties were frantic with jealousy. Finally, after a couple of months, one of my girls cornered me for a heart-to-heart talk.

"Pauline," she said, "the girls are mighty bitter about the tricks Louise is pulling every night."

"What do you mean by tricks?" I asked. "She works hard, minds her own business, and seems to be pleasing the trade."

"It's the kid clothes she wears, the pigtails, the whole juvenile bit that we don't like. She comes on like the kid next door. She's got the customers fooled into thinking they're getting a genuine piece of young teen-aged ass."

"What can I do about it?" I asked. "Every girl has her special tricks for turning a guy on. Louise just happens to play the part of a young virgin."

"That's the trouble," the mouthpiece for my bewildered, irate beauties wailed. "We can't compete with that kind of an act. You've got to make her quit wearing that kid stuff and dress up like all the rest of us."

"What if she refuses?" I asked.

"Then we're going to go on strike against unfair competition. If we refuse to work, you'll soon find out that it takes more than one phony virgin to keep a house going."

I didn't take the strike talk seriously, but I was worried about the bitter feelings that were upsetting the routine of my house. Furthermore, I realized the other girls had a legitimate gripe. Louise's virginal role was a tough act to top. I finally agreed to have a talk with our over-aged "Lolita."

The next day I carefully explained the problem to Louise. I told her the other girls insisted that she wear grownup evening clothes, use makeup, and stop cavorting about in pigtails. For the first time, Louise resisted.

"It's not fair," she cried. "They've got all the beauty. What more do they want? It's silly for them to think they can't compete with my kid act."

"That's how they feel, though. And we've got to do something to humor them."

Louise morosely agreed to think it over, but she wouldn't make any promise to change her act. After two weeks of waiting, she still was playing the teenie-bopper role to the hilt. The other girls kept nagging me to take some kind of action. In turn, I could only give them vague assurances that Louise had agreed to "think about" their demands.

At the end of the third week of this war of nerves, my girls decided there had been enough stalling. That evening Louise, clad in a simple, girlish skirt and blouse, was the only one to show up in the parlor. The four other girls in my stable remained in their rooms, announcing through locked doors that they were on a sitdown strike. Tacked to the wall of the upstairs hallway was a cardboard sign, announcing in big letters:

WE'RE ALL SITTING DOWN ON THE JOB. WE WON'T STAND FOR ANY
MORE EXCUSES, AND WE WON'T LAY DOWN FOR ANYBODY UNTIL
OUR TERMS ARE MET.

PROFESSIONAL PROSTITUTES UNION, LOCAL NO. 1

At the time, I wasn't amused. I roared with indignation at the thought of having a bunch of girls trying to dictate the terms on which I could run my business. I paced up and down the upstairs hall, giving vent to a truly eloquent display of my extensive vocabulary of profanities. "You girls aren't going to tell me what to do!" I hollered. "You can sit in your rooms 'til your goddam asses turn to concrete!" Then I stormed downstairs to attempt to placate a steadily growing throng of impatient tricks.

Louise worked diligently, but she couldn't begin to handle the night's traffic. Some of the customers even went upstairs and pleaded with the girls to abandon their strike. The girls just hooted derisively. "Pack up your hard-ons and get lost," they cried defiantly. "There's no action here tonight." At last, about eleven o'clock, I sent the unhappy customers on their way and locked up for the night.

The following evening the girls were still locked in their rooms. By nine o'clock, with an unruly crowd of disgruntled customers threatening to break down the doors, I capitulated. I ordered Louise to her room and told her to remain there until she was ready to work in the standard evening gown uniform of the house. I ripped up the strike sign in the hall and told my sitting girls that they had won their battle. With lusty cheers, my beauties emerged from their rooms in full uniform. They charged down the stairs and pounced on the waiting lineup of tricks, eager to make up for their lost earnings. Business on Clay Street was back to normal.

After sulking briefly in her room Louise returned to the arena the next night. Instead of simple schoolgirl attire she wore high heels and a chic blue evening gown which unfortunately had no curves to cling to. Instead of a fresh-scrubbed, freckled face, she had skillfully applied all the customary makeup of her profession. Instead of beribboned pigtails, her nondescript brown hair was groomed in the latest upsweep fashion. And instead of the illusion of a virginal teen-ager, she presented the pitiful reality of a plain Jane prostitute surrounded by beauty with which she never could compete.

Louise hung on stubbornly for a week, but her spell was broken. Finally she packed her bags, said good-by, and drove out of our lives, doubtlessly in search of a new, unsuspecting house where she could once more revert to her teen-age fantasy. With her departure, I breathed a sigh of relief. Peace again had been restored—at least temporarily—among the girls in the house on Clay Street.

*The 'tricks'*

## The 'tricks'

Through the years I've been asked all sorts of questions about life in a whorehouse. Oddly enough, most of these questions have come from respectable women—curious females who, after learning the nature of my business, avidly seek as many spicy details as possible about the oldest profession.

On the other hand, except for trying to find out why a prostitute gets into the business in the first place and how much she can earn once she's in it, men ask far fewer questions, probably because most of them know damned well what goes on in a brothel. Women are by far the most pestiferous snoopers to plague a madam.

A female whose sexual experiences have been limited by strict adherence to the code of monogamy can ask some of the silliest questions imaginable. And even the more sophisticated matron is mighty naive about the lives and customs of her fallen sisters. Generally, though, all women outside the profession ask the same questions about four subjects which seem to puzzle them most:

How does a prostitute prevent getting pregnant when she has intercourse so frequently with so many different men?

How many times a night can a prostitute "do it"?

Does a prostitute frequently experience a climax?

And the question which really bothers a lot of women: what kind of men go to a whorehouse?

I'll deal with the first three points of curiosity before I get down to the key question with which this chapter is mainly concerned—the "tricks," the men whose dollars make a prostitute's life worth living.

On the question of pregnancy, I recall a tough, grizzled master sergeant from Camp Campbell who was a steady patron of my house during World War II. He was a veteran of more than twenty years in the army, a hard-bitten soldier with a huge paunch which betrayed a monumental capacity for beer.

One evening in the parlor, several of my girls were teasing Ol' Sarge about his beer gut. "I do believe you're pregnant, honey!" one girl joshed.

Ol' Sarge looked at her with a wry grin. "Baby," he said, "when you've been in the army as long as I have, and you've been screwed by the army as many times as I have, you're bound to get knocked up sooner or later!"

The old soldier's joke was ironically applicable to one of the basic job hazards of prostitution. All girls, of course, use birth-control devices because a baby is the last thing on earth they want. In fact, many of them work in a house to support children they acquired during ill-fated marriages or bungled romancing. Most of my girls used a diaphragm or a vaginal jelly. Today, I imagine, more and more prostitutes are using the "pill."

In any event, there is no foolproof birth-control method. Despite all precautions, a girl occasionally becomes pregnant. In such cases, girls and madams know where to contact an abortionist. Most of these illicit practitioners are doctors who, because of personal birth-control convictions or the desire for an easy buck, are willing to overlook the ethics of their profession. Some, however, are nonprofessionals who have acquired abortionist skills. In the Bowling Green area, for example, the top abortionist for many years was a Negro woman who combined a smattering of medical knowledge with seemingly effective "country-folk cures" handed down to women in her family from one generation to another since the days of slavery.

Next question: how many times in one night? The answer, of course, depends on how many hours a girl works, how busy the house traffic is, and how "long-winded" her customers are.

I once read a book about San Francisco in which the author claimed that some of the more popular girls in the notorious Barbary Coast "cribs" handled a hundred or more customers a night. Maybe so, but I'd have to see it to believe it. I'd say that, even if she's servicing a "quick-like-a-bunny" customer, it takes an absolute minimum of fifteen minutes for even the most skilled prostitute to process a trick once he's in her room. Most of the time, though, a routine party—from the moment a customer enters the girl's room until he leaves—lasts twenty to thirty minutes. Aside from the action in bed, other time-consuming details must be attended to. The customer's money must be collected and safely stored with the rest of the girl's receipts for the night. Both parties must undress completely. The girl must apply soap and water to make sure the trick is clean. Before the ultimate activities commence, a certain amount of preliminary love play is indulged in. And after the action has ended, the girl again must clean the customer and tend to her own essential hygienic tasks before they both get dressed and return downstairs.

I never undertook a "time study" in my house, but I doubt if any of my girls ever serviced more than three tricks an hour. As for a full night's work even during our most hectic wartime period when soldiers from Camp Campbell and Fort Knox mushroomed our customary heavy traffic, I can't recall a girl handling more than thirty men during a single shift. And believe me, that was a long, busy, fifteen-hour Saturday night.

Next, what about climaxes? Even if she if she were blessed with an endless series of skilled, considerate lovers—a rare masculine bird, I assure you—a prostitute could not permit herself the luxury of repeated orgasms. In the first place, a girl's income depends on the number of customers she can satisfy. She can't spare the time usually required for attainment of female sexual satisfaction. Secondly, no woman can stand the emotional strain of experiencing repeated orgasms night after night. It's too exhausting.

A skilled prostitute develops to a high degree the art of simulating passion and fulfillment, for most tricks like to bolster their masculine egos with the thought that they've been man enough to satisfy a beautiful, experienced woman. However, while going through all the expected writhings, clutchings, moans, and exclamations of pleasure, a prostitute often is busily thinking of her personal problems or plans, or wondering impatiently how long it's going to take the stud to finish his business. It's only occasionally that a prostitute, seeking relief for her own tensions, will permit herself the emotional luxury of a climax. And this generally occurs during a long, leisurely date with a good-paying customer whom she finds sexually appealing.

Finally the all-important question from a female point of view: what kind of men use the services of a whorehouse?

The answer, of course, is that you can't lump all tricks in one category any more than you can say all prostitutes are nymphomaniacs, lazy sluts, or feebleminded. The customers of a brothel come from all walks of life, from the highest to lowest positions in our society. Patrons of my house have included multimillionaires, men in powerful political positions, important industrialists, businessmen and bankers, men in the professions, actors, athletes, teachers and students, law-enforcement officials, farmers, salesmen, and plain everyday workingmen. Once the forbidden fruits of my house even attracted a preacher who turned out to be an enthusiastic, exceedingly energetic customer.

One frosty January afternoon the doorbell of my colonial country house chimed. As usual, I answered the door. Our visitor was one of the most handsome men I'd ever seen. He appeared to be in his early thirties, tall, broad-shouldered, with curly blond hair and nearly classic features. He was a newcomer to my house, and even though he was a beautiful hunk of man, I had to make sure of his credentials as a customer. An experienced madam doesn't let strangers in the house without first asking questions.

"I'm looking for Miss Pauline," the stranger said.

"You're looking at her," I replied. "But how did you happen to get my name and address?"

The stranger politely introduced himself and said he had been referred to my house by one of my trusted bellhop tipsters. That was a good enough reference for me. I invited our new friend into the parlor. He was immediately surrounded by my girls. Evidently they had spotted his arrival through the windows and were eager to meet such a handsome prospect.

"Charlie," as the stranger had identified himself, mingled easily with the girls, utilizing a ready gift of blarney to compliment them on their beauty and their gowns. He seemed especially smitten with Pam, a blond gal blessed with all of Mother Nature's deluxe accessories.

"Could I have a date with Pam?" he asked, his politeness reminding me of some of the boys who used to call at my home to ask my mother for permission to squire me to a school dance.

"Honey, if Pam strikes your fancy, it's sure all right with me."

An hour later, they returned downstairs. "Charlie" looked as contented as a fox after a successfully appetizing henhouse raid. And Pam had a moonstruck look in her eyes as she showed him to the door.

"He was absolutely wonderful," Pam sighed after her Adonis had left. "He even gave me a tip. I wonder if he'll ever be back."

"Who was he—what does he do?" the girls wanted to know. "Does he live in these parts?"

"I don't know," Pam replied. "I didn't want to be nosey and get him sore at me."

The identity of the handsome stranger didn't remain a mystery for long. When the next day's paper arrived, page one prominently featured a story about a well-known evangelist coming to town to lead a two-week revival meeting. Accompanying the story was a picture of the evangelist. The noted preacher was none other than Charlie, our handsome stranger.

One of my girls, after staring wide-eyed at the newspaper story and picture, hurriedly summoned Pam from her upstairs room. She thrust the newspaper into Pam's hands, pointed to the story and exclaimed, "Now look what you've done, Pam—you've led a God-fearing preacher to sin!"

Pam read and reread the story and studied the picture. "Well," she said softly, "if he's half as good a preacher as he is a lover, he's quite a man in the pulpit."

After seeing who our Charlie really was, I was certain he'd never be back. A whorehouse is just about the last place a visiting evangelist should include in his itinerary. About an hour later, however, the doorbell rang. Charlie was back for an encore.

This time, I ushered him into my private sitting room for a personal talk before the excited girls could get their hands on him.

I didn't fool around with formalities. "Reverend," I said, "the cat's out of the bag. Everyone here, and everyone in town, knows who you are. Isn't it kind of risky for you to be coming to my house?"

Charlie didn't seem to be upset. "I'm very careful not to be seen," he said. "Besides, your place is out in the country, with no close neighbors."

"But you're a preacher," I said. "Doesn't it bother you to come here and then go back to town to preach the gospel?"

Charlie shook his head firmly. "I'm a man of God, but I'm also a mortal man with mortal hungers. Unfortunately, I have a very strong sex drive which I'm not strong enough to resist. I have no remorse, for I'm sure God will forgive my weakness of the flesh."

"Why don't you get married?" I asked.

"Oh, I am married," the Reverend explained. "But my wife has been an invalid for several years. I've had to look elsewhere for sexual gratification. Every time I reach a new town, I locate a fine quality house like yours, one that has a maximum of privacy."

I was still terrified at the idea of having a man of the cloth as a customer. I could picture the scandal that would erupt if he were caught in a raid on my house. "I still think it's terribly dangerous for you to come to a brothel," I protested. "Couldn't you pick out one of the young ladies in your church, explain the situation, and have a private affair?"

For once the handsome Reverend was shocked. "Of course not," he exclaimed. "That would be a sin!"

Well, you can't argue with that kind of cockeyed logic. I reluctantly agreed to continue accepting Charlie as a customer, as long as he arrived early in the afternoon before we normally opened for business.

"If you think it's okay with your Big Boss, I guess it will be okay by me," I said.

"I surely do appreciate your kind hospitality," the Reverend said. "Things get mighty lonely for a man in a strange city."

One thing is for sure. The Reverend didn't suffer from loneliness during his stay in Bowling Green. Except for two Sundays, which he apparently devoted to spiritual matters, he visited my house every day, enthusiastically pursuing pleasures of the flesh. His wayward gamboling didn't seem to affect his powers as a preacher. When his two-week revival ended, the local newspaper commended him on the eloquence and fervor of his "stirring messages against sin."

Despite his steady patronage and generous tips, I was relieved when the Reverend departed for another city and another flock of sinners. His presence in the house, of course, was a risky, scandal-threatening proposition. But beyond that factor I could see that Pam was falling in love with him, a one-sided infatuation which could only end on a sad note.

Charlie had sampled several of my girls, but Pam was his favorite. She, in turn, became increasingly smitten with the virile preacher. And after his departure she mooned around the house like a lovelorn schoolgirl. Finally I had to put a stop to her romantic fantasies.

"Pam, this nonsense has got to stop," I said. "The Reverend is gone. Forget him!"

"I try to, but I can't," Pam sighed. "He really got to me."

"That's ridiculous," I snapped impatiently. "You know there's no place for love in this business. If a girl falls for a guy, she quits and gets married. But you can't even do that. The Reverend already has a wife."

"I know he does. But I'm sure he cares for me. I don't know what to do."

I hated to disillusion Pam, but I had no choice. I told her how the Reverend had confided to me that he patronized prostitutes because he believed he'd be committing a sin if he indulged in sex with a "good" woman.

"In other words," I said, "he looks on a prostitute as a low form of life that he can screw and forget, with no worries about sinning."

Pam's shock at hearing this news was quickly replaced by anger. "That no-good, hypocritical bastard," she raged. "Making love to me, and all the time seeing me as some kind of animal." She stormed up to her room and never again mentioned the Reverend.

Unfortunately not all affairs of the heart which occasionally plague a whorehouse are so easily resolved. As a madam I've had my share of headaches trying to build defenses against Cupid's arrows. Prostitution is a mercenary business, but its practitioners and the men who patronize them sometimes let their emotions blot out the grim reality of love for sale. I repeatedly warned my girls to (1) never encourage a trick who showed signs of falling in love with them and (2) above all, never let themselves become emotionally involved with a customer.

"Always remember that you're not in a house to be made love to," I cautioned them. "You're here to provide a sexual service for which you get paid. Fuck 'em where you find 'em, and leave 'em where you fuck 'em. That's the only sensible way to operate in this cockeyed business."

Despite such warnings, however, the "love bug" still invaded the house from time to time. And it always brought troublesome complications. Once they decided they were in love, a girl and a trick usually attempted to keep their big romance a secret. The secrecy, however, soon was broken by several telltale signs easily recognized by an alert madam. The trick would arrive at the house, learn that his lady love was busy with a customer, and start muttering angrily, pouting, or indulging in other forms of ill-concealed jealousy. Such outbreaks of jealousy also would tip the girl's secret crush. She would begin quarreling with other girls whom she suspected of trying to move in on her man. Occasionally these spats would erupt into hair-pulling scraps. Other enamored girls would manage to curb their tempers, but I'd catch them in lies or learn that they were secretly seeing a customer on the outside although such meetings were forbidden by the rules of my house.

Elsie was one of the girls who resorted to outside trysts. She had fallen for one of my married customers, a young businessman, but I suspected nothing until the affair was seriously out of hand. One Saturday night Elsie told me she planned to go to church the following morning. I thought nothing of it, for my girls had permission to attend church whenever they felt the need for spiritual comforting.

Early Sunday morning, however, a delivery boy from a local florist came to the house on Clay Street with a large gardenia corsage for Elsie. I gave her the flowers when she came downstairs for breakfast before leaving for church.

"You must have a secret admirer," I remarked suspiciously.

Elsie blushed. "Oh, no," she said. "My brother just remembered my birthday." And she hurried off to church without even finishing her coffee.

After Elsie had left, another girl at the breakfast table eyed me quizzically. "Pauline, I hope you didn't fall for *that* line," she said.

I admitted that the delivery of the corsage and Elsie's birthday story had bothered me. "What do you know that I don't?" I asked.

"Those flowers are from Elsie's Lover-Boy," the girl replied, identifying the boyfriend as one of the regular customers of my house. "They've had a big thing going on the sly for several months."

"That damned wench told me she was going to church," I exclaimed heatedly.

"Oh, she's going to church, all right," my informant said. "Elsie is going to church because Lover-Boy's baby is being christened this morning!"

"She's going to a christening service? She's going to be at church, right in the middle of that jerk's wife and family?"

"That's right. She said her Lover-Boy insisted that she come."

"That man's a goddam fool," I said disgustedly. "But she's an even bigger sap. She's going to get her ass in more trouble than she ever bargained for."

I never did learn whether or not Elsie attended that christening service. The ensuing events that day gave me no time to really question her and attempt to set her straight. Shortly before noon Lover-Boy arrived at the house, asking for a party with Elsie.

"She's gone to church," I said tersely, fighting back the urge to lambaste him for his idiocy in becoming infatuated with a prostitute. I decided it would be wiser to wait until he had left before having a showdown with Elsie.

Elsie returned a short while later, unconvincingly expressing surprise at finding Lover-Boy waiting for a Sunday "nooner." They went upstairs hand in hand like a couple of silly teen-agers in the throes of puppy love. It must of been quite a party because it was at least two hours before they returned from their bedroom frolicking. As soon as Elsie said her fond farewell to Lover-Boy, I cornered her.

"Where's the money, Elsie?" I asked.

"What money?" she countered with an air of injured innocence.

"Elsie, don't play games with me," I said, resisting an impulse to belt her. "You were upstairs with that Lover-Boy of yours for two hours. Now hand over the money!"

"There's no money," Elsie replied. "I didn't ask for any. Today's party was on the house."

"On the house!" I yelled. "Hell's bells, do you think this is like a goddam gas station? We don't give trading stamps, we don't give gift certificates, and we sure as hell don't give away a piece of ass!"

"But this is Sunday," Elsie protested feebly. "I thought it would be nice to give a good customer a free party."

"Who in the hell are *you* to say anyone can have a party on *my* house?" I added a few other choice endearments and told her to pack up and get out. In my indignation over being confronted by a whorehouse "giveaway," I never did get around to chewing Elsie about her romancing with a customer. In any event, she apparently didn't linger around town very long. In about a week I heard that Lover-Boy was reconciled with his wife. It was almost a year before he returned to my house to renew his extramarital adventuring. And you can be sure he never got another free party on Clay Street.

Generally, though, a whorehouse love affair doesn't end on such a ridiculous note as a free party. A madam often can nip romance in the bud by having a heart-to-heart, no-nonsense talk with the girl. At times, though, it is necessary to sit down with a love-stricken trick and explain the facts of life.

The Professor was one of these romantically blinded males. He was an intelligent, mature man—a respected instructor at Western Kentucky University—until he met Madge. After a couple of upstairs parties with her it was evident that, even though the Professor was an expert in his field of study, he had a distressingly low I.Q. as far as the female of the species was concerned.

It wasn't that the Professor was naive or inexperienced. He was a widower in his early forties. And he had patronized my house for several years without losing his head or his heart. Then one evening he had a party with Madge, a newcomer to my stable. Never was there clearer proof that love is a funny proposition. Madge was an attractive woman "nearing thirty," according to her count—a veteran of nearly ten years on the sex circuit. Certainly there were far more beautiful, more desirable girls in my house whose goodies the Professor had sampled without going ape. But after one session with Madge he was practically a basket case. He started showing up three and four times a week for a date with Madge, a rather heavy drain on a college teacher's salary back in those days. And when she was occupied with another trick, he would sit morosely in the parlor, eating his heart out with dark thoughts of his lady love sharing her "all" with another man.

The Professor's lovesick symptoms didn't bother me at first. Madge had assured me that as far as she was concerned he was just another trick. Unless he caused trouble, I decided, it would be safe to let the infatuation run its course. I was certain that after a few weeks the Professor would come to his senses, forget his grand passion, and begin playing the field once more.

A telephone call, however, put an end to that bit of wishful thinking. Madge, I learned, was meeting the Professor on the outside when she went into town for her weekly medical checkup. The informer, a friend of mine who clerked in a downtown drugstore, told me tnat for more than a month Madge had been dropping in for a coke and sandwich. Minutes later the Professor, sporting dark glasses as a disguise, would saunter in and join Madge at a table. And after billing and cooing like a couple of kids, they would leave the store arm in arm.

"I know you don't allow your girls to meet men outside the house because it can cause trouble," my friend said, "so I thought I'd better let you know what's going on before there's a lot of nasty gossip."

When I confronted Madge with this report, she made no attempt to deny it. "Nothing has *really* happened," she said. "We don't do anything but talk."

"That's plenty," I said. "All I need is for some nosey biddies to see and recognize the two of you. The word will spread fast that Pauline is letting her prostitutes mingle with the rest of the town, and before long my ass will be in a sling."

Madge was distressed. "Pauline, I've got a problem. The Professor is a real nice guy, but he sure doesn't turn me on. He keeps insisting he loves me and wants to marry me, and he won't listen when I tell him he's acting foolish."

I eyed her suspiciously. "Are you on the level? Are you positive you aren't giving this poor dope a come-on?"

Madge shook her head. "Believe me, Pauline. This is a one-sided romance. I don't know what to do. I've never met a man with such a one-track mind."

"Okay, honey," I said. "I guess the time has come for me to have a talk with the Professor."

The next evening when the Professor arrived at the house I was ready for him. When he made his customary request for Madge, I told him she was busy upstairs.

"I'll wait," he said.

"I'm sorry," I told the Professor, "but you'll have to choose another girl."

The Professor was horrified by my effrontery.

"I don't want anyone else," he exclaimed. "I want Madge, the same as always."

Not wanting a scene in the parlor, I invited the Professor to my private sitting room so we could discuss the problem frankly. Once the door had closed behind us, the Professor asked with a worried frown, "What's the trouble? Is Madge sick, or has she left town?"

"Madge is just fine," I said. "It's just that I don't want the two of you having anything more to do with each other."

The Professor was enraged by my interference in his love life. "Now see here, Miss Pauline," he sputtered. "Madge and I are adults. We don't have to take orders from you."

"You do as long as you're in my house," I said.

"Then I'll take Madge out of here right now. I wanted her to leave a long time ago."

I sighed wearily. A mule is a sweet-tempered, reasonable critter compared to the male animal when his mating instincts are aroused. "Professor," I said, "you just hold your horses a minute and listen here to me."

Patiently, as if I were lecturing to one of the Professor's classes, I set out to teach him the ABCs of life in a whorehouse. I told him bluntly that Madge was free to leave the house with him whenever she wanted to give up her job as a prostitute.

"The point is that Madge doesn't want to leave with you," I said. "She likes you, but not enough to take a chance on marrying you. She's been a prostitute for a long time. She's taken good care of herself and saved her money. In another year or two, before she's too old, she's going to have enough money to quit and invest in a good business of her own some place where folks don't know about her past.

She's not going to risk all this on a marriage that's got about as much chance of lasting as a snowball in hell."

"That's preposterous," the Professor protested. "I'm deeply in love with Madge. It would be a splendid marriage."

"Professor, you're talking through your balls right now," I said. "You think that Madge is the greatest thing that ever laid down on a mattress. But after marriage Madge will soon become just a plain old wife, and you'll start remembering the hundreds and hundreds of men who have been there before you. It just won't work. You'll both end up unhappy as hell, hating each other's guts."

"You're not giving me any credit for decent feelings," the Professor insisted. "I love Madge, and I'm broadminded enough to accept and forget about her past."

"That's a bunch of crap," I said indelicately, "and deep down you know I'm right. You've just been thinking about yourself all along, not worrying about who gets hurt. You've been a customer here long enough to know I don't allow my girls to meet fellows on the outside. You know damned well that the folks of Bowling Green won't stand for my girls gallivanting around town. Yet you've jeopardized Madge's job and my house by insisting that she meet you. How long do you think you'd last at the university if you married a known prostitute? The only reason the word hasn't gotten around now about your big romance is because Madge is new in town. You've just been lucky."

"I don't care what you say," the Professor angrily proclaimed, "I'd marry Madge tomorrow if she'd have me."

"Then you're a bigger fool than I thought you were," I snapped. "As far as I'm concerned, it's up to Madge. If she wants to accept your proposal, it's her funeral. But I'm telling you one more time—as long as she works for me you can't date her."

The outraged teacher stormed out of my house, insisting that he'd "take Madge away from all this." For several weeks he tried all manner of subterfuges to get a chance to plead his case with Madge, but she refused to see him. He never returned to my house, and about a year later he moved on to another college. And as for Madge, she eventually retired from the business, moved to Florida, and bought a gift shop.

Madge was smart in refusing to be lured into marriage with an infatuated trick. I've known many prostitutes who married successfully and raised families after their retirement. But seldom have I seen anything but disaster in a marriage between a girl and one of her customers. Like the Professor, the man may start out with the best intentions in the world. However, the egotistical male rarely can endure for long the secret torture of knowing that his wife is "soiled merchandise." The ghosts of past lovers soon blot out the fragile spark of passion, leaving only bitter ashes on love's hearthstone. There's a lot of common-sense truth in the old female adage: "what a man doesn't know won't hurt him."

Most men who patronize a brothel have one thing in common besides the sex urge. They're lonely men, seeking the warmth of human companionship. Probably this is one of the basic reasons why tricks like the Professor sometimes lose touch with reality and imagine they're in love with one of the girls. This legion of lonely hearts isn't restricted to young singles, confirmed bachelors, and widowers. A surprisingly large number are married men, buying an illusion of the passion which their wives are unwilling or unable to provide. In fact, I'd say from experience that a big share of business in a whorehouse is the end result of wives who are so occupied with homemaking, children, jobs, and outside activities that they can't be bothered with sex. They can't seem to understand that once the "Old Man" realizes his love life is last on his wife's list of priorities he's going to look for his pleasure outside the home. Even though a house may not be a home, it's a substitute for one in the eyes of many husbands.

One of these straying husbands almost didn't make it back home to his family one night. John was a successful lawyer, a man in his fifties who, for a number of years, had been finding a substitute in my house for his wife's fading libido. At least once a week he would sample my tasty "tarts" with the same enthusiasm he devoted to his torts during working hours.

One night, however, he apparently became too enthusiastic in his pursuit of pleasure. His date for the evening called me frantically from the top of the stairs.

"What in the world's the matter?" I asked when I reached her, huffing and puffing from the exertion of rushing upstairs.

"Something terrible has happened," the frightened girl whispered. "My date just topped out on me. He's lying unconscious on the bed, limp as an old wet dishrag."

I hurried downstairs to phone the doctor who handled the weekly medical checkups of my girls. Then I rushed back upstairs to help the girl dress the still-unconscious trick. The amorous attorney was "respectable" when the doctor arrived. After an examination, the doctor said John had suffered an apparently light heart attack.

"We'll have to get him to the hospital," he said, promising he'd make sure no one knew where the heart attack really had occurred. By this time John had regained consciousness and agreed on the need to cover up his tracks. He suggested a story that the had become ill while driving and stopped at the doctor's office for help. It was a believable alibi, but it made it impossible to summon an ambulance to Clay Street. So I helped get the stricken man into the doctor's car, and they rushed off to the hospital. Then to complete the ticklish logistics problem I drove the lawyer's car to the doctor's office, parked it, and left it there, returning to my house by taxi with another scandal luckily averted.

It was several months before John was well enough to risk a return to action at my house on Clay Street. When he showed up for the first time, he thanked me profusely for the tactful way in which the doctor and I had dealt with his delicate dilemma.

"What would have happened if I had died upstairs?" he asked, giving voice to a morbid question which, without doubt, had been bothering him.

"Honey," I said, "there's only one thing we could have done. We'd have carried you out of the house, put you in your car, and driven it to some lonely country road. We'd have left you there in the car for some passerby to discover."

"Would you really have done that to me?" the lawyer asked, seemingly shocked by such a cold-blooded attitude.

"I sure as hell would," I said, "not only to protect my house, but for the sake of your wife and children. And," I added, "for the sake of your own reputation."

The attorney thought this over. "You're right, Pauline," he finally admitted. "I never before thought about it this way, but a madam does have to think about other things besides making money. What happens in this house can affect a lot of lives and reputations."

In his idle musing, the lawyer put his finger on the key to success for a bordello. The customer's privacy and reputation must be protected at all times. A whorehouse can't operate for long if this code of secrecy is violated, any more than it can stay in business if it flaunts its illicit trade in the face of the community. That's why a smart madam makes sure her girls don't gad about in their free time. That's why a smart madam will tolerate no trouble-making customers.

Trouble-makers—the drunks, the rowdies, the males with brutal instincts—are among the major worries that beset the daily life of a madam. During my first year in the business I learned through several unhappy experiences to turn away as diplomatically as possible all sloppy, belligerent drunks even when they were regular, good-paying customers who had fallen off the wagon. Although I permitted my customers to bring their own bottles and mix their own highballs, I never allowed my girls to drink on the job. And I always made sure my imbibing customers knew I would stand for no heavy boozing in my house. The reason for such precautions is simple. One or two unruly drunks can create chaos in a house.

Rowdies sometimes are a bigger problem than drunks. Fortunately, I had a well-known reputation as a "tiger" in dealing with unwelcome guests. I recall one night when four wild bucks from Kyrock, a small town near Bowling Green, came pounding at the door of my house on Clay Street. They not only were rowdies; they were drunk.

"We've come for some of your pussy," one of them bellowed.

"Not tonight, boys," I said. "You know I don't let drunks in the house." I slammed the door in their faces.

Two of the unwelcome visitors drove away, but the other two prowled around outside the house, shouting obscenities and banging on doors and windows. I watched their wild antics from a downstairs window. Twice, within a few minutes, customers drove into my parking lot, saw these drunks whooping it up, and promptly departed.

"My God!" I thought. "Those bastards are driving all my customers away. I've got to do something."

Suddenly I had an inspiration. I remembered two large Roman candles I had saved from a Fourth of July celebration. Armed with these fireworks, I went out to the yard. I lighted the candles and went charging toward the two drunks. Finding themselves under fire, they turned and fled. I was right on their heels, bombarding their singed rumps with salvos of fireballs spurting from the Roman candles. I chased them about a hundred yards down the road before my ammunition was exhausted. I didn't need a new supply. The drunks kept running, disappearing into the night. I never again had trouble with those Kyrock hoodlums.

Aside from drunks and rowdies, a house also gets its share of unpleasant customers—the men with nasty personalities who'd find something to complain about even if they were serviced by the Queen of Sheba. And, of course, there is the perennial problem of peeping Toms.

Generally, the peepers are kids, curious teen-agers looking for a free show. But every once in awhile a house has problems with adult voyeurs. One in particular kept returning periodically for almost a year. We never seemed to be able to trap him and put an end to his visitations.

I was in the kitchen one night when I heard a noise in the yard. There was considerable cash in the house at the time, and I was worried about burglars. I got a flashlight and a loaded revolver from my bedside lamp table and went into the yard to investigate. I quickly determined the source of the noise. A shadowy figure was standing at a rear bedroom window, peering intently through a gap in the curtains. He was so engrossed with the action in the bedroom that he didn't realize he had company until I switched on the flashlight.

What a scene it was! Standing there, blinded by the sudden glare, was one of the town's most prominent businessmen. His trousers were unzipped and one hand still was lovingly clutched around his erect organ.

"Go ahead and finish your business," I suggested icily. "It's going to cost you twenty bucks, so you might as well have your fun before you leave."

The businessman hurriedly stuffed his quickly wilting apparatus back into his trousers. Struggling to regain a semblance of dignity, he stood rooted to the spot, staring bug-eyed at my pistol, which was pointed at his rotund belly.

"Can't you put that gun away?" he finally managed to squeak.

"I'll put it away as soon as you fork over twenty bucks," I replied.

The businessman briefly forgot his embarrassing predicament. "Twenty dollars!" he blustered. "What for?"

"Mister, this is my place of business. Men who come here pay for our services. If you want to play peeping Tom at my house, it's going to cost you money. Twenty bucks, to be exact!"

"You realize that this is robbery at gunpoint," the now-indignant peeper protested.

"Why don't you come in the house and phone the police?" I suggested sweetly. "I'll even let you use the phone free."

There was no more quibbling. The businessman quietly handed over a $20 bill and vanished into the night. He never returned to my house to indulge in his appetite for sex as a spectator sport.

Although I finally got rid of our problem peeper, we never were completely free from the harassments of obnoxious customers. One whom I will never forget was a big-time movie star, an eighteen-carat conceited slob. He had been on tour, and for some vague reason he showed up at my house in Bowling Green after making personal appearances in Louisville.

For several hours he disrupted business in the house. He settled down in a big chair in the parlor and began entertaining customers and girls with tales of his Hollywood escapades. He was a considerable hunk of man, and my girls practically ignored the other waiting tricks as they vied for the honor of servicing a genuine star, a hero of God only knows how many movies. At last, with the grand air of a feudal king, he made his selection from my "harem"—a luscious, bosomy blonde named Karen.

Karen had been upstairs with the movie star for about fifteen minutes when, to my surprise, she returned alone downstairs and summoned me into the hall for a private conference.

"Pauline, that damned actor is giving me fits," she complained.

"What's the problem?"

"When we got to the room, I asked him for the money before we got undressed. But he refused to pay. He says he should get it free, and he says he won't leave my room until I give it to him."

"That goddam phony expects a free piece of ass in my house!" I exclaimed. "Who in the hell does he think he is?"

I marched upstairs with Karen, my rage increasing with each step. We found the movie star, still fully dressed, lounging casually in a chair in the bedroom.

"What's this crap about a free party?" I raged. "What kind of a cheapskate are you?"

The movie star favored me with his famous devil-may-care grin. "You should be honored to have me patronize your house," he said. "Just think, after I've gone on my way you'll be able to tell everybody that a real celebrity has screwed here."

"I don't care who you are," I yelled. "Nobody, not even the President of the United States, gets free pussy in my house."

"It's not the money, it's the principle of the thing," the movie star insisted. "I've never had to pay to get laid. I don't intend to spoil that record in Bowling Green."

"Then, by God, you ain't going to get laid in Bowling Green," I roared. Ignoring his size and his outraged protests, I grabbed the surprised actor by the collar, hustled him downstairs, and gave him my deluxe bum's rush out the front door. I can't remember any other time when playing the part of a bouncer gave me so much pleasure. I damned near had an orgasm as I shoved him sprawling onto the porch.

Even more drastic action was required to get rid of a couple of other obnoxious tricks. One was a chronic grouch—a creep who never was happy unless he was complaining about something or giving stupid orders on how to do things properly.

For several years this old goat, an office manager by trade, came to my house three or four times a month. My girls dreaded his visits because of his endless complaints, his caustic criticisms, and his bossy manner which he even carried into the bedroom. Finally, after wearying of his constant carping, I told my girls they could have the rare privilege of turning down this particular customer.

The next time the old grouch came to the house he happened to arrive in the midst of a slow evening. Reluctant to turn down a trick, Marjorie agreed to date him despite her unhappy memories of past parties with this infuriating man. They'd been upstairs only a short time when howls of pain echoed through the house. I ran up to Marjorie's room and found our perennial pest hopping up and down in the middle of the room. His face was twisted agonizingly and he was gently dabbing his sorely damaged penis with a handkerchief, trying to stop the flow of blood.

Marjorie was sitting on the edge of the bed, crying. "I'm sorrry, Pauline," she sobbed. "He wanted a blow job. He kept criticizing me, and telling me how to do it. Then he started hitting me and I lost my temper. I bit him good and hard."

"You're damned well right," the old grouch moaned. "She bit me, and her teeth are sharp."

I found it impossible to sympathize with the suffering customer. "Hell's bells, if it had been me, I'd have bitten the damned thing off and fed it to the pigs," I told him before I fetched medications to patch his wounded organ. That was the last time that old grouch came to my house.

Archie, one of the town's merchants, also was an obnoxious S.O.B., a vain, overbearing bully with crude sex techniques and a talent for treating all women—including his browbeaten wife—like they were dirt. He was a good-paying customer, but my girls hated the very sight of him. They disliked his bullying ways, found his crudities distasteful, and were frightened by his quick, explosive temper. Still, he was a generous tipper, so they accepted him as one of the unpleasant aspects of their jobs.

I never attempted to coddle my girls. Except in such an extremely nerve-wracking case as the old grouch, who was more trouble than he was worth, my girls were expected to handle all types of tricks—the uncouth, unpleasant characters as well as the nice guys. Whenever a prostitute came to work for me, I would tell her frankly that she was working for one main reason, to please the customers.

"Different men get their kicks in different ways," I would say in my introductory lecture. "When a girl takes a man to her room, he can stand her on her head and spin her like a top if that happens to be his pleasure. Whatever the customer wants is all right with me as long as he can pay the price. There's only one place where I draw the line. I won't let any man, no matter who he is or what he's willing to pay, physically abuse my girls. This house wants no part of sadistic bastards."

Archie, of course, ranked in the lower levels of acceptable customers, mainly because of his willingness to "pay the price." It wasn't until he paid an unusually big fee to get me to relax my rules and permit him to have an afternoon date at a motel with one of my girls that he crossed the forbidden line.

The girl, Mary, returned from the motel date looking like a refugee from a street brawl. She had displeased Archie by refusing to extend the party a few more hours, and he had roughed her up. Her new custom-tailored suit was ripped beyond repair. Her cheek and arms were bruised and an eye was blackened.

"He lost his temper and slapped me around," Mary cried. "Don't ever ask me to date that pig again."

"Don't worry, honey. That creep will sure as hell never date another one of my girls. What's more, I'm going to make sure he pays for your suit."

I immediately got busy carrying out my promise. And for once I wasn't worried about a customer's reputation. I telephoned Archie at his home. He was furious.

"What in the hell's the idea of calling me here?" he wanted to know.

"Don't you get on your high horse, you no-good bastard," I said. "You slapped Mary around, and you ripped the hell out of her expensive suit."

Archie showed no signs of remorse. "She had it coming," he growled. "She got nasty with me."

"Bullshit!" I said. "I'm coming out to your house. You owe Mary a hundred and fifty dollars for that suit, and I'm coming out right now to collect it."

"Don't you dare come here," he said, a note of alarm in his voice. "My wife is home."

"Okay, then you or one of your people at the store get down here right away with the money. I'll give you an hour to pay up."

"I'm not going to do any such thing!" Archie snorted.

"Well, buddy, you'd better have the money ready when I drive up, because I'm leaving for your house *now!*"

"The hell with you!" he yelled, banging the receiver in my ear.

About twenty minutes later I parked in the driveway of Archie's large home, walked up to the front door, and knocked. The door was opened by one of the clerks from Archie's store, a Man Friday who doubled as a chauffeur and handyman. I pushed him aside without a word and went storming through the house in search of Mary's assailant. I found him in a bathroom, off a long central hallway, helping his young son bathe his pet dog.

Archie obviously would have enjoyed killing me. But with his wife busy in the kitchen preparing dinner and his son looking on curiously, he had to maintain at least a semblance of domestic tranquillity. He pulled me back into the big living room and whispered a hoarse-voiced threat to have me arrested if I didn't leave his home immediately.

"Call the cops," I replied, not caring who heard me. "But remember this—we'll go to jail together because I've got all the proof I need to file charges against you for assaulting Mary and ripping her clothes."

Archie abruptly capitulated. "All right, all right," he said, still keeping his voice low. "I'll pay the money, but you'll have to wait until morning. I'll have it delivered to your house." He cast a desperate glance over his shoulder to make certain no one was witnessing our scene. "Now, for God's sake, get out and leave me and my family alone."

"Okay, I'll leave," I said. "Just remember, if that hundred and fifty doesn't arrive, I'm going to file assault charges against you."

The money was delivered early the next morning—$150 in cash. Archie never came to my house again. In fact, he left Bowling Green about a year later and opened a successful chain of stores in Louisville. A few years later, after he had become a big-shot businessman, he had the nerve to telephone me, asking if I could line him up with an all-night date for a $250 fee. "Archie," I said, "you can go to hell!" And this time *I* banged the receiver in *his* ear.

Mary's experience was bad enough, but Polly—another of my girls —barely escaped with her life during a party with a real psycho. The customer involved in this terrifying incident was a newcomer to my house, but his credentials were impeccable. He was a wealthy landowner from another part of the state, a member of an old-line, socially prominent Kentucky family.

However, Polly hadn't been upstairs with the new trick more than a half hour when I had one of those hunches that I'd get occasionally, a premonition that something was wrong in the house. I left the parlor and quietly climbed the stairs. At first, everything seemed in order. But as I tiptoed down the hall, I heard a strange mumbling and threshing noise coming from Polly's room. Silently I opened her door an inch or two and peered in.

It was like a scene from a horror movie. The trick was lying on top of Polly, but he wasn't engaged in the customary bedroom activities. He was choking her. Polly's eyes were bulging, and she was clawing frantically at his hands, trying to break his grip on her throat.

I ran into the room, screaming for help in a voice loud enough to rattle windows all the way downtown. I grabbed his arms, but I couldn't budge him. I grabbed his legs and tried to pull him off the struggling, gasping girl. No matter how hard I tugged, though, I couldn't move him an inch. The violent customer paid no attention to me. He just kept choking Polly and muttering some kind of insane gibberish. By this time, three or four of my girls and their dates, aroused by my screaming, had rushed into the room. One brawny trick, naked as a jaybird, wasted no time asking what the trouble was. He picked a heavy reading lamp off a nearby table and smashed it across the head of Polly's assailant. The psycho collapsed, loosening his grip on Polly's throat. We pulled her safely off the bed and set about reviving both the nearly strangled girl and the unconscious, blue-blooded customer who had tried to kill her.

Polly recovered first. Almost incoherently, she told us that everything had been proceeding normally when the trick suddenly, with no provocation, began to choke her. "I was helpless," she said. "I thought I was a goner."

A few minutes later her nearly fatal date regained consciousness with apparently nothing more serious than a big lump on his head. At first he was indignant to find the room crowded with people, all of them but me as naked as he was. But after we angrily told him what had happened and showed him the livid bruises on Polly's throat, he was stricken with remorse.

"My God!" he said in a voice heavy with despair. "It's happened again!"

When I asked for an explanation, he told me that for several years he had been having periodic blackouts during which his actions were either highly erratic or violent. "But there's never been anything this bad before. I know now that I've got to see a doctor and get help."

As long as neither Polly nor the customer was injured badly, there was no need to summon the police. No one wanted to be involved in a scandal. Before he left the dejected trick apologized profusely to Polly, dug into his wallet, and handed her two crisp $100 bills. After he had departed, Polly looked at the money and sighed. "All I can say is that it's a hell of a tough way to earn two hundred bucks," she said.

Fortunately for my sanity, obnoxious and dangerous customers like the gentleman farmer, Archie, and the grouch were not an everyday occurrence. Most of the customers of my house were normal, pleasant males looking for companionship, a few laughs, and a good time in bed with a pretty girl.

My mind is filled with memories of hundreds of tricks and the silly antics in which they sometimes indulged. I recall, for example, the skinny corporal from Camp Campbell who tried to screw one of my girls in a backyard hammock.

It was a hot summer weekend during World War II, and my colonial country house was packed. All the bedrooms were in use, and this corporal volunteered to bed down in a hammock with Sue, the only available girl. She agreed to the experiment, and they hurried into the yard with a couple of pillows. A few minutes later I heard a blood-curdling scream. I ran into the yard and found the hammock twisted out of shape. Sue and the corporal were on the ground under the hammock, still busily engaged. I quietly retreated to the house, knowing that Sue still had the situation well in hand. The scream apparently had just been one of alarm when they fell out of their temperamental love-making "couch."

"It was the damnedest sensation I've ever had," Sue told me later. "That hammock was jiggling and swaying like mad. Suddenly it flipped over and we hit the ground." Sue giggled with delight at the memory. "That skinny ol' soldier was holding me so tight that even when we were falling and rolling on the hard ground he didn't miss a stroke!"

Of all my memories of the tricks, though, I guess my favorite ones are centered around the kids in the fraternities at Western Kentucky University. Now, I guess these young men generally couldn't be classified as tricks because not many of them had enough cash to patronize a brothel regularly. Nevertheless, they were always welcome in my house during off hours. They would talk with me and the girls, play cards, put money in the jukebox, and dance. During working hours, however, no student loafing was permitted. If they came to the house then, it was as paying customers.

In time, Pauline's house became sort of a legend on the campus—a legend bolstered by the school's fraternities. The frats required every group of aspiring initiates to visit my house, talk with me and my girls about the facts of life, and return to campus with a personal letter, signed by me, attesting to the successful completion of their mission to a palace of sin.

Ultimately, the initiates were required to return to campus with more exotic evidence in addition to my testimonial—a pair of panties donated by one of my girls. This became a rather costly custom, for my girls, like almost all prostitutes, had a weakness for frilly, expensive lingerie. Finally, I jokingly wrote a letter to the college.

"For God's sake," I wrote, "take up a collection to buy my establishment a few dozen pairs of women's panties. The fraternities have been taking them for years now, and my poor girls are down to their last pair of pants."

Some unknown jokester on the campus saw my letter and mailed me a package filled with two dozen cheap pairs of panties. Enclosed was an unsigned note: "Here are 24 pairs of panties bought for 50 cents each at the dime store. Give these to the kids in the frats. They won't know the difference."

However, it was one of my girls who really wowed the frats with an idea for a new custom. After being pestered by a group of initiates for a pair of panties, she told them she'd give their frat a far better love token. She went upstairs, promising to be back with her mystery gift. When she returned, she handed the young men a token which, for a long, long time, occupied a prominent display space on that particular fraternity's bulletin board.

The token was devastatingly simple. It was a generous swatch of curly, coal-black pubic hair, elegantly tied with a thin red ribbon. Attached to the ribbon was a card bearing this message:

"A Token of Love for the cutest tricks we've never laid, from the girls down at Pauline's."

*The big-time spenders*

# *The big-time spenders*

A properly operated brothel, like a large department store, is set up to cater to a wide range of tastes and budgets. Its "basement store" and "regular departments" offer basic sex entertainment (such normally popular male pastimes as a "straight" lay and, for tricks seeking an extra thrill, the routine "trip-around-the-world" or the more sophisticated "frenching" party) at nominal prices. These services provide a house with a major share of its day-to-day business.

However, every top-quality house also has its "exclusive shops"— special sex services set up for the big-time spenders, the affluent gentlemen who demand more than the mere basics enjoyed by the masses. Included in this exclusive category are *very special*, and *very expensive*, "boutiques" which feature all sorts of exotic perversions for customers who are ready, willing, and able to pay the price. It's these big spenders, the well-heeled gents who delight in pampering their sexual appetites, who provide the all-important extra frosting for the cake that is a brothel's profits.

During my long-ago apprenticeship, Miss May briefed me at length on the importance of carefully catering to the fancies of the big-money clientele, the men who can afford to rent a whorehouse for an entire weekend or indulge in other costly sexual frolics. She and her girls also opened my eyes to some of the more prevalent customer hangups and to the excellent revenue-producing possibilities inherent in servicing these perversions as specialties of the house.

"Always remember, there are two kinds of big-time spenders in a whorehouse," Miss May had said. "First, there's the guy with a big bankroll who wants everything in a deluxe package. And then there are those with perverted tastes who are willing to pay big to have their hangups serviced. You can make these freaks pay outrageous prices because most of the time they have nowhere else to go to get their kicks."

Miss May's advice was sound. However, nothing that I learned at her Clarksville house and nothing that I experienced in subsequent years prepared me for one big-time spender who came calling one day at my colonial country house. When I answered the doorbell that afternoon, I found myself confronted by an attractive middle-aged woman, smartly and expensively dressed. This matronly type introduced herself as Roberta So-and-so, and after determining that I was Pauline, she asked if she might have a private talk with me about a very personal matter.

I showed the stranger back to my private sitting room, wondering what she wanted. Most female callers at my house were job-seekers. But this woman obviously was not in such a nubile age bracket. Perhaps, I told myself, she was some married biddy who had decided to confront me after learning that her husband had been straying in my sinful pastures.

My guess wasn't even close. Roberta settled herself in a comfortable easy chair, tugged modestly at her skirt as she crossed her somewhat heavy nyloned legs, and lighted a cigarette after daintily affixing it to a delicate ivory holder.

"It's rather awkward," the woman said in a deep but pleasant voice. "I just don't know how to begin."

"How about at the beginning?" I suggested.

"Well," Roberta blurted hastily, "the problem is I'm not a 'she,' I'm a 'he.' "

"You're a what?" I asked, staring at her like she'd lost her mind.

"I'm a transvestite—a man who enjoys wearing women's clothing and adopting a woman's ways," Roberta said, nervously fluffing her, or his, shoulder-length hair.

"My God, I've seen everything now," I finally managed to mutter. "But what in the hell do you want in a whorehouse?"

"I know it sounds strange, but I want a date with one of your girls." The he in she's clothing giggled self-consciously.

I wasn't amused. It sounded damned peculiar to me. "How come you want a piece of tail?" I asked. "I always thought guys who dressed up like dames were pansies."

Roberta quickly assured me this was not so. "Most transvestites remain normal males sexually even though we like to live in a feminine world," he said. He claimed that he had led a normal male life—owned his business, was married, with grown children—until his wife died three years before.

"Ever since I was in college, I have enjoyed dressing up as a woman," Roberta said. "After my wife died, I sold my business, had my beard and leg hair removed by electrolysis, moved to another state, changed my name from Robert to Roberta, and started living a full-time life as a woman."

"And now you want to get laid?" I asked.

"Occasionally I still get the urge real bad, and it makes things awkward," Roberta said, claiming he was stuck in Bowling Green for several days on a sales trip for a lingerie business he'd started after "turning" female.

I looked at the stranger's smooth complexion, long eyelashes, enameled fingernails, and fair-sized bosom. "Dammit," I said, "I think you're pulling my leg, whoever you are. Those knockers look mighty real to me. Are you sure you aren't some goddam freaky lesbian looking for a party?"

Roberta snorted indignantly at the lesbian idea. He pushed his well-kept hands against his swelling bosom. "These breasts are the result of hormone shots and padding," he assured me. "Underneath all this female finery I'm still a man."

"Well, by God, you're going to have to prove it to me before I let you touch one of my girls," I exclaimed. "I've got to see it to believe it!"

Blushing a deep beet red, Roberta stood up, lifted the chic skirt, struggled with girdle and panty belt, and finally stood exposed. He was a he, all right—a well-hung male.

I laughed until my sides ached. The sight of Roberta's male apparatus dangling grotesquely amid the tangle of feminine dainties was too much. "I don't see anything so damned funny," Roberta growled, momentarily forgetting his feminine role as he struggled modestly to rearrange girdle and skirt.

"Well," he finally said, smoothing down his skirt one last time, "do I qualify for a date?"

"Honey, you sure do," I said, adding quickly, "provided you care to invest one hundred bucks in the party."

Roberta didn't blink an eye. He pulled a wallet out of his purse and handed me five twenties. I summoned Terry, the best of my girls in dealing with the freak trade.

"Roberta would like to have a party with you," I told Terry, adding none of the essential details.

"A party!" Terry exclaimed after giving the well-dressed matron a hasty glance. "Pauline, you know I don't have nothing to do with lesbians."

"I guarantee that Roberta's not lez," I said. "In fact, Roberta's a man who likes to dress up in woman's clothing. Right now, though, he wants a piece of tail."

Terry was still skeptical. But on the strength of my assurances she took Roberta upstairs for a party. When the action was over, and Roberta had departed for whatever never-never-land transvestites favor, Terry informed me: "That guy may be a freak about women's clothes, but he's sure a horny old stud in the sack. A real man!"

To my knowledge, I never met another freak like Roberta. I don't know whether he knew what he was talking about when he claimed that most transvestites are normal males when it comes to sex. But one thing I can tell you—Roberta was one he in she's clothing who was all man when he squirmed out of his girdle and panty belt.

At least Roberta's hangup turned out to be relatively wholesome compared to some perversions I've encountered through the years. I recall my first experience with a freak a few months after I started business in the house on Smallhouse Road.

He seemed to be a normal, handsome young man. He waited quietly in the parlor until the only one of my girls with long hair entered the room. He immediately selected her and away they went. About a half hour later, after the trick had departed, his date excitedly told me of their strange party.

"Everything was okay at first," she said. "We got undressed and I washed him. Then when it was time to get into bed, he asked me to let down my hair so he could brush it."

For the next ten or fifteen minutes, the girl said, the trick brushed her long hair, ran his fingers through it, buried his face in it. Finally, with an ecstatic moan, he climaxed without even once engaging in normal sex.

"It sure was an easy way to earn two dollars," the girl said.

"Two bucks?" I asked. "Is that all you charged this freak?"

"Sure," the girl replied. "It wasn't as messy or strenuous as a regular piece. All he did was monkey with my hair until he unloaded. It wasn't worth more than two bucks."

"I don't care how easy it was," I said. "That guy was a freak, and in my house freaks have to pay more to get their kicks."

"How much should I ask if he ever comes back?" the girl wanted to know.

That was a good question. It was my first dealing with a perversion, and I had no idea how much I could ask. "Try ten bucks," I suggested, pulling a figure out of the air.

"Ten!" the girl exclaimed. "He'll never go for that. He'll walk out." She was wrong, however. The trick with the odd-ball hair fetish paid $10 without a murmur the next time. And he continued to patronize my house at this rate until I closed up and moved to Indiana. This experience taught me a lesson I never forgot: the perverts of this world will pay fantastic prices, even far more than they can afford, to have their weird appetites satisfied.

And believe me, some of those appetites defy the imagination. One of my girls made a lot of money off one well-to-do old goat in town by the simple process of jabbing a greased candle in and out of his rear end. At the time, we had a hard rubber "dick," which the girls could strap around their waists and use when a customer requested a "rear-end job." But I guess this one freak was old-fashioned. He insisted on candles. I imagine the local dime store wondered for years what in the hell we were doing with all those candles I used to buy to keep Connie's freak happy.

Another of my off-beat customers was a handsome, virile man—the type you'd least suspect of freakish tendencies. And, for a strapping six-footer, his hangup was a dilly. This big yo-yo liked little girls —or, at least, pictures of them.

It was after his first and only date at my house on Clay Street that Phyllis, his girl for the half-hour party, handed me a $50 fee she had collected.

"Another weirdo?" I asked, surprised. "He sure didn't look like one."

Phyllis explained that, as soon as they got to her room, this trick had pulled a movie magazine from his coat pocket and turned to a centerfold spread of photographs of child stars—girls ranging in age from five to ten, I suppose.

"He told me he got his kicks pretending he was screwing a five- or six-year-old girl," Phyllis said. "He had a strange expression in his eyes. Said he wanted to hold the magazine over my face while we were screwing so he could look at a little girl's picture and imagine she was the one he was doing it with."

Phyllis shuddered at the memory. "He made me sick, just describing it in his wild way," she said. "I didn't want any part of that kind of a freak, so I told him a party like he had in mind would cost him fifty bucks." The girl shrugged. "The freak paid it, and I had to go through with it. I thought I was going to smother with that magazine jammed over my face. God, I still feel dirty."

I never saw this freak again. But I took no chances. I violated my code of silence, telephoned police, and gave them a full description of this trick and his sickening sexual hangup for little girls. He certainly seemed to have all the earmarks of a potential child molester, and I couldn't have slept with him on the loose unless I at least had reported the incident to authorities. Perhaps this freak went through life just play-acting out his perverted taste for sex with a small child, like he did in my house. However, I wouldn't bet on it for the difference between play-acting and brutal reality in some perversions is dangerously thin.

Sadism—the so-called exquisite torture of the whips—is a prime example of the thin line that frequently divides perverted "dabbling" in the Marquis de Sade's black arts and murderous, maniacal actions which can erupt during the catering to this lust for pain.

In my house, and, I imagine, in most high-class brothels, the whip is by far the most popular of the bedroom sports indulged in by the freak clientele. It is also one of the most profitable perversions for, unlike a number of other hangups which are seldom encountered, sadism is fairly common, and most sadists seem to return frequently once they've found an establishment which caters to their unique kicks. And, I might add, this type of freak generally is well-to-do and quite able to pay exorbitant fees for his pain parties. Sadism, I assure you, is not a poor man's sport, at least when it is indulged in at a brothel.

For years, my house was equipped with several sets of whipping straps, illegal items which are sold mainly by the so-called sex novelty distributor firms. One strap was composed of several strong, long

nylon lashes attached to a leather handle. This strap was the whip, the "instrument of divine torture." The other straps were of heavy leather, an inch or two wide and covered with a soft, nonabrasive cloth. Only a sturdy metal buckle was exposed at one end of each of these straps, with metal rimmed holes at the other end for hooking onto the buckle. These buckled, padded leather straps were used to securely tie the sadistic freak to the bed, face-down and spread-eagled, so he couldn't break loose and turn on the girl during his pain-filled sexual frenzy.

Brothels are strictly a one-way street for sadists. In a house servicing this type of perversion, a sadist can have as wild and as long a whipping party as he wants, as long as he is the target. But under no circumstances is he permitted to lay a hand on the girl. Thus, the precaution is taken to strap the freak to the bed before the whipping begins. The reason is basic: most sadists not only enjoy perverted pleasures in experiencing pain, but find equally intense sexual satisfaction in inflicting pain on others. A pain freak quite possibly would turn savagely on the whip-wielding girl if he wasn't securely tied.

The list of practitioners of sadism serviced by my house through the years is fairly long, and the indentity of many of these men would shock an awful lot of people in Kentucky, and other states, too. As noted previously, sadism is an expensive hobby, and a surprising number of the freaks turn out to be highly respected men from positions of authority. From my observations, quite a few are overbearing, despotic males, but a surprising number are seemingly mild, pleasant men—the last type in the world you'd suspect of harboring a lust for pain and violence.

Jeffrey was one of the quiet, reserved, superefficient-type executives. A wealthy industrialist from Northern Kentucky, he generally flew his own plane into Bowling Green for a whipping party two or three times a month. His procedure never varied. He would telephone me several days in advance so I could make arrangements to close the house on Clay Street to all other customers during the afternoon whipfest. This shutdown of other business for several hours (one of the factors involved in the $300 tab the captain of industry paid for his party) was essential. A madam can't afford to have other customers on hand—men with normal, healthy sex urges—when the entire house is reverberating with the screams, groans, moans, and weird, ecstatic howling of a freak undergoing the delights of the whip.

Anyhow, Jeffrey would start the afternoon party innocently enough. He would sit in the parlor for about a half hour, leisurely discussing all manner of things with the girls and me. At last, after paying his fee in cash, he'd always choose the same two girls to accompany him upstairs.

In the large bedroom, the girls undressed, then stripped Mr. Moneybags and strapped his hands and feet tightly to the bedposts. The girls then took turns lashing Jeffrey across the back, buttocks, and legs with the nylon whip. When one was using the whip, the other would stand close to Jeffrey's head, screaming all types of vile curses at him—an additional defilement he requested which seemed to give an extra zest to his perverted kicks.

After switching back and forth from the arm-wearying task of whipping to the throat-straining cursing several times over a period of perhaps twenty to thirty minutes, the girls would succeed in beating Jeffrey into an agonizing, roaring climax. With his mission accomplished, he would lie on the bed, trembling violently while the girls would gently apply a soothing ointment to his whip-welted posterior. Once Jeffrey had quieted down, the girls would release the four belts, clean him, and help him struggle painfully into his clothes. By the time he left the house the once-howling, yelling pervert from upstairs again had reverted to his calm, precise executive ways, once more ready to flaunt his VIP image for all the world to admire or envy.

I know there are many theories about what kind of incident or influences, dating back to childhood and even infancy, lay the groundwork for mankind's perversions. I've heard quite a few self-pitying diagnoses from freaks who have frequented my house. Roberta, the transvestite, for example, told me he first got the urge to play the part of a woman when, as a teen-ager, he secretly tried on his older sisters' clothing. The freak with the hair fetish claimed that his mother, whom he adored, would let him brush her long, shimmering hair each evening. She died when he was still a child, and he always associated the brushing and fondling of a woman's long hair with the most exquisite of sex thrills. And Jeffrey, the industrialist, said in one of his rare moments of self-revelation that he was convinced that severe whippings administered by his mother during his childhood produced his sadistic quirk. Now perhaps all of these gents were right; I have no way of knowing. But I do know that while under the influences of their perversions, they were nuttier than a fruitcake.

As one of the girls who participated in Jeffrey's whip parties once told me: "If you could see the terrible glaring look in Jeffrey's eyes and his violent twisting and snarling when he's being whipped, you'd know he's crazy. I'm terrified every time I'm with him."

As our experience with another sadist proved, the girl had good reason to be terrified. For several months one of our regular customers was a prominent horse-breeder from another Kentucky county. He was a large, fine-looking man with graying hair—a stud who seemed as normally lusty as the stallions on his big horse farm. One of my girls, however, seemed to sense that behind this façade of normalcy was lurking a sadistic yen. Thinking of the extra money involved if her hunch was right, the girl—a husky, big-bosomed brunette named Ernestine—hinted that our house had the "very latest" in whipping devices.

The trick leaped like a hungry fish after a fly. "You mean to tell me a guy can get a whip job in Bowling Green?" he asked.

"That's right," Ernestine said. "Of course it costs quite a bit because we have to close the house down for just this one party."

"How much are you talking about?" he asked.

"Well, if you use just one girl it's two hundred and fifty, or three hundred if you want two girls."

"Hell, that's cheap," the horse-breeder exclaimed. "I've paid as much as five hundred bucks for whip parties in places like New York and Chicago."

As a result of Ernestine's ability to recognize a freak in square's clothing and her capable sales job, we ended up arranging a three-girl whip party for the Kentucky horseman the following afternoon, at a $350 fee because of the extra girlpower.

As the appointed time drew near and the freak's car pulled into our parking lot, I told one of the girls to "put the milk can" in the middle of our driveway entrance. For years, this big, old-fashioned milk can, attached to a big tree with a long length of chain, was an important symbol for my customers. When the can was placed beside the driveway, it signaled that the coast was clear. But when it was in the center of the driveway, it warned my customers to stay out—the house was closed.

Anyhow, with the milk can warning presumably in place, Ernestine and two other girls—the trio who would be swinging the whips —took the horseman upstairs for his pain party, going through the customary precaution of buckling his legs and arms to the bedposts before starting to work him over.

Never have I heard such noise. This large freak bellowed, screamed, cursed, and, at times, even seemed to nicker like an excited horse as the three girls diligently applied the whips. And right in the midst of this ear-shattering bedlam, the doorbell rang.

"My God, it's a raid," I thought as I ran to the front window and peered cautiously out from behind the drapes. But it wasn't the gendarmes. It was a customer. The girl had neglected to put out the milk can as I had ordered. I hurried to the door, desperately groping for some kind of story. The customer, as soon as he entered, asked in an awed voice, almost drowned out by the monumental volume of the outcries from upstairs:

"Good grief, Pauline! What's happening? Is somebody being murdered?"

"Nothing that bad," I said. "One of the fellows got boozed up and he's got the DTs. Thinks he's seeing snakes and vampires and stuff like that. I've got him locked in a room until the doc gets here."

"Well," the nervous trick exclaimed, "I guess I'd better get out of here until things quiet down." He ran to his car, and I was right behind him, ready to shove that damned milk can into the middle of the driveway where it belonged at a time like this.

By the time I got back to the house, a new disaster was threatening. Girls' screams were now mingling in shrill terror with the sadistic horseman's insane yelling. Upstairs, the bedroom looked like D-Day on Normandy Beachhead. While the girls had been flogging him, the broad-shouldered, powerfully built freak had ripped off the bedpost to which his right arm had been tied. Seconds later, he apparently unbuckled the restraining strap on his other arm. When I arrived, he had Ernestine clutched under one arm and was brutally beating her with his fists while the other girls lashed him furiously in a futile attempt to make him stop.

In desperation I grabbed a heavy antique bedroom water pitcher and shattered it across the frenzied horseman's head. It didn't knock him out, but the blow did seem to bring him to his senses. He surveyed the hysterical girls, he looked at Ernestine's badly battered face and the splintered ruins of the bed. He offered no excuses, no apologies. He dressed quickly, knowing that we four women weren't about to attempt to stop him.

At last, before leaving the room in which his unbridled, perverted passion had nearly exploded into murder, the well-to-do horse-breeder turned to me and said:

"Send a bill for all this to my attorney. I'll make sure he pays you to avoid any embarrassing publicity."

I sent a sizable bill, and it was paid promptly with no questions asked. But the next time I saw that horseman in Bowling Green, I told him in no uncertain terms to stay away from my house. And never again did I permit a muscular freak to enjoy the ecstasies of a whip party in my house. I wanted no more wayward, oversized perverts rampaging through my house.

The devotees of the whip, because of the violence of their hangups, are always a potential danger in the operation of a brothel. But there also are various other perversions, several of them extremely bizarre, which turn up at a house from time to time. Two of these perversions are as completely revolting as any I know. I mention them only because I have been told that they are (quite understandably) among the rarest of mankind's perversions, and the odds against both occurring in a town the size of Bowling Green must rate something like a million-to-one. Yet they both happened, not only in Bowling Green, but in my house on Clay Street.

In fact, for several years there were three Bowling Green practitioners of one of these stomach-churning perversions. These freaks followed the same routine. When one came to the house he would select a girl, and go through the customary undressing and hygienic processes. Instead of climbing into bed, however, he would stretch out, face up, on the floor, with a padding of absorbent towels under his head and shoulders. Once the trick was set, his date would squat over his head and, as quickly as nature permitted, would urinate in his face, using his mouth as her "toilet." Without fail, the freak would experience an orgasm during these unorthodox sewage-disposal proceedings.

A closely allied perversion, which I've encountered only in one person, is even more nauseating. This particular freak, a prosperous professional man active in civic and club affairs, patronized my house regularly, paying mighty fancy fees, for a number of years. Despite the size of his payments and his reputation for being a good tipper, it was always difficult to find a girl willing to service him. In view of the truly sick nature of his hangup, the girls' reluctance was understandable. Finally, I had the girls service him on a rotation basis—not too arduous a schedule inasmuch as he generally indulged in his secret vice about once a month.

This freak (we called him Cookie for reasons which were self-evident) would arrive at the house after setting up an appointment a day in advance so that the girl could be primed for her key function in the proceedings. With him he would bring a sack containing a half dozen large oatmeal cookies.

In the bedroom, after the preliminaries of undressing and cleanup had been taken care of, Cookie would begin a strange ritual. He would carefully lay out his six oatmeal cookies and a butter-spreading knife on the nightstand. Then he would carefully place two towels on the floor beside the bed. With these "housekeeping" chores completed, he'd stretch out on the bed and watch with intense rapture as the girl squatted over the towels and, with self-conscious grunting, struggled to produce a bowel movement.

Sometimes, despite the advance notice, the poor girl would draw a "blank," and another replacement would be called into action. Sometimes it would require three or four girls to produce a successful BM. When this occurred, the freak would groan with pent-up desire, use the knife to neatly spread the results on his oatmeal cookies, and munch greedily on his "shit delicacies." Inevitably, this "feast" was accompanied by a steadily expanding erection, followed by a king-sized ejaculation. Somehow, I'm sure, this isn't exactly what our Creator had in mind when He invented the human sex processes.

Fortunately not many perversions are as sickening as these. Some, in fact, range from the ridiculous to the funny. We had one trick, for example, who insisted that his date be dressed in black lace bra and panties, black stockings, and black patent-leather shoes, and that she use Chanel No. 5 perfume. This freak, a businessman with wife and children, would stretch out on the floor while the girl paraded around him. He'd ogle the black undies and sniff like a dog at her black patent-leather shoes, and before long he'd have his climax. Still another freak with a similar lingerie fetish would have a girl spread out a pair of her panties beside him on the bed. Then bypassing any attempt at normal intercourse, he'd have the girl massage his organ until he climaxed on her panties.

Looking back, though, I guess the funniest freak to patronize my house was a middle-aged judge who hit upon a comparatively safe way to satisfy his tastes for voyeurism.

This gray-haired gent came to my house on Clay Street one evening and requested a private conference with me. He handed me his card, and I almost fainted when I saw he was a judge from another part of the state. I figured I was in some kind of legal hot water.

However, the Judge quickly put my mind at ease. "Pauline," he said, "some very influential people have told me you can be trusted completely. That's why I've come to you."

The Judge had a real problem. During the past year he had found himself the victim of an uncontrollable urge to be a "peeping Tom."

Even though the logic of his legal mind told him he was jeopardizing his career, his family, and his reputation, he still found himself prowling the streets at night occasionally, seeking a good prospect for his peeper activities.

"I just can't control this impulse," he said. "And I'm afraid if I sought psychiatric help the story might get out and I'd be ruined."

"Well, Judge, I sympathize with you, but I don't know how I can help you."

The Judge, however, had a plan. As a legal expert, he was dismayed to suddenly find himself in the grip of one of the riskiest of sexual compulsions—voyeurism. For not only is a peeping Tom rather easily detected by police patrols but he also presents a vulnerable target for the guns of families who happen to catch him in action. After several frighteningly close calls during his nocturnal prowlings, the Judge devised his scheme for a "safe" system of peeping.

"Pauline," he said, "to satisfy this urge, I want you to hide me in the closet of one of your girls so I can watch in secret while she takes care of a customer. That way I can be a peeper without worrying about being arrested or being shot."

I looked at the Judge in slack-jawed amazement. "I've never heard of anything so outlandish in my life," I exclaimed. "Who ever heard of a whorehouse renting out a closet to a peeping Tom?"

However, the Judge was insistent. "Look, Pauline," he said, "I know you cater to a lot of weird freaks here, including whipping parties. By comparison, my hangup is rather mild, I'm sure arrangements can be made to take care of my needs."

If this had been an ordinary trick, I probably would have continued to resist the idea. But even outside the courtroom it doesn't pay to argue too strenuously with a judge, not even one with a freakish hangup. "Okay," I said. "I'll see what I can work out, but it's not going to be cheap."

"Don't worry about price—just worry about setting up a safe arrangement," the Judge said.

I discussed the Judge's odd request with several of my more reliable girls, and Sue finally agreed to give the plan a tryout. Her room had a long closet along one wall. It was decided that we would conceal the Judge in the closet behind Sue's well-stocked wardrobe of long evening gowns. By leaving the sliding closet doors open a few inches, His Honor would be able to peer carefully from between Sue's gowns and witness the unsuspecting customer in action.

I described the plan to the Judge and set a price of $60 for his boudoir box seat. He promptly agreed to both the plan and the price.

"But for God's sake be careful," I cautioned. "Don't do any sneezing or coughing, and don't get too excited and knock something down. If a customer catches you, God knows what he'll do to you!"

"Don't worry, Pauline," the Judge said. "I'll be as careful as if I were sitting on the bench."

"You'd damned well better be," I replied. "Because it's your neck —and mine, too—if anything goes wrong!"

The big preview night arrived with the Judge on the scene early. We hid him in Sue's large closet, skillfully camouflaged behind a long row of colorful gowns. We even managed to squeeze in a narrow vanity stool so the Judge could peep in comfort when he got tired of standing.

The Judge's preview was perfect. From his closet hideaway, he had practically a ringside seat as Sue frolicked with four tricks, none of whom suspected that they were performing for an audience. After the fourth date's departure, the Judge evidently decided his appetite for voyeurism was satiated for the night. He quietly returned downstairs while Sue was in the parlor awaiting another customer, waved goodby to me from a hall doorway, and vanished into the night.

A week later, he was back for a $60 encore. In fact, for nearly two years he patronized my house—or, to be more accurate, Sue's closet— three or four times a month. During this period, I'm sure, he gained a firsthand knowledge, from a spectator's point of view, of all manner of sexual acrobatics. I'm equally sure that in the process he saw enough big-shots in action to add some mighty juicy tidbits to his secret political dossiers.

Nevertheless, the Judge's "safe" peeping Tom scheme almost ended in disaster. One evening after sitting through four splendid performances, he was toying with the idea of calling it a night when Sue entered the room with another trick. But this was no ordinary customer. He was a national VIP politician, and he obviously was deep in his cups. The Judge could scarcely contain his excitement as the action got underway with the VIP drunkenly confiding to Sue considerable inside dirt about bluegrass-brand politicians. Then, as the Judge cautiously inched forward in the closet to obtain a better listening post for the VIP's lowdown, he knocked a clothes hanger off the rod.

The hanger fell to the floor with a "thunk-thunk-thunk," a noise that echoed in the Judge's ears like a doomsday bolt of thunder.

The VIP, just commencing his manly exertions, was equally alarmed. "What in the hell was that?" he roared as he leaped out of Sue's receptive embrace and stared suspiciously around the room.

"You mean that funny bumping noise?" Sue asked nervously, tugging at her alarmed stud's arm in an effort to get his mind off strange noises.

"Yeh, I mean that bumping noise," the VIP said. "It sounded like it was something *right here* in this room."

Sue managed a convincing giggle. "That's just the *old plumbing* in this house," she said. "The pipes are right behind the walls in this room, and lots of times they make loud noises when someone turns on the water in the bathroom."

"I don't know," the suspicious VIP growled, perching on the side of the bed. "Maybe I ought to see if we got a snooper."

Sue leaped playfully on the customer's back, smothering him with kisses. "Don't be such an old fogey," she cried, adding a few more enticing caresses. "This is a place for lovin', man. Let's get busy!"

In the face of Sue's amorous onslaught, the VIP soon forgot about suspicious noises. But an hour later, after the big-time politician had departed, the Judge crept downstairs, still ashen-faced and trembling.

"Never again, Pauline," he said. "I thought for sure I was done for tonight, and I'm certainly not going to press my luck again." The Judge never returned to my house. Perhaps he gave up his voyeuristic flings, or perhaps he devised another "safe" plan to enjoy his kicks as a sex spectator. If so, he was never caught, for his political fortunes continued to flourish, perhaps abetted by some of the spicy facts he'd collected from his box seat in Sue's closet.

Undoubtedly freaks like the Judge and other perverts, with their willingness to pay ridiculously high prices to have their hangups serviced, are important sources of income for a brothel. But for sheer money power, there's nothing to compare with a big-time spender who's hankering to rent himself a whorehouse to entertain his friends with a good, old-fashioned screwing, drinking, and eating party.

I've encountered a lot of big spenders in my time, but I guess the most frantic money-to-burn period for my house came during the oil boom up in Kentucky's Greensburg-Camelsville region. It turned out to be a shallow pool, and before long the boom turned to bust. For a number of months, though, there were at least four chickens in everybody's gold-plated pot, and well-heeled wildcatters were howling for female entertainment.

Generally there were few refinements in the parties thrown by the newly rich Kentucky oil speculators—just babes, booze, and boasting about their next big strikes. I recall one speculator who took over my house for three days after peddling an oil lease for better than $100,000. During those three days, the oilman and two of his associates, cavorting with three of my girls, ran up a tab of nearly $3,500, which they paid in cash when the party was over.

The big-time oil and natural-gas executives were a different, more polished breed than the boom-or-bust wildcatters. They flew in from various parts of the country from time to time for parties at my Clay Street house. However, their parties had more class—plenty of liquor, but no one getting obnoxiously drunk and no one chasing screaming girls through the house. Also, they would usually fly in with supplies of quail, for serving on toast for breakfast, and huge amounts of thick, frozen steaks for midnight "snacks." With gargantuan appetites for both sex and food, I was never quite sure whether I was operating a whorehouse or a restaurant when the petroleum boys came zooming into town.

One of my favorite big-spenders was the owner-operator of a cross-country natural-gas pipeline. During the last week of each May, he would reserve my house for two days. At this time, he and nine of his friends would fly to Bowling Green from Texas for a two-day sex party before proceeding on to Indianapolis for the famed Memorial Day 500-Mile Race. This group had a special tradition. The ten men in the party requested ten girls, no more and no less. At the outset of the party, they'd assemble around my kitchen table and cut cards. The lucky high man would have first choice of the girls, and on down the line. After the first sex session the men swapped bed partners. It was a point of honor that, after the two-day clambake had ended, each of the ten men had bedded down with each of the ten girls.

In addition to sex, food, and liquor, big-stake poker games often enlivened the festivities. I've seen considerable gambling in my time, but these Texans were a breed by themselves. They'd sit through pots containing thousands and thousands of dollars, joking, drinking, and bragging like a bunch of the boys having a ball at penny-ante poker. Once I managed to coax a couple of the oil barons into my favorite game—cut-throat pinochle—but after I'd racked up winnings of $400 or $500 they returned disgustedly to what they described as "a gentleman's gambling game."

Next to the oilmen, politicians were the biggest spenders in my house as far as private parties were concerned. There's quite a difference between the two groups, however. The oilmen mix business with pleasure, indulging in wheeling and dealing in the midst of their fun and games. Even so, there seems to be a carefree, what-the-hell spirit attached to this dealing, and their main objective appears to be a rollicking, sex-saturated good time with no strings attached in a fine quality house where they can be assured of privacy.

Politicians, on the other hand, seem for the most part to be an uptight group, incapable of having a really good time because they're always fretting about the reactions of other people. As a madam, I've witnessed the pomposities, buffooneries, and idiocies of many hundreds of politicians, big and small, within the walls of my houses for nearly four decades. There have been a few fine men among them, but for the most part they seemed to be a rather shabby-souled, shallow-minded lot.

Few politicians indulge in the financing of costly sex parties for the fun of it. They are, in most cases I've observed, using sex and booze as tools to either influence key people they are hoping to use or to pay off political debts to people who have done them special favors. Then, of course, there are the politicians who are guests at big brothel blow-outs bankrolled by special interest groups—the lobbyists, who also rank near the top on a madam's list of big-time spenders. The political guests of these lobbyists are really a low form of life. For in accepting the wining, dining, and wenching of a brothel party, they're taking bribes, selling out their public trust for pieces of ass rather than pieces of silver.

To be as fair as possible, I must point out that my low opinion of politicians is based only on those I've seen cavorting in my house and many of those with whom I've had to deal as the operator of an illicit business. So I really can't say that *all* politicians are fools or charlatans. Perhaps my low opinion is the product of oafs like the senator who delighted in running around my house naked, wearing a grotesque Halloween mask and bursting gleefully into the rooms of busily engaged couples; or the governor who, while enjoying the tongue-tickling frenching talents of one of my girls, would telephone the Statehouse and chew out his subordinates for goofing off the minute he left town on business.

Whatever my feelings, though, I managed to play the part of the hostess with the mostess. Through the years, I maintained friendly relationships with the political camps, one of the factors which I'm certain helped me stay in business for so long. When in Rome, I did as the Romans did. I played politics to the hilt, and it paid good dividends. It's only now that I'm retired that I can wonder out loud how our country has managed to endure as long as it has with the type of people we so often elect to office.

A lot of folks have asked me what these big-time parties cost. Really, it's impossible to say. Beyond a flat fee per day for taking over the brothel, there's no bargaining on prices. These big-moneyed gents give lavish tips, and—in leaving—the leader of the group hands the madam a cash-filled envelope which always adds up to an exceedingly healthy sum. Needless to say, their patronage does wonders for a brothel's bank account.

Aside from the two- and three-day brothel parties, there are other lucrative forms of big-spending that brighten a madam's days. There are, for example, the "stag party" and the "pillow party." The stag party is an all-male affair arranged by a group of fellows who, for some special reason, want to have a real whiz-bang blowout. The main ingredients for such a blast are girls—lusty wenches who'll dance in the nude and indulge in sex play with the guests. And generally the main sources for such girls are brothels.

I recall one stag party in particular. One of Bowling Green's leading doctors was moving to another state. His fellow medics, after renting several large suites of rooms at a local motel for the party, sent one of their group to consult with me on the critical question of girls. I supplied the party with three girls for nude dancing and sundry other services. One of the girls, a tall, graceful, dark-haired beauty named Penney, really caught the fancy of the stag-partying medics.

"She was one of the most exquisite dancers I've ever seen," one of the doctors told me later. "She danced in the nude, but there was nothing vulgar about it. It was a great natural talent. She ought to have professional training."

Unhappily, although no one suspected it at the time, poor Penney needed medical help more than she required professional dance lessons. Within a year she became ill quite suddenly, and in a few months this lovely, talented girl was dead of cancer, quite possibly a fatal memento of a young marriage to a brutal man from whom she eventually fled into a life of prostitution.

A "pillow party" is a different sort of proposition. It is an exhibition, usually staged and financed by some hefty-bankrolled trick who is eager to demonstrate to everyone in the house his prowess as a stud. Other times, of course, a group of customers—after tiring of the boasts of one of their buddies about his rare sexual capabilities—will pool their money and offer to pay the tab for a public exhibition by the braggart.

I vividly recall one such pillow party. Bucky was a regular patron of my house, a married man with six kids and endless stories of his female conquests. As a self-proclaimed great lover, he wasn't much to brag about. He was a scrawny man, about 5-foot-7, with wispy hair, a long, horsey face, and big ears. But he was no shy violet. He loved to talk, especially about himself and his astounding endurance records in the field of sexual intercourse.

Early one evening Bucky was expounding on his favorite theme to a group of tricks and girls lounging in the parlor. He had just completed a story of engaging in a three-hour, nonstop screwing session when one of the tricks snorted derisively.

"Bucky," he said, "we've been listening to your horseshit for months now. Frankly, I think you're all mouth. You're probably the worst excuse for a stud in the whole damned state!"

"Goddam it," Bucky screeched indignantly. "I can outscrew a jerkoff like you any day in the week!"

Bucky's challenger, a husky ex-football star, wasn't impressed. "Let's take up a collection and have a pillow party," he said. "We'll each take two girls, so we can switch back and forth, and all the folks can sit around and watch and see who is the best man."

Bucky agreed promptly. He and his challenger each put up $20, and then I passed the hat among about fifteen customers who, by this time, were packed into the parlor. The total ante was more than $100, so we moved into the larger living room for the great Battle of the Studs. Spectators sat in chairs and sofas, or on the floor, around the sides of the room. In the center of the room, we spread a number of pillows, and the "arena" was ready for action.

At this point, four of my girls volunteered (for a fee of $10 each in addition to a split of the collection) to service the two studs. After stripping, two of the girls stretched out on pillows in Bucky's half of the arena, while the other two flopped down on the challenger's pillows. Next, the contestants undressed. The challenger was a thickset stallion, hairy-chested and well hung. He towered over the loud-mouthed Bucky in all aspects but one. Scrawny, flabby muscled Bucky was endowed with an enormous penis that seemed to dangle halfway to his knobby knees. Adding to its frightening appearance, Bucky at one time or another had engaged the services of a tattoo artist. A luridly colorful snake, with fangs bared, was twined in tattooed splendor around a goodly portion of Bucky's amazing tool.

Anyhow, after a few more preliminaries—including placement of bets by the more sporting members of the audience and the customary soap-and-water cleansing of the contestants' private parts—Bucky and his challenger leaped into action. It soon was evident that both were capable swordsmen. They'd change from girl to girl every few minutes, while the audience cheered them on. Finally, after about twenty-five minutes, the husky challenger apparently lost control during one of his shifts. He suddenly tightened up, indulged in a few final spasmodic thrusts, and rolled off the girl, cursing his bad luck. Bucky, however, was still going strong fifteen minutes later when I put an end to the show.

"You're the champ, Bucky," I said. "There's no use continuing."

"But I'm still not finished," he protested.

"Well, you're finished down here," I said. "I can't tie up business in the house any longer. If you want to keep going, take a girl upstairs, pay her, and get back in the saddle again."

Bucky shrugged, gathered up his clothes, and took one of the girls upstairs to finish his marathon session. From that time on, no one challenged his stories for they had seen the champion stud in action.

For a number of years, a group of public officials from a nearby state would show up twice a year at my house for a two-day private party. It was always the same seven-man group—a county judge, a postmaster, a police chief, a county coroner, two state legislators, and a city engineer. And they always arrived with a motorboat, loaded with fishing gear, attached to the rear of their station wagon.

These out-of-staters, after paying handsomely for their two days of partying, would leave for home with their fishing gear still packed. After several visits, during which the routine never varied, I asked about the boat and fishing gear which they never seemed to use.

"It's this way, Pauline," the postmaster explained. "We're all getting up past forty, but we'd still rather fuck than fish. The only problem is, we need an excuse to get away from our wives for a few days so we tell 'em we're going fishing."

"But what happens when you get back home with a dry boat and no fish?"

The county judge chuckled. "On the way home, we stop and put the boat in the lake for awhile, do a little fishing, and then stop at a place where we can buy all the fresh-caught, live fish we need to take home."

"Well," I said, "if I ever get married again I'm damned sure going to tag along every time my husband goes fishing!"

Some folks have asked me, from time to time, what I believe was the strangest party ever held in my house. Well, there have been a lot of weird ones, a lot of funny ones, and a lot of lavish, supercostly ones. But, now that I'm retired, I guess I can finally reveal the story of my favorite party.

When I purchased the house on Clay Street after the burning of my place in the country, I spent several hard, expensive months completely remodeling and landscaping the property. I spared no expenses in rejuvenating the old brick relic. But with the help of two extremely talented interior decorator friends of mine—a couple of lovey-dovey "gay" boys—the job was finally completed.

With the house scheduled to open for business on Monday, I made a final tour of inspection of the establishment on Saturday, accompanied by the gay ones. They seemed especially thrilled by the large upstairs bedroom, a lavishly decorated and furnished boudoir for VIP customers.

"Miss Pauline," one of the gay boys stammered nervously. "We'd like to ask a favor."

"What's that?"

"Well," he said, "we'd simply *love* to spend just one night together in this beautiful room before the house opens."

I gazed at the lovebirds in amazement. The idea of a house being used by a couple of queers had never occurred to me. But inasmuch as the opening of the Clay Street house still was about thirty-six hours distant, I began to sense the possibility of a profitable deal.

"I'll tell you what, fellows," I said. "I'll rent you the room—the entire house—just for tonight. It can be your brand-new love nest, but it's going to cost you a hundred and a half in advance."

The gay boys were delighted. They paid the $150 and moved in. They emerged early Sunday afternoon, hand in hand, and thanked me profusely.

"You don't know how much it means to us to be able to tell *our friends* we spent a night together in a whorehouse," one of the gay boys said.

And that is how the notorious house on Clay Street received its baptism—with a nightlong $150 party by a couple of queers!

*The law—and the outlaws*

## The law—and the outlaws

The Sheriff was riding tall in the saddle, enjoying a brisk evening canter on as fine a $5 filly as ever came prancing out of Pauline's corral, when the door to the room burst open with a splintering crash.

Two young deputies, who minutes earlier had pushed their way into my house and sneered at my warning they were heading for trouble, leaped into the bedroom, shouting: "This is a raid! You're under arrest!"

Temporarily dazed by such an unexpected interruption in his weekly workout at my Happy Bottom Riding Academy, the Sheriff slowly dismounted and turned to face the vice raiders.

"Who's under arrest?" he roared.

The young deputies' eyes bulged and their faces paled. They had thought they would boost their careers by raiding a new whorehouse. Instead, they ended up busting into the room where their boss was having himself a party with a cute blond chick.

"Jeeezuz Keerist!" one of the young deputies managed to croak. "We're sorry, Boss. We had no idea we'd find *you* here."

The barrel-chested Sheriff for the first time realized he was naked —that his once splendid "Colt .45" had, in the excitement, deflated to toy water-pistol dimensions. He hurriedly grabbed a sheet from the bed, wrapped it around his midsection, and with mounting rage, screamed, "Who in the goddam hell gave you nitwits the orders to pull a raid?"

"Nobody," one of the deputies admitted. "A whorehouse is illegal, and we thought it was our job to arrest lawbreakers."

The Sheriff rolled his eyes heavenward as if seeking some sort of divine strength to keep him from committing violence on the two naive deputies. "What kind of idiots are we getting in the department these days?" he yelled. "You get your stupid goddam asses back to the station, and you sit there the next four weeks telling yourselves that in this county, by God, nobody pulls a raid unless the Sheriff says so!"

The frightened deputies beat a hasty, apologetic retreat. The Sheriff, with his anger finally receding, climbed back into bed to see if his good ol' "Colt .45" could be rejuvenated for a return to the saddle. And Pauline Tabor's house, after one of the shortest, most farcical vice raids in history, resumed operations as usual.

This hilarious incident occurred shortly after I opened one of my houses years ago. A similar incident, with different results, temporarily put my house in a tizzy some years later. This time, a pair of eager young patrolmen pounded on my door and announced that the house was raided.

Again, I cautioned the patrolmen that they were heading for trouble, but I was told to shut up. So I let the lambs head for the slaughter as they started to empty the rooms of girls and customers.

In the first room they barged into, they discovered our county's top political boss in bed with a frisky redhead. Before they recovered from that shock, the county politician's buddy—disturbed by the racket while frolicking in an adjoining room—showed up, wrapped in a towel, to see what in the hell was going on. And the newcomer turned out to be *Mr. Big* in Kentucky politics, a man with enough clout to make the young patrolmen wish they'd never been born.

In spite of my indignation at being raided, I couldn't help feeling sorry for those two rookie cops. They were like a hunter who grabbed a wildcat by the tail—afraid to hang on and afraid to let go. They could only stare wide-eyed at the two political powers and wait mutely for the ax to fall.

However, Mr. Big had reached his exalted position because he was a man with rare political savvy. He never overlooked a chance to make friends, especially the type that might be able to do him a vital favor some time. So instead of pulling his "muscle" on the two patrolmen, he turned to them with a friendly grin.

"Say, boys," he told them, "you look like a couple of young bucks who'd enjoy a tumble in the hay. Why don't you pick out a couple of girls and have a party? I'll pick up the tab."

"But, sir, we're on duty," one of the patrolmen protested weakly.

"Hell, don't worry about that," Mr. Big said, turning to the county politician. "I reckon we can take care of that, can't we, Jim?"

The county political boss nodded, and added a grimmer, thinly veiled warning. "I guess there's a lot of things we can take care of if we have to," he said.

Confronted with this situation, the young patrolmen picked out two girls and started upstairs. "Just a minute, fellows," I said. "In my house, you've got to check your artillery at the door." Sheepishly they removed their holstered revolvers and ammunition belts and handed them to me before continuing upstairs for their politically donated parties. I was raided on other occasions after that, but never by those young patrolmen. In fact, they became customers of my house, showing up during off-duty hours several times a month to *pay* for dates with my girls.

It seems to me that these two incidents illustrate a point which still holds true in most law-enforcement areas: a young, ambitious officer who takes it upon himself to raid a place without first getting a go-ahead from higher authorities is likely to end up deep in the official doghouse, even though he has been upholding the law. The reasons for the conflicts that sometimes exist between the law as it stands on the books and the actual enforcement of that law are not difficult to understand once you accept the concept that, under the administration of our code of justice, some folks—for various reasons—are more equal than others.

I know there are a lot of legal beagles who will indignantly protest my cynical views on justice. To them, I can only say that for nearly forty years I operated outside the law and I operated openly with the full knowledge of all law-enforcement agencies and with only occasional, relatively minor legal harassment. And, I assure you, I was just *one* of *thousands* of illicit operators throughout the nation to enjoy such immunity. The question, of course, is why?

First, in almost any city, town, or county in the United States, a few favored illicit businesses—mainly gambling, brothels, call girl houses, and after-hours drinking spas—are permitted to operate relatively unmolested while similar unfavored illegal operations in the same area are raided repeatedly and frequently put out of business. The answer is that (1) the favored illicit operators have influential friends in high places, (2) influential people in the community own a piece of the action, (3) the illicit operators spread protection money around in the right places, or (4) the illicit operators have convinced some *very* important people that they know where some *mighty* embarrassing skeletons are buried.

Second, in many of the larger U.S. cities, the big-time crime syndicates are deeply entrenched in both legal and illegal enterprises, spreading nets of corruption that reach high into every facet of government, and even within some labor unions and other sectors of our everyday lives. In such cities, syndicate businesses operate and flourish, while any outside competition is quickly and effectively throttled.

And third, in smaller cities and towns like Bowling Green, local officials prefer to have a few people they know and trust operate illegal businesses rather than have the big syndicates move in and take over. In addition, many of these officials believe that a few well-run, clean brothels benefit a town in several respects: they provide an outlet for sexual energies, thus cutting back on the incidence of rapes and other sex crimes; and they help reduce the veneral disease rate by taking much of the sex trade away from the uncontrolled, uninspected bar girls and streetwalkers.

I've been asked many times how I managed to stay open for so many years with relatively little interference in a town like Bowling Green. Well, let me set one thing straight right at the beginning: any operator of an illicit business who claims he's never had to pay out a single cent in protection money just isn't telling the truth.

I will say this, though. Except for my ill-fated venture in Indiana, I never had to make a payoff to law-enforcement officials. If I had operated in larger cities, I'm sure I would have been forced to buy protection from crooked cops, but I was lucky to be able to work with honest, decent lawmen in Bowling Green. However, a payoff doesn't have to be anything as crude as a sealed envelope filled with cash, handed to a cop on the beat or slipped quietly to a bagman from police headquarters. I learned through the years that there are other forms of payoffs which a madam must face—payoff demands which do not emerge from police headquarters, but from other key sources of power within a city.

Most of these other sources are political. Rarely are they so crude as to demand direct weekly cash payoffs for protection. Usually the pressure is more subtle. If it's around election time, the boys start dropping around for campaign contributions, not once but several times. And each time you dig down and give to both parties, figuring that no matter who wins you've got to have a friend in City Hall. Believe me, this kind of friendship can carry a mighty high price tag at times.

Aside from political payoffs, there are countless other pressures. As a madam you may be a social outcast, but whenever a fund-raising drive is launched your place is one of the first to be solicited. The town dowagers may snub you on the street, but they never turn up their noses at your money when they're shilling for their favorite charity. Lots of times I've felt like telling these respectable biddies to get lost, but I've held my temper and paid, figuring it was just another of the operating costs of my sex-merchandising business.

Actually, however, I don't believe that such payoffs were a major factor in my successful career as a madam. In fact, some of the roughest times I've had have been from politicians who were constantly at my door with their hands out. No matter how much you gave this breed of political polecat in phony contributions, he seemed to think he could scare more out of you by giving you a rough time just to teach you a lesson.

I would say that my good fortune in being able to operate a brothel for so many years with a minimum of law-enforcement trouble was due to three main considerations:

First, I was a home-town girl from a good, trustworthy family, and I had the benefit of a number of influential friends in the community.

Second, I maintained tight control over my house and my girls. I screened my customers carefully to avoid troublemakers whenever possible, and I made certain that all my girls underwent thorough medical checkups once a week. Also—except during the big-money private parties—I allowed no excessive drinking in the house.

And third, as the operator of a brothel with a high-type clientele I was privy to many secrets that could have rocked the town to its very foundations. In fact, I'm certain that many officials were convinced that I knew far more than I actually did. Needless to say, I never sought to set them straight on this score. As a result I had a reputation as a gal who knew where all the bodies were buried—a bad woman to tangle with.

Of course, occasionally I'd be subjected to a raid just to show the respectable folks in town that our law-enforcement people were really trying to do something about suppressing vice in Bowling Green. In the case of such token raids, I'd be tipped in advance by friends in the police or sheriff's department, so there would only be myself and one or two girls to face the music when the law arrived. We'd go to court, pay our fines, return to the house, and open for business again a few days later.

One time, however, a couple of candidates for mayor played dirty pool. I had contributed close to $1,000 to each of their campaigns. Nevertheless, as Election Day drew near they both began screaming about the need to wipe out vice in Bowling Green—a political ploy obviously aimed at wooing the Holy Joe vote. Under this stimulus, the crusaders went into action. My house was raided, and I found myself on the witness stand in a crowded courtroom.

I said hello to the judge, an elderly, longtime friend of my family. Then I looked out over the courtroom. I waved to the prosecuting attorney and called out, "It was sure good to see you down at my house last week, Tom. I sure hope you'll be back real soon!"

The attorney leaped to his feet, raging over my remarks and demanding that I be cited for contempt of court. "What do you have to say about that, Miss Tabor?" the judge asked gravely. "Frankly, your remarks did seem uncalled for."

"Well, Judge," I replied sweetly. "After looking over the folks in this courtroom, you seem to be the *only* one who hasn't been a customer in my place." And I started pointing here and there in the audience, naming a few Toms, Dicks, and Harrys in the process. Never before was a courtroom emptied so quickly. When the excitement finally subsided, the judge rapped his gavel and proclaimed: "Case dismissed!"

On another occasion, a doctor on the State Board of Health, for reasons which never were completely clear to me, set out on a long and bitter campaign to close my house on Clay Street. He wrote "scare" letters to the newspaper and made speeches around town, claiming there was a serious increase in venereal disease, a health menace which he blamed on the girls in my house.

My doctor—the one who examined my girls each week—tried to refute the Health Board official's claims by producing week-by-week records showing my girls had an extremely low rate of V.D. However, his records received little publicity, and the barrage of scare material continued. The ultimate blow came when the State Health official produced a document stating that one of my girls was infected with gonorrhea and had passed the disease on to a number of men in the last few weeks. This document resulted in a State Board of Health order directing me to appear to answer the charges that my house was a health menace and should be closed.

Faced with this crisis, I summoned my doctor and we confronted the supposedly infected girl in her room. Tests disclosed no traces of gonorrhea or any other venereal infection. We called in two other reputable doctors, and their tests were equally clean.

At that point I started grilling the girl. "Something's rotten here, Laura, and I want the truth," I said. "How come you signed that doctor's paper, stating that you had gonorrhea, when you knew damned well you're as clean as a whistle?"

"Please, Pauline, don't ask any questions," the girl cried. "I'm scared to death."

"You're going to be a damned sight more scared if I throw your ass in jail for signing a false affidavit," I said.

Finally Laura leveled with me. She had been dating the Health Board doctor on the outside for more than a month. After several weeks of trysting in motels around town, he told her he was out to close down my place and run me out of town because he hated brothels. He started the phony V.D. scare campaign, then coaxed Laura into helping him. She went to the Health Board clinic three times for gonorrhea treatment, signing the document attesting to the medical aid she had received. And, she said, after each V.D. treatment she and the doctor had a sex party in a motel.

By the time the Health Board hearing was set to open on Monday morning, my attorney was ready. He had the affidavits of three doctors attesting to Laura's good health; he had Laura's signed and witnessed account of the story she had told me; and he had affidavits and guest registration records establishing proof of the motel liaisons between the doctor and Laura at a time he claimed she was diseased.

Before the proceedings started my attorney suggested a private hearing in the judge's chambers among all concerned parties.

"This is rather unusual," the judge observed. "But I guess we'd better see what you have in mind."

In the chambers my attorney turned to the Health Board doctor. "Your affidavit shows that the girl in question received three treatments for gonorrhea last week," he said. "Would you say the disease was in a highly infectious stage at that time?"

"Definitely," the doctor snapped.

"Then," my attorney said brusquely, "I assume that you also are undergoing treatment for gonorrhea!"

The judge's chamber exploded in a furious uproar. At last the doctor was able to make his indignation heard. "I demand an apology," he yelled. "How dare this . . . this shyster insinuate such a thing!"

Even the hearing judge was outraged. "That's a very serious accusation, sir. The doctor isn't the person on trial here."

My attorney moved in for the kill. He produced the records showing Laura was disease-free. He produced Laura's admission that the doctor had asked her to falsely attest to a gonorrhea infection and her account of her romance with the doctor. And he also produced proof of their motel trysts at the time she was being treated for the nonexistent disease.

"Gentlemen, shall we proceed with the public hearing, or shall we quietly call the whole rotten frameup a secret and drop the charges right now?" he asked.

The vote was unanimous. The Health Board quickly dropped the charges against my house on Clay Street, and the crusading doctor slipped out of town, unwept, unhonored, and unsung. As I noted earlier, I never could be sure why he went to such ridiculous lengths to try to frame me. But in the light of subsequent happenings, I began to have some nasty suspicions that he may have been acting for a group of racketeers in an attempt to put me out of business so the mob could take over without a struggle.

For some time there had been rumors that a big-time crime syndicate was getting ready to move in on the Bowling Green area. There were signs around town that this might be so. Several liquor stores, taverns, and restaurants were bought by strangers from out of town. I discovered three syndicate girls in my stable—including Laura, the doctor's "girl Friday"—and I promptly got rid of them. Laura, in fact, told me that she had been sent to my house to work with the doctor in an attempt to frame me. Then, after the doctor's frameup failed, I received a call from a suave, fast-talking gent who drove up to my house in a red Cadillac convertible with Illinois license plates.

"A group of associates I represent is interested in buying your business," he told me. "I'm sure we could come up with a very attractive deal."

"Sorry, but I'm not interested, no matter what figure you offer," I said.

"Miss Tabor," the stranger said in a quietly menacing voice, "my associates don't like to take no for an answer. Perhaps you'd better think this over, and I'll call you later in the week."

"Buster," I said, "I don't have to do any more thinking. I want nothing to do with a bunch of cheap hoods like you. Tell your boys if they come messing around me, I'll get out my shotgun and shoot off their goddam greasy nuts!"

It was brave talk, a lot braver than I felt inside. Twice during the next few days I received threatening telephone calls. Then on four straight nights homemade bombs were thrown in my yard from passing cars, shattering windows, causing other minor damage, and completely disrupting business in my house.

After the fourth night of bombs, one of the town officials came calling. He suggested oilily that the syndicate was too big to fight. "Sell out to 'em, Pauline," he said. "They'll give you a good price, and they'll let you stay on and run the place for 'em."

"Well," I snorted, "it's plain to see that you've gone over to the other side."

The town official shrugged. "There's no use fighting that kind of mob power. They play rough. I guess they've already got half the town sewed up."

"We'll see about that," I said, reaching for a phone. I called some key people in the police and sheriff's departments, the county attorney's office, and the No. 1 power behind the scenes in Bowling Green. I briefly explained the situation and they promised to hurry over for a conference.

As I hung up after the last call, the local turncoat was edging toward the door. "Where in the hell do you think you're going?" I asked.

"I've got an appointment downtown," he muttered.

"Sorry, but you've got one appointment, and that's right here in my parlor," I said. I picked up a shotgun which I had earlier placed beside my rocker, and I pointed it at the public official's chest. "You make one move toward that door, and I'm going to splatter whatever guts you've got all over this room." The official, pale and trembling, perched nervously on the edge of a chair, keeping a cautious eye on the shotgun which I now nestled in my broad lap.

Within half an hour, the "general staff" of Bowling Green's antisyndicate forces was in session. I described my period of harassment, from the Health Board doctor's attempt to frame me to the bombings, the threats, and the turncoat official's efforts to coax me to sell out to the mob.

I also revealed the turncoat's boast that the racketeers already had half the town in their pockets. My friends promptly began to cross-examine him, with a bit of arm-twisting and face-slapping added to refresh his memory. Within an hour they had a sizable dossier on the identity of the mob—a bunch of hoods from the Chicago-Peoria area—as well as a rundown on the local officials, businessmen, and hoodlums who already had joined forces with the Illinois racketeers.

The task force really went into action—especially the honest police officials. There wasn't a word of publicity. They called on the out-of-state hoodlums, worked them over a bit, and kicked them out of town as undesirables. Then they visited the local citizens who had been in cahoots with the mob invaders and taught them a few hard facts of life. The turncoats who were on the public payroll, including police officers, were suspended or fired. Other citizens were told they'd be kept under close surveillance to make sure they didn't start playing games with hoodlum elements again. Within a week the town was cleared of mobsters, and the crime syndicate's invasion was smashed, with few citizens of Bowling Green even aware of the battle that had been waged behind the scenes.

That's what infuriates me when I read news reports of how the Mafia and other racketeers are so deeply entrenched in a city or a state that it is almost impossible to break their control. In my business I've encountered quite a few big-shot racketeers, and without exception they've been human scum. But, bad as they are, they're not as low as the public officials who are on their payrolls. The so-called syndicate couldn't exist for a week if it wasn't for the crooked officials —including corrupt police, judges, legislators, and shyster attorneys —who serve them. I'm certainly not the vigilante type. But at times I feel that the only way to get rid of this organized riffraff is for a group of decent folks to round them up and exterminate them like clearing a house of an invasion of cockroaches.

Somehow, our police always seem to be on the ball when it comes to clamping down on small-time brothels or bookies, or raiding stag parties or after-hours booze joints. But when it comes to the multi-million-dollar looting of our big air terminals, the hijacking of valuable truck cargoes, the swindling of small investors on phony land or stock deals, the loan-shark rackets, the flooding of our country with narcotics and pornography, and a lot of other such mob-infested enterprises, our law-enforcement and judicial officials for some reason seem helplessly inept.

The threat of a takeover by the big crime syndicates isn't the only worry that plagues a brothel-keeper. Far more serious is the ever-present danger of holdups, for a busy whorehouse with a large intake of cash every night presents a mighty tempting target for larceny-minded hoodlums.

During the years I guess my houses have been robbed at least twenty times. And on a number of occasions other holdup attempts have failed. On one occasion I answered the door and found myself staring at two men armed with pistols. I slammed the door in their faces, fetched my shotgun, and went galloping out onto the parking lot in time to see a car start pulling out. I let go with both barrels. The car drove off, but I heard some man scream in pain so I guess I winged at least one of the worthless varmints. In fact, my reputation as a top marksman—a handy gal with any kind of a gun—was well known. This reputation, I believe, did discourage a lot of would-be holdup men.

Another time a couple of Western Kentucky University students helped avert a holdup. These husky young fellows—one later became a famous singer and the other a dentist—were playing pinochle with me one afternoon in my private sitting room when the doorbell rang. I left the game and answered the door.

The customer was a nice-looking chap, a husky man I'd seen in the house several times in recent months. He came in, dawdled around the front parlor for awhile, and finally picked his date. During this period I had a special system for collecting money. The girl would collect from the trick before undressing. Then she'd come to the head of the stairway and call me, and I'd get the cash and stash it away safely, keeping records so the money could be divided squarely at the close of business. Earlier each girl had kept her earnings in her room until the end of the night, but this proved to be too easy a target for holdups.

Anyhow, the newcomer and his date went upstairs. Fifteen, then twenty, minutes passed with no word from my girl. Finally I shouted up from the foot of the stairs: "What the hell's going on up there? Toss me some money!"

"I can't. I'm having problems," the girl shouted frantically.

I rushed upstairs. The trick, still fully dressed, had an arm wrapped around the girl. His other arm, with clenched fist, was waggling menacingly in my face. "I need money," he said, "and I need it now."

"Well," I said, "you sure as hell aren't going to find any money upstairs."

"Then take me to wherever you've got it hidden, or I'll beat both of you to death," he snarled.

With the trick still holding the girl, I led the way downstairs and along the hall to my private sitting room. As we entered, my two brawny student friends—both members of the Western Kentucky football squad—leaped to their feet and rushed to our rescue.

Faced with two unexpected male guests, both of imposing proportions, the would-be robber turned and fled from the house, speeding away in a car he had parked in the driveway. However, that wasn't the last we heard of him. The next day I opened the paper and there was a picture of our larcenous trick. He was a former policeman from Hopkinsville, Kentucky—a copper who had gone wrong. And the previous evening he had been captured while robbing a gas station out on the Louisville Pike, shortly after being chased out of my house by my football-playing buddies.

The final clincher came the next morning. That damned excop, who was all set to rob me, had the nerve to send a note to me from the jail asking for $5 for cigarette money. Lots of times I'd send money to folks in jail because I felt sorry for them. But as far as this S.O.B. was concerned, I just sent him a note telling him to drop dead!

Of course, I wasn't always so lucky when it came to being victimized by criminals. Several times my house was hit heavy. And in each of these cases police later learned that it was girls working in my stable and secretly associated with pimps on the outside who engineered the heists.

In hiring girls I always tried to make certain they were not involved with pimps. In my book a pimp is vermin, an utterly worthless human who lives like a parasite off the women he manages to lure into lives of prostitution. Yet an amazing number of men seem to be able to hold this power over some women—either through fear, love, or some other weird fascination, or through the supplying of dope. These tragically hooked girls not only turn over practically all their earnings to their pimps but seem to obey them like trained dogs. In other words, a hooked girl has only one loyalty—to her pimp. For this reason I would immediately get rid of a girl if I discovered a pimp lurking in her background. A few, however, weren't discovered until it was too late.

For a period of several weeks during the Korean War, a big, flashy character, who always arrived in a white Stetson hat, patronized my house on Clay Street. He was a good spender and he dated several of the girls, but he always seemed to be especially enamored with a slender redhead named Roxie, a girl who had joined my stable several months before.

One night he showed up with two buddies. They each picked a girl and went upstairs. This time, however, he bypassed Roxie for another date, and Roxie went upstairs with another trick a few minutes later. After awhile, when there was no word from the girls, I became suspicious and went upstairs to investigate. The first door I opened revealed a girl stretched on the bed, her hands and feet and mouth taped tightly, and the room's contents methodically rifled. And standing near the door with a revolver pointed at my sizable bulk was the flashy, big-spender type.

"No nonsense, Pauline," he ordered. "I know where you keep the night's receipts downstairs, so let's get going." Out in the hall, he knocked on two other doors and his buddies joined him with assurances they had looted their girls' rooms of everything worth taking. Downstairs, they marched me to my back bedroom, reached under the bed, and pulled out the wooden box I used for the night's receipts. They pocketed that cash, then forced me into my private sitting room where they took my prized coin collection from my cedar chest. Then they taped my hands and feet and mouth, left me lying on the floor, and fled.

Minutes later I managed to get loose, call the police, and hurry upstairs. I found three other girls, one with a customer beside her, tied up and robbed. I ran to Roxie's room. Her trick was stretched out unconscious, a purplish lump on his head and his wallet missing. Roxie also was missing. Her window was open, and a rope made of sheets disclosed her escape route. Obviously she had set me up for the holdup and had fled with her buddies once the job was finished.

Their total take, including my coin collection, was well over $1,500. However, they didn't have long to enjoy it. They were picked up by State Police near the Illinois border and were sent away for a long vacation in the penitentiary—a place where, I'm sure, Roxie's services for her handsome pimp came to an abrupt halt.

Aside from the professional holdup men, my house also was beset constantly with "shoplifters"—customers who delighted in filching mementos of their visit to a brothel. The girls' undies and stockings, of course, were favorite loot for these amateur thieves. But they'd also take jewelry (the dime-store variety, for no girl was fool enough to blossom out on the job with real gems), small radios, knickknacks, ash trays, pictures, and any other souvenirs they could conveniently carry away. For some reason earrings became a big item among the shoplifters at one time. Even though they were inexpensive, the loss of five or six pairs a week to thieves ran into a goodly sum. At last the girls complained to me.

"The answer is simple," I said. "If you're going to wear earrings, have your ears pierced. It'll be kind of hard for 'em to swipe your entire ear." Most of the girls took my advice. After that, the theft rate of earrings dropped rapidly.

One cold winter night, when schools had been closed by snow and ice for several days and everyone was bundled up like an Eskimo, I noticed three young fellows head out the front door with overcoats bulging with all sorts of hidden contraband.

I hollered at them to stop, but they started running, or—I should say—waddling awkwardly with their concealed loot. I grabbed my trusty shotgun and began the pursuit across the icy parking lot. My first shot knocked out a rear tire of their car. The second shot went thundering inches above the hood of the car. No further artillery fire was needed. The three young shoplifters piled out of the car and lined up facing me and my shotgun.

"Okay, boys, off with the overcoats," I ordered.

Off came the overcoats, and all manner of items from the house—ranging from bottles of perfume to a butcher knife from the kitchen and a framed Currier and Ives print—tumbled to the snow.

"Okay, fellows, now off with your pants and shirts," I said.

"Hell, Pauline, we'll all freeze to death," one of the culprits complained.

I lifted the shotgun a bit higher and pulled back a hammer with an ominous click. "I'll give you five seconds to get started," I said.

Before long the three shivering thieves had stripped down to their long johns, unloosing still more loot in the process. With the thermometer down in the low 20s, they weren't exactly dressed for comfort. But still I took no pity on them. "Okay," I said, "now get those damned long johns off!"

All three screamed in protest. In reply, I fired another shotgun blast—this one over their heads. They got the message. Within seconds they were standing ankle-deep in snow, as naked as the day they were born. And, believe it or not, the removal of their long johns disclosed still more loot, including four pairs of panties, two bras, a garter belt, and one of my old kimonos.

With the loot scattered on the snow, I ordered the naked, snow-frosted trio to get dressed again. When that bundling-up task was finished, I made them carry the loot back into the house. With that job done, I let them thaw out in the kitchen, gave them a few cups of hot coffee, and sent them back out into the bitter cold so they could change their shotgun-blasted tire and return home. I assure you, I never again had shoplifting troubles with that group of pilfering young bucks.

One of them told me several years later: "After going through that striptease in the snow, it was damned near July before any of us thawed out again."

Actually there was only one shoplifter who really got my goat. He was one of Bowling Green's up-and-coming young businessmen, a regular customer of my house who frankly admitted he had ambitions to become mayor.

Now as I've mentioned previously, my house on Clay Street was filled with antiques from many parts of the country. Included in my collection were two fairly expensive milk glass toothpick holders. One morning they turned up missing, and one of my girls said she had seen the merchant stuff them in his pockets the previous night.

Figuring that he had been a bit juiced up the night before and in a prankish mood, I telephoned the businessman at his store and asked if he would please return my antique toothpick holders because they were among my prized possessions.

"I would have asked you last night, but I didn't want to embarrass you," I said.

"I don't know what in the hell you're talking about," he snarled, banging down the phone without another word.

I didn't pester him again, but I didn't forget the incident. A few months later, the daily newspaper reported that the shoplifting merchant had announced his candidacy for mayor of Bowling Green.

Again I telephoned him. "I see that you're running for mayor," I said. "Don't you think it might be wise to return my antique toothpick holders?"

"Are you trying to threaten me?" the merchant blustered.

"Sweetie, I'm just telling you that the whole town's going to know what kind of a petty thief you are unless you return my antiques."

The aspiring politician laughed nastily. "Pauline Tabor," he said, "I've got the support of all the top people, including the biggest man in Bowling Green. And when I'm elected the first thing I'm going to do is run your big ass out of town."

"Okay, buster, if you want a fight you're going to get one," I replied, banging down the receiver. I telephoned Bowling Green's Mr. Big—a man who had been one of my most trusted friends for many years—and told him the entire story. I never got back my antiques. But, on the other hand, the sticky-fingered businessman never received his expected nomination for mayor. In fact, from that time on he was politically dead in Bowling Green.

With good friends in the various law-enforcement offices, I'd usually be tipped in advance when a raid was going to be staged. Sometimes, when the grand jury was in session, I'd be warned that the "big heat" was on and told to close down for a spell. On these occasions, I'd declare a vacation, send the girls away, and go gadding about the country for a month or two. Then when I received word that the heat was off, I'd come back to Bowling Green and reopen my sex mart.

Most of the time, however, the raids were purely temporary harassment, intended to keep the Holy Joes happy. In such cases my big worry was keeping an eye on several of the town cops who weren't above pocketing anything that wasn't nailed down. Once I lost several hundred dollars during a police raid, and another time an entire set of whips and straps turned up missing. This whip apparatus never showed up as evidence at headquarters, either. I guess one of the cops just wanted it for his own private whip parties. Needless to say, despite my bitching to police officials nothing was ever returned. In fact, looking back to that long-ago raid on my Indiana house, I'm sure it was the cops who looted the place after we were hauled off to jail. No professional burglars would have wasted time hauling off groceries in addition to money and other valuable loot.

Nevertheless, in spite of such unhappy experiences, most lawmen I've dealt with have been decent, standup sort of guys. Many of them have been customers of my house, and always on a *paying* basis. At times they'd call me to arrange parties for visiting law-enforcement officials, and even these VIPs would pay. No one, not even politicians, expected or received free "rides" at my house.

I've had as customers a number of important law-enforcement officials from out of town, including several FBI agents and two Internal Revenue Service men who, during a ten-day investigation of some firm in town, spent every evening relaxing in my establishment. Among all of these guests I can recall only one who was really a bastard.

It was during some sort of law-enforcement conference, and that evening my place was crowded with lawmen from various places. Midway in the festivities one of my girls came downstairs with her trick, a weasel-faced little squirt from out of state, grasping her tightly by the arm.

My girl was crying. "Miss Pauline," she said, "this man says he's from the FBI. He's asked me all kinds of questions. He says we're part of the syndicate, and he's going to put us all in jail."

One of the Bowling Green officials heard this and bellowed with rage. He grabbed the self-styled FBI agent by the collar and shook him like a rag doll. "What the hell are you trying to pull, you two-bit Indiana police sergeant?" he yelled. "What's the idea of scaring this girl with this FBI horseshit?"

"I was just having some fun," the Indiana policeman whined. "It was just a joke."

The Bowling Green officer slapped the jokester three or four times across the face, then threw him out of the house. There was no more trouble at our party that night from our phony FBI agent. Presumably, he returned, with no good-bys, to the land where the moonlight's always fair along the muddy, stinking Wabash.

The strangest tip I ever received came from Washington, D.C., about midway during World War II. The call was from a member of Congress from Kentucky, a longtime friend and customer.

"Pauline," he said, "I'm afraid I'm the bearer of bad news, and it's urgent or I wouldn't be phoning you."

"What in the hell's the trouble now?" I asked. "Everything seems quiet here."

My Congressman friend hurriedly explained that during the past year there had been steadily increasing pressure nationally from mothers, wives, members of the clergy, and assorted other do-gooders to force the War Department to close down all brothels near military posts.

"The pressure finally got so bad that Roosevelt's ordered an immediate military clamp-down on all prostitution," he said. "I understand the big drive starts tomorrow, and your place—between Camp Campbell and Fort Knox—is high on the list. So you'd better beat 'em to the punch."

I was dismayed at the thought of being forced to close my beautiful colonial country place. It was a gold mine, and business had been increasing steadily under the impetus of the wartime boom. "Isn't there anything that can be done?" I asked. "It seems to me that clean places like mine are a lot better for the soldiers than having them get themselves mixed up with a lot of diseased streetwalkers and barroom whores."

"You're absolutely right, Pauline," the Congressman said. "But the politicians are running scared, so the military has no choice but to go along with them. There isn't a chance in hell of you or any other house staying open."

With that advance warning I hurriedly closed my country house, paid off the girls, and sent them on their way. Two days later, when a contingent of Military Police arrived on the scene, I was a lady of leisure presiding over a gracious country manor. I escorted them through the house, served them ice tea, cokes, and cookies on the patio, and waved a cheerful farewell as they disgustedly drove away.

After that visit I called a neighbor woman to help me clean the big house before I closed it for a vacation. She was cleaning wax off the hardwood hall floors with white gasoline when there was a sudden explosion. I don't know what touched off the blast, but the flames spread like wildfire. I managed to get the cleaningwoman safely out of the house and summon the volunteer firemen. Then I returned to the house and removed a few of my more valuable antiques, pieces of furniture, and personal possessions. But by the time the firemen arrived the entire house was ablaze. Within an hour it was burned to the ground.

The combination of the crackdown by the military and the destruction of my big colonial house really knocked me for a loop. The years since my return to Kentucky had been highly profitable, but they also had been hard. I was well fixed, my sons and mother had plenty of security. The idea of retiring began to appeal to me more and more. So I set out on a leisurely trip around the country to think about my future away from the home-town pressures.

I guess it was at least six months before I returned to Bowling Green. One of the first persons I met was the mayor. He asked me up to his office for a private talk.

"Pauline," he said, "we need you back in business."

"What's the problem now?" I asked. "I thought the military bosses ruled that screwing is off limits."

The mayor cursed heartily. Since the military crackdown, he said, the town's venereal disease rate had risen to alarming proportions— and the same thing had happened at the military posts.

"The town, and the entire county, have been flooded with cheap little chippies," the mayor said. "They solicit openly on the streets and in the bars, and we have no way of running medical checks on them. Even worse, a lot of them are working with pimps, clipping suckers for their entire bankrolls. We've had several men, including a couple of soldiers, badly injured."

"Well, mayor, I'm real sorry to hear all this, but after all I didn't close my house because I wanted to."

"I know," the mayor said. "But now a lot of us around town—including some of the military brass—are wondering if you'd be willing to open again."

"I'm kind of enjoying retirement," I replied. "I've got enough money, and I don't know why I should get back in the business with all its headaches and all the shit I had to take from two-bit politicians over the years."

"Pauline, we know there's been a lot of trouble for you in the past," the mayor said. "But what's happened in Bowling Green since you were closed down by the army has opened the eyes of a lot of people. I think you'll find things will be different in the future. This increase in V.D. has really got folks scared."

"Seems to me I've heard that song before," I said. "You sweet-talkin' politicians tell me everything will be fine and dandy, that the town needs my house and I'll have no trouble at all. And the next thing I know I'm raided or the grand jury's going to put the heat on, and my house is closed again. Now, even the Army is in the act, claiming there's nothing in the world too good for our boys except a piece of ass."

The mayor shrugged. "Pauline," he said, "I won't try to kid you. Sure, there are elements in this town that will always be out to get you. Sure, you're going to run into trouble from time to time. But doesn't the profit make the risk worth taking?"

"In other words," I said, "you claim the screwin' I get is worth the screwin' I get." I then proceeded to list a few facts of life about whorehouse economics. To reopen a brothel, I'd have to start from scratch, digging deep into my savings for a new house and new furnishings, and then start rebuilding my customer lists once again.

"The type of house I operate requires a big investment," I told the mayor. "I'm not getting any younger, and I've worked damned hard for what I've got. It seems to me I need a real good reason for getting back into the sex rat race again."

"Pauline," the mayor pleaded, "the town needs your house. If you'll open up again we'll make damned sure you'll have a minimum of trouble. We'll even keep the military in line as much as possible."

In the face of such a plea, I surrendered. "Okay," I said wearily. "Against my better judgment, I'll open another house. But if any son-of-a-bitch starts giving me bad trouble, I'm going to close my doors—and this time it's going to be for all time."

That is how, after my early retirement, the town's mayor finally sweet-talked me into opening my house on Clay Street—an establishment which kept me in the sex-merchandising business for another twenty-five years of my long and lurid life.

*Special friends—and enemies*

## Special friends—and enemies

It is ironic that so many of the world's lonely, unloved men turn for comfort to the lonely, unloved prostitutes on the back streets of society. It is, I suppose, a meeting of kindred souls—a fleeting grasping for warmth and understanding, a desperate searching for a meaning to the often ridiculous business of living.

To be sure, the love, warmth, and understanding bought at a brothel are only illusory—a temporary easing of the ache of loneliness. But I wonder if it is any more temporary or counterfeit than the so-called true love of many present-day marriages? In fact, I believe that the bond of passion which so briefly joins a prostitute and her customer is, despite its commercial aspects, more meaningful than the perfunctory couplings which make a farce out of so many marriages. Who is the more compassionate human—the prostitute who makes the effort to bolster the male ego with cries of ecstasy she doesn't feel, or the unresponsive wife who dutifully yields to her mate's embrace with scarcely concealed boredom or contempt?

I will admit that, as far as textbook education is concerned, my credentials as an expert in human relations may be sadly lacking. I have never studied Kraft-Ebbing, with its profound explorations of the perversions of mankind, nor have I browsed through Dr. Kinsey and other latter-day studies of human sexual behavior. But I believe I've got some vital advantages over these so-called experts on sex because, for most of my adult life, I've lived in the harsh, day-to-day world of sexual experiences in which they've only dabbled as students.

Many of these experts seem to view prostitutes and madams as a special kind of human animal—as a breed apart from the rest of society. This is not so. We are no different than the rest of God's children. We are subject to the same emotions, the same ambitions, the same despairs, the same pain, the same weaknesses, the same hungers. The only basic difference is that the society from which we come puts us in a different, untouchable category—an ostracized class of "fallen women" who, if we are lucky and make our fortune, magically are socially cleansed and become respectable once again.

No one who has not lived through the transition between the world of respectability and the world of vice can understand or appreciate the sudden army of enemies who surface once convention has been flaunted. I guess that, in making the break from normal society, it was this hostility which proved to be the most difficult pill for me to swallow. Oddly enough, many of these foes turned out to be kinfolk and past friends, persons on whom I had counted for at least a measure of understanding and compassion.

The most soul-shattering snub came a week or so after I had opened my first house on Smallhouse Road. All my life I had been a faithful churchgoer, from Sunday school classes as a child to adult worship and the teaching of Sunday school. I was a good friend of the minister and his wife, and an admirer of his sermonizing on the need for Christian tolerance and forgiveness. One day I met the pastor and his wife on the street. In view of my new profession, I didn't expect an enthusiastic welcome, but I wished them a pleasant day. They didn't respond. They looked the other way, and scurried across the street as if to avoid contamination. I hurried home and wept bitterly. Since that day I have never been inside a church. I still have my faith, but I cannot tolerate the hypocritical attitudes of so many of our churches and the pastors who so rarely practice what they preach.

There's just one more case I'd like to cite on the subject of churches. Two years ago, when my husband of more than twenty-one years died, a minister came out to our farm to offer his condolences and any help he might provide in my time of sorrow, even though he knew neither of us personally. A month later this kind pastor was dismissed, and one of the reasons cited for his firing was the sympathy he so foolishly had shown to a notorious, retired madam in her time of grief.

As far as my immediate family was concerned, I know I caused them much grief and humiliation. But never once did they turn their backs on me. My sons, growing up in the same town, had more than their share of scraps defending me against the jibes of their schoolmates. But I stayed as close to them as possible in my role as a "part-time" mother. Both matured into good, law-abiding men with fine families and profitable businesses. Other of my kinfolk, however, were not so understanding. For years many of them refused to recognize me in public or to have anything to do with me in private. I must say, however, that this "coventry" by my relatives didn't extend to refusing to accept my money. Whenever times were tough or there were hospital and medical bills, they'd get word to my mother or sisters, and I'd end up paying the bills. In time it got to be kind of a joke. Doctors and hospitals didn't bother billing my kin. They'd just send the bills to me, knowing I'd take care of the costs. I'm glad I've had the money to help, but it would have been nice to get a thank you note once in awhile.

There are other kinds of foes, too—the kind that pose as friends until they've used you for one purpose or another. I've been taken a number of times, especially in my younger years as a madam, because I was a soft touch for a hard-luck story. I recall one businessman, a frequent customer of my house who eventually moved to Louisville to invest in a new shoe store at a large shopping center.

Several years later he showed up at my house. His face was haggard, his eyes red and puffed as if he hadn't slept for weeks. I got him a cup of coffee and asked what was troubling him.

"I'm in deep financial trouble," he said. "A couple of investments went sour. I'm flat busted, and I don't know how long I can hold on to my store."

"Aren't there some relatives or friends who can help you out?" I asked.

The businessman shook his head. "I've tried, but they all have excuses," he said. "Once you're down, they don't want anything to do with you."

I felt sorry for him. I'd known him for several years, and he had always seemed to be a decent, honest type. "I'll tell you what I'll do," I said. "I'll loan you a thousand dollars, and you can pay me back when you get on your feet again."

The businessman pocketed my check and thanked me with tears in his eyes. "Pauline," he said, "I'll never forget this. You'll get your money back as soon as possible."

That was at least fifteen years ago. The businessman now owns a chain of shoe stores and other enterprises in Northern Kentucky. But he's never repaid my $1,000 loan or even acknowledged my letters asking for payment. Frankly, I wouldn't lower myself to try to collect this debt in court. I just figure that persons like this deadbeat have helped teach me a valuable lesson in turning a deaf ear to hard-luck stories.

Another type of foe is the hypocrite, the kind who smiles friendly as all hell when he faces you and then can't wait to get out his knife and stab you when your back is turned. The woods are full of these worthless characters, of course, but I remember one in particular.

He was an up-and-coming bank clerk when I first knew him, a skinny, balding young man who frequented my house on Smallhouse Road regularly. The first time he showed up, he was as nervous as a caged cat. "Pauline," he said, "I don't know what they'd do to me at the bank if the word got back that I was seen in a whorehouse."

"Quit fretting, Jake," I said. "Whorehouses stay in business because nobody tells secrets beyond these walls. Just relax, pick out a pretty girl, and have yourself a party."

Jake, the young banker, took my advice. He selected a girl, had himself a ball, and was back later in the week for an encore. After several visits, he thanked me warmly for helping him get over his nervousness.

"I wanted to come when you first opened," he said, "but I was too scared. I finally got up enough nerve to come out here, and you helped me see it through."

This young chap was a regular trick for several months. Then after being promoted to a junior executive position at his bank, his nervousness returned. "Pauline," he said, "in my new position at the bank I can't risk being seen here. I wonder if you could arrange it for one of your girls to meet me secretly at the hotel two nights a week. I'll double the usual fee, and that way I won't run the risk of being seen here."

It was against my rules, but Jake was a good customer so I agreed to his request. For several weeks this arrangement ran along smoothly. Then one day I had occasion to go to the bank where Jake worked, a bank which I generally did not patronize. Jake was at a desk in the lobby when I entered. He took one look at me, and—apparently figuring I was there to visit him—he leaped from his chair and raced out the back door. Later, after finishing my business, I left the bank and found myself approaching the jittery Jake. He quickly hurried to the other side of the street.

A couple of days later Jake telephoned, asking for a girl for a date at the hotel that evening.

"Jake," I said, "I don't like to get personal, but it seemed to me you gave me the brushoff a couple times the other day. I want you to know that neither my girls nor myself have to take that kind of treatment in public."

The banker sputtered indignantly. "Pauline," he said, "you ought to know that a man in my position can't afford to be seen talking to a . . . a . . . a *whore* in public."

I exploded. "You lousy bastard," I shouted. "Don't ever call me for another girl, and don't ever show up at my house again, or I'll shoot off your worthless, scrawny ass!"

That wasn't my last experience with Jake. He was one of the leaders of the Holy Joes who finally succeeded in forcing me out of Bowling Green the first time. And in later years he led other crusades against my house. Today he's a big-shot banker, but in my book he's still a hypocritical, narrow-minded S.O.B.

The Holy Joes, of course, were perennial foes. Dried-up, frustrated jerks like the banker, busybody females, sexless old maids, zealous pastors, crusading editors, and a host of other do-gooder types could always be counted on to periodically start beating their breasts and crying out against vice in our town. Normally they were merely a nuisance, although sometimes they'd be in cahoots with an ambitious county attorney or scare up some political support and force me to close my doors for a month or so. Nevertheless, I always managed to evade facing a grand jury, and after my Indiana fiasco I never spent another night in jail.

Although I was never able to prove it, I'm reasonably certain that my worst outbreak of trouble was stirred up by a group of Holy Joes who started a vicious whispering campaign on Western Kentucky University's campus against me and my house on Clay Street.

For some time there had been a number of nasty stories in circulation, including a terrible lie that I was hiring coeds from the university as part-time prostitutes. Anyhow, someone or something got a group of more than a hundred students, mostly girls, stirred up one evening. Bearing signs and armed with rocks and bricks, they paraded down from the Hill, past Fountain Square, and on through town to my house on Clay Street. A large contingent of police followed them, but it wasn't until the kids started bombarding the house with bricks and rocks and screaming demands that I be jailed that the police stepped in and put an end to the uprising before the mob could break into the house. A number of windows were smashed, and several customers were scared out of their wits, but there fortunately were no injuries or no serious damages.

Neither police nor newspaper reporters ever were able to find out what caused this student attack on my house. All I can say is that it was the only trouble I ever had with Western Kentucky students. So I find it difficult to believe that this particular attack was not deliberately organized and provoked in another effort to close my sex-peddling establishment.

It's easy to stir up old grievances against old foes—the biddies who delighted in spreading untrue rumors; the local newspaper owners, two brothers who conducted endless vendettas against my house; self-serving politicians who tried to use me as a stepping-stone for their careers; and many others who spent much time and energy in futilely plotting my downfall.

Nevertheless, it is much more pleasant to remember my friends—the men and women who, even though they frequently despaired of my choice of a career, stood squarely beside me in good times and in bad.

I recall, for example, one over-aged gossip who telephoned a businessman friend of mine one day with a real blockbuster bit of news. She reported that she had been told by a reliable source that the businessman's college-age son was spending his evenings in Pauline's kitchen, playing cards.

"That's wonderful news," the businessman maliciously told the astonished gossip. "I'd rather know that my son is there than a lot of other places around town. When he's out at Pauline's, I at least know he's safe, and he's sure not drinking because she limits the college kids to cokes."

"But what about all those immoral women?" the gossip gasped.

The businessman chuckled. "It looks like my boy's inherited his old man's good taste for first-class fillies," he said, hanging up to put an end to the gossiping.

Sometimes, through an unexpected turn of events, a foe would become a friend. The operator of the town's leading beauty salon was included in this category. For a number of years my girls and I used this shop even though the owner pointedly told us on several occasions that she wished we'd take our business elsewhere.

"You girls give my place a bad reputation," she complained on one occasion.

"Baloney, Grace," I'd replied. "We spend more in a week here than most of your customers. You've got the best place in town, and we're willing to pay your prices, so what are you bitching about?"

"My husband and I just don't think it's right," Grace insisted. "Why, the other day one of your girls had the nerve to ask my husband to bleach her pubic hair so she could be blond all over."

"Did Fred handle the job?" I asked innocently.

"He did not," Grace snapped. "I did the job myself, and I charged her twenty-five dollars."

"Then what are you bitching about?" I asked. "My girl got a yellow snatch, and you got twenty-five bucks for about ten minutes work. So shut up."

That's the kind of armed truce Grace and I lived under for years. She was contemptuous of us and our profession and went out of her way to be nasty. But no matter how indignant she got, she never turned down our money.

One day when several of us went to the shop, my favorite operator was absent. "Where's Betty?" I asked.

"She's in the hospital, real sick," another of the operators told me. "I guess she's going to have to have surgery."

I was dismayed. Betty had worked on my hair for years. She was a widow in her forties and had several youngsters to support. I knew she was having a struggle, so I wrote out a check for $200 and gave it to the operator.

"Please see that Betty gets this to help with the expenses," I said. "If she needs more, let me know."

Later, as I was leaving the shop, I saw Grace hurrying toward me, check in hand. I figured that in her typically belligerent manner she was going to return my check as an unwanted charity. However, for once I misjudged Grace.

She was crying, and she clasped me in her arms. "How can you ever forgive me for the way I've acted?" she sobbed. "I've treated you and your girls like dirt, but you've been the only one of my customers to have the kindness to help Betty when she needed it."

We both had a good cry, and from that time on Grace was our friend. At times she'd even drop out for a visit at the house on Clay Street for coffee and a chat and to pass on the gossip she'd heard at her shop.

In fact, several of my women friends, respectable matrons whom I had known since our childhood, also defied convention and would drop in for visits during the mornings or afternoons. They also kept me well informed about the gossip in town and were especially helpful in letting me know the latest vice drive plottings by the Holy Joes. One of these friends, a lively, fun-loving woman, told me she had a special ambition—she had always wanted to visit a whorehouse at night to see what is was like when things were busy.

"Honey, you come on out any time you like," I said. "Just don't be shocked if one of the customers asks a good-looking gal like you for a date."

"Don't be silly, Pauline," my friend giggled. "I'm as old as you, and God knows that's mighty ancient!"

A few weeks later my friend telephoned and asked if she could come calling that evening to see what went on in my wicked, wicked world. "Come ahead, Celia," I said. "But you'd better wear your chastity belt!"

Celia had a great time. She mixed with the girls and the tricks, danced, joked, and swapped tall tales with them until the early morning hours. But the highlight of her evening came when I fixed it up with one of the handsome young customers to ask my friend for a date. He cornered Celia in the parlor and whispered a few sweet nothings in her ear.

Celia hugged the young stud and roared with laughter. "Don't tempt me," she said, "but you're about twenty years too late!"

In addition to these kind, loving people—the men and women who defied convention to keep in contact with me through the years—there were my *special friends*. These, of course, were the men I've mentioned previously—the VIPs who did so much behind the scenes to help me stay in business. They represented a cross-section of the town's life: law enforcement, politics, business, industry, and the professions. Most of them were men I had known for years, and never did they betray my trust even though many of them were not in agreement with my choice of profession. In fact, as the years passed and my savings grew, several of these friends urged me to invest in other enterprises. Quite candidly, I do not believe that any madam can operate successfully without reliable friends in important places. I certainly know that I couldn't have succeeded without their help.

Beyond these influential friends, I had one *very* special friend—a man who for nearly twenty years was the biggest influence in my life. This gentleman was the head of one of the largest businesses in Bowling Green, a well-educated, cultured man whose heaviest burden was an unhappy marriage. Yet because of his personal moral code and his reluctance to hurt his children, he never considered divorce.

I first became acquainted with Bill when I was selling cosmetics and hosiery from door to door. For some reason he took an interest in me and became my best customer, keeping both his wife and his current mistress well supplied with my products. During my year-long affair with the Colonel, my long illness, and my ultimate opening of the house on Smallhouse Road he remained a good friend. He was one of the men who helped me get started; he was the one who set up my contacts in Indiana; he was the one who came to my rescue with bail money when I ended up stranded in the Hoosier jail; and he was the one who helped me set up my Louisville call house.

During these years our friendship gradually matured into a far more intimate relationship. Sex, however, was never the dominating factor, for there was a wide difference in our ages. We enjoyed each other's company, shared many common interests, and spent hours in my private sitting room discussing all sorts of things. I know that it was Bill, more than any other person, who taught me the finer points of power plays in politics—the intricacies of playing both ends against the middle to attain important objectives.

Also, he was the one who helped me select properties and remodel them; the man who first roused my interest in interior decorating and antique collecting; the man who guided me in investments and taught me the importance of living within my means. He was, in brief, a wise, good, and loyal friend who helped shape my life.

At times he would discuss the sorrows that shadowed his life. He had attained fortune and a position of power in the business world. But his personal life had disintegrated. His wife was a self-centered female who cared only about her social position. His three children, off at private schools, were seldom home, and then paid little attention to their parents.

"It's an empty world, Pauline," my friend once told me. "But I've got to see it through to the end. I've got money and power, but the only contentment I find is being with you. And even that's a hopeless situation."

When Bill died, I wept long and bitterly—not just in grief, but over the tragic truth that, whatever a man accomplishes, his life is empty unless it is blessed with a decent, true, and lasting love. As for Bill, he left me something to remember him by—$65,000 in cash gifts spread over a period of several years. It was a generous gesture, but it really wasn't necessary. I could never forget Bill and the loyal, uplifting friendship with which this lonely man blessed and enriched my life.

As I've noted before, we members of the oldest profession are just as human as any of our other fellow passengers on this sorry old earth. We have the same weaknesses, the same aches and pains. And despite our constant dealing with the seamier aspects of sex, we also slip occasionally and fall in love. My long relationship with Bill was not a love affair. It was, perhaps, something deeper and rarer—the close, enduring friendship between two lonely people which survives the fires of passion and the torments of love.

Nevertheless, I did fall in love twice after my starry-eyed marriage as a naive eighteen-year-old, the marriage which ended in divorce seven years later. Once early in my career as a madam I fell for a handsome stud and married him. It was a dreadful mistake, for he was an out-and-out bastard in every respect. I got rid of him quick, via the divorce court, before I yielded to the temptation to fill his worthless hide with buckshot. There's no point going into details. It was a mess and I was lucky to get out of it.

My next, and last, chance with romance came some years later when I was in my forties, and oddly enough the object of my affections was a man I'd known casually most of my life.

He was about five years older, enough so we rarely mingled as children. He came from a fine Bowling Green family, but by the time he reached college he was considered one of the wild kids whom we good girls of the town were forbidden to date.

While he was a student at Ogden College he was striken with spinal tuberculosis, a disease which left him in frail health the rest of his life and, for a time because of the pain, a morphine addict, a medical curse which he finally overcame.

As his health improved he drifted into business as a bookmaker. However, it wasn't until years later, when I was operating my colonial country house, that I really met him. He arrived with a group of four or five other men looking for a good time, but he ended up spending the entire evening talking with me in the parlor.

Two nights later he was back again. Once more we spent the evening talking about everything under the sun. We seemed to have just about everything in common—a love for travel, an interest in antiques and gardening, a liking for the same kinds of foods, a sharing of memories of a lifetime in Bowling Green. Added to these shared interests, we both were divorced and we both operated illicit businesses.

After a few more meetings—when that foolish old heart of mine was ringing all sorts of alarms—he suggested that we might consider marriage. At this point I told him of my long affair with Bill, an affair from which sex had long vanished.

"However," I said, "as long as Bill is alive I can't hurt him by marrying. He's a dear and loyal friend, and I'll stick with him to the end."

My new love agreed, again exhibiting his rare talent for understanding. Within a few months Bill was dead, and several weeks later my colonial house burned to the ground. Again I received a marriage proposal, and again I put it off, telling my suitor I had to get away by myself for awhile to think things through clearly.

"Marriage is a big step," I said. "This time I've got to be sure."

Actually, I was fibbing. I already had made up my mind to marry him. But before becoming a bride again I wanted to get myself in shape.

He was a handsome, slender man—quick-witted, shrewd, and blessed with a sense of blarney that could twist you around his little finger and still leave you thinking you were getting your own way. On the other hand, I was a veritable battleship of a woman. I was heavy, quick-tempered, stubborn, outspokenly blunt, profane, and impatient.

Nevertheless, with marriage on my mind I was determined to take drastic action in seeking to regain a semblance of my long-lost girlish figure. Without confiding in anyone, I packed a couple of suitcases and headed for Barnarr Macfadden's famous health resort in Danville, New York.

For six weeks, I went for broke. I took steam baths and sauna baths. I submitted to rubdowns and massages. I pedaled bicycles and groaned my way through all sorts of exercises. I ate like a canary—a few bits of tasteless health foods, assorted juices, and enough raw carrots to supply half the nation's rabbit population. At the end of six weeks I climbed on the scales. I had lost a grand total of eighteen pounds, which figured out to about $125 per pound. At that point I decided the gentle art of reducing was too expensive a hobby for me. I returned to Bowling Green and told my fiancé of my unhappy attempt to reduce before our marriage.

"Hell," he laughed, "why all this stewing about losing weight? If I had wanted a skinny wench, I could have found plenty of them."

And so, as the saying goes, we were married and lived happily ever after. Oddly enough, that saying held true as far as we were concerned. In the nearly twenty-two years of our marriage, I never had cause to regret our action. He was a man I admired and respected, a man whose love and devotion I never had cause to doubt.

We were married in Tipton, Georgia, and took off on a madcap six-month honeymoon around the country. We drove up through New York state and into Canada, stopping for fishing expeditions and antique-shopping in out-of-the-way villages. From New England we headed down along the Atlantic Coast to Palm Beach and Miami Beach, then across to New Orleans where my husband could indulge in his favorite spectator sport—cock fighting.

I recall sitting alone in a New Orleans restaurant one afternoon when a friend joined me at the table.

"Where's your husband?" he asked.

"He's gone to a cock fight," I said.

Our friend raised his eyebrows. "A cock fight?" he said.

"Yeh," I replied. "I told him he was wasting his time going to a cock fight when we could have a helluva one right up in our hotel room. But I guess that wasn't exactly what he had in mind!"

Anyhow, from Louisiana we headed back to New York City to take in some Broadway shows and do our Christmas shopping. I even found time to indulge in more antique-hunting before we headed back to Kentucky for the holidays.

In Bowling Green we found quite a few persons shocked by our marriage. One woman, a doctor's widow who had been a friend of mine for years, bluntly asked:

"What on earth ever possessed you? How can the two of you ever hope to find happiness?"

"Well," I said, "I may be a madam and he may be a bookie, but we've got one thing going for us. We love and respect each other, and we don't give a tinker's dam what the rest of the world thinks about us. I'm proud to be seen with him, and he's proud to be seen with me, and nothing else matters."

Actually, when we returned to Bowling Green I had no intention of opening another house. The mayor, however, made his big pitch about the community needing my brand of sex merchandising. I discussed the situation with my husband, and he agreed that I should try one more venture and see if the politicians would carry out their word to leave me alone.

"But," he warned, "don't expect me to help you out in the house once it opens for business. I've been a lot of things in my time, but never a kept man—never a pimp. I'm going back to work as a book-maker!"

"Honey," I said, "I wouldn't want it any other way." And that's how we solved our problem as a working couple. I ran a brothel with a first-class stable of girls, and he concentrated on the betting odds connected with stables of thoroughbred horses.

*Christmas in a whorehouse*

# Christmas in a whorehouse

As the old Yuletide saying goes, Christmas comes but once a year, and when it comes it brings good cheer. Maybe so, but these holiday joys don't necessarily apply to life in a whorehouse.

As matter of fact, Christmas in most brothels is strictly dullsville —a time when most tricks are either abstaining from pleasures of the flesh because of the holy season, too busily engaged with their families, or too broke from the rigors of holiday shopping. On the other side of the street, most girls are given the holidays off to spend Christmas and New Year's with their families. This leaves most houses with just a skeleton staff: the madam, a few girls who have no family to celebrate with, and a few part-time prostitutes seeking to bolster their holiday budgets by helping handle the tricks who like some extra frills added to the mistletoe routine.

One Yule season my girls decided that our house needed some good, old-fashioned Christmas spirit. It all started early in December with a story in the local newspaper listing poor families in the city who needed a helping hand for the holidays.

"Hey," one of the girls exclaimed, "why don't we adopt a family for Christmas?"

We all agreed it was an excellent idea, something that would give us a chance to join in the spirit of the holiday season. I telephoned the newspaper—one of the most implacable foes of my sex emporium—and announced that we wanted to adopt a needy family for Christmas.

The editor was momentarily shocked. "You mean to say you want to help out in our Christmas drive?" he finally managed to squeak.

"What in the hell do you think I'm calling about?"

"Well," he muttered, "this is highly unusual. I'll have to speak to the publisher. I just don't know what he'll say about a brothel contributing to our Christmas charity."

"Look," I said, "you tell that damned old skinflint that if he doesn't want my help I'll start my own Christmas charity drive and make him look sick."

Ten minutes later the editor was back on the phone. "It's okay," he said. "We've assigned you the family of so-and-so. They've got twelve kids, and the old man is out of work. It's a real hardship case."

"Don't worry," I said. "We'll take care of them."

I investigated and discovered that the sly old publisher had really handed us the toughest of his charity cases, a Negro family existing on the brink of starvation. Father, mother, and a brood of twelve children, ranging in age from seventeen to a babe in arms, were packed into a ramshackle six-room house down in niggertown. There was scarcely any food, no coal for heat, and only a few pieces of furniture. Obviously this wretched family couldn't wait until Christmas for assistance.

I enlisted the help of several of the girls, and we went into action. I called the coal company, ordered a couple tons of coal, and told them to send me the bill. Then I called my very special friend, and he lined up a full-time job for the father of this huge brood. I dispatched the girls to lay in some food for the family, and I visited a few of the new and used furniture dealers, told them the hard-luck story, and got them to contribute some much-needed pieces of furniture to our good cause.

After those basic necessities were taken care of, we started Christmas shopping for the family. Each of us contributed money and took turns shopping and gift wrapping. It was a wonderful experience—assembling clothes, books, toys, games, nuts, candy, and fruit, a veritable mountain of gifts for a family of twelve kids and two adults. We planned to deliver the gifts on Christmas Eve, and earlier that day we labored in the kitchen, baking a turkey, a ham, and batches of holiday cookies.

Suddenly, as our chores were nearing an end, one of the girls exclaimed, "We've fogotten the most important thing. We don't have a Santa Claus!"

"Good Lord, that's right!" I said. "We've got to find us a Santa Claus!"

"How about Elmer?" one of the girls suggested, referring to a hefty, 200-plus-pounds city fireman who traditionally performed as Santa at several local lodge parties each year.

"Perfect," I said. I telephoned Elmer at the fire station, explained the situation, and he happily agreed to serve as our Santa Claus. It took two cars to carry all the gifts, foods, Christmas tree, passengers, and Santa. But it was worth all the labor and expense to see the happiness shining in the eyes of those children when Santa burst into that house with a sack of toys and loud cries of holiday cheer.

Later on, we returned to the house on Clay Street to our own Christmas tree, the exchanging of gifts, and special brandy-laced eggnogs. We asked Santa to join the party, and he agreed, sprawling in an easy chair and sipping on an eggnog. While he was relaxing after his arduous chores, one of my girls whispered in my ear:

"Miss Pauline, don't you think it would be nice to give Santa Claus a present?"

Carried away by the holiday spirit, I agreed. "I think it would be a wonderful idea," I said.

With my approval, the girl went over and sat down on Santa's lap. She whispered a brief message to him, and the Old Boy's eyes sparkled and his false whiskers quivered eagerly. Then, laying his finger aside of his nose, up the stairway he rose, accompanied by as nice a blond Christmas package as ever was given as a gift. Thus, Santa became the one and only patron of my house to get a present from me of a free party during forty years of sex merchandising—and then only because I got carried away by the holiday spirit.

Anyhow, that particular holiday season began a long Christmas tradition for us. Each Yule season we would adopt at least one needy family and take care of their needs. Later, as my house became increasingly prosperous, I tried to extend a helping hand to the needy at other times of the year as well. For example, one day I happened to drive through Delafield, a poor school district, and I noticed that, despite the cold weather, many of the children were inadequately clothed.

I telephoned the school, talked with the principal, and identified myself. "I don't want to shock you," I said, "but I noticed today that a number of your children are poorly clothed."

"I'm afraid you're right," she said. "Many of our parents are too poor to dress their children properly. It's a shame, but there's nothing we can do about it."

"Well," I said, "if you won't feel insulted, my girls and I would like to help out. Take the children who really need clothes down to the store, get them whatever they need, and send the bills to us. The merchants know that we're good for the money. In fact, if some of the folks are really desperate for food or fuel, take care of that, too, and send us the bills."

After that, Delafield became another of our pet projects. We never sought to publicize it, but Miss Mattie of Delafield School always went out of her way to stop and chat with me and my girls wherever we happened to meet. And you can be sure that, through her, people in the right places knew what we were doing.

In fact, I sometimes thought that Miss Mattie did too good a job in spreading the word. Throughout the years we were asked by numerous organizations—including churches and clubs that did everything possible to cut us behind the scenes—to help out on their charity drives. Generally we'd chip in, but mainly we concentrated on our own projects, some of which arose quite unexpectedly. I recall one particularly vicious siege of winter when, right after the holidays, Bowling Green was cut off from the outside world. Temperatures had dropped to twenty below, snow was knee-deep, trains, airplanes, and all highway traffic were hopelessly stalled. Even telephone and Western Union communications were knocked out.

In the midst of this storm two young G.I.s from Camp Campbell showed up at the house almost frozen to death.

After I thawed them out with some hot coffee, they told me they had hiked from the downtown bus station—where they had been waiting to return to Camp Campbell after their holiday furlough—because several hundred tourists were stranded by the storm in the bus and train stations and needed help.

"They're in a bad way," one of the soldiers said. "There's no food, not much heat, and the stations are packed. We thought you might be able to help out."

The two soldiers pitched in and helped. We got a couple hams and a couple roasts out of the freezer, as well as a dozen loaves of frozen bread. We made stacks of sandwiches, two large bowls of potato salad, two twenty-four-cup urns of coffee, and other foods. We packed it into my car along with paper plates and cups and plastic utensils and set out for the bus station. We made it through the storm, fed the people, brought a few elderly, ailing tourists back to my house, and then repeated the process for those stranded at the train station. By the time the second trip was completed, we had twenty-four elderly and infant tourists bedded down in my house along with the two G.I.s and my stable of weary girls who had labored as cooks for hours during the emergency.

The next day the storm continued unabated. The soldiers shoveled the drifting snow from the driveway and sidewalks, and we hauled another load of food into the bus station only to learn that other agencies finally had gotten busy and had the emergency under control. We returned to my house and, with the stranded passengers, spent the next two days playing pinochle and other games and tending to squalling infants. At last, after the third day, transportation was resumed and our guests departed, few except the two G.I.s suspecting that they had been stranded for seventy-two hours in a notorious bordello.

About a week later the doorbell rang. It was a Military Police lieutenant.

"I'm looking for Miss Pauline Tabor," he said.

"Well, sonny, you don't have to look any further," I said. "I'm Pauline, and what can I do for you?"

"I'm just checking out on the stories of a couple of soldiers from Camp Campbell," he said. "They were AWOL for three days in getting back from their holiday furloughs. They claimed they were stranded at your house for three days because of the storm. They said you and your girls put them to work helping feed and take care of other stranded travelers."

"That's the honest to gosh truth," I replied. "In fact, if those boys hadn't hiked out here through the storm, we never would have known the trouble they were having at the bus and train stations. We never would have been able to help out when we were needed that first night."

The MP lieutenant shook his head sadly. "What a break," he said. "Two G.I.s get snowbound in a whorehouse. How much luckier can they get?"

"Well," I said with a laugh, "at least they had to work—they didn't get to sample any of the merchandise."

"How can you be sure of that?" the lieutenant asked. "The way they tell it, they damned near screwed themselves to death out here."

"Very simple," I replied. "All my girls slept upstairs, and I bedded down the soldiers in a downstairs parlor. Every night I sprinkled talcum powder on the steps leading up the stairs to show up any footprints. And to be extra safe I slept on a cot at the foot of the stairs. There's no man living—not even a combat veteran—who can sneak across my two hundred and sixty pounds without knowing he's been in a battle."

The lieutenant laughed. "So those damned lying G.I.s spent three days in a cathouse without a single piece of ass. Just wait until I get back with that story! Three friggin' days without a single score!" And the lieutenant drove away, still chuckling at the misfortune of the hapless, assless G.I.s who had the bad luck to end up broke in a whorehouse for three days.

One Christmas Eve, my oldest son received a valuable lesson in some of the little-known facts of a brothel operation. He was in his twenties then, and had stopped by to pick me up for a family holiday get-together.

"You're early, son," I said. "I've got a car loaded with Christmas baskets for the poor. How about giving me a hand? I could use a good strong arm."

It took us three trips to get rid of all the Christmas baskets. I guess my son saw streets and hovels that night which he had never dreamed existed. After returning from delivering the last load, I could tell he was really shook.

"Mother," he said, "I've lived in Bowling Green all my life, but I never realized anyone was as poor as some of the people we've visited tonight. I've never realized conditions were so bad for some families in this town."

"Son, wherever you go in this world you'll find poverty and misery if you take the time to look."

"When we went from place to place, it seemed like these people were expecting you," he said. "Like you were their one hope for a decent Christmas."

"Well," I said, "I've been delivering these baskets every year for a long time—ever since I could afford to help the poor. After all, I've known some tough times, too. I know what it's like to be poor, and it sure as hell isn't pleasant."

My son shook his head in bewilderment. "I've never known any of this," he said. "I had no idea you've been doing so much for other people."

"It's something you don't go around bragging about, not if you're sincere about trying to help," I said. "I've done a lot of things I'm not especially proud of. But I'm not a phony. I've never claimed to be something I wasn't. I'm glad you had a chance to help me tonight because it may help you understand me better. But I wouldn't want the rest of the world to know because it would make me look like a phony, seeking sympathy."

As I noted earlier, most of my regular girls would take off for the Christmas holidays. We'd usually have our party, complete with tree and trimmings, a sumptuous feast, and an exchange of gifts before they would leave to join their families for the holidays. Then I'd start the task of interviewing part-time girls to take over during the slack holiday season.

I recall one part-timer who really put on a show in downtown Bowling Green one busy Christmas season. This girl was a young brunette from Nashville, a good-looker except for a hick town wardrobe that looked like something out of Tobacco Road.

"I guess you'll do," I said. "But I'll have to take you downtown for some new clothes and a medical checkup."

The girl, who claimed her name was Patricia, got a clean bill of health from the doctor. After that, I bought her a couple of dresses and evening gowns, then took her into a store for some shoes. That's when the fun started. The shoe clerk measured her foot, and Patricia, with legs sprawled apart, hoisted her skirt to midthigh. The clerk's eyes bulged, and his face reddened. He scurried back to look for a few pairs of shoes. Before long, four or five other clerks were clustered around, enjoying the unexpected holiday scenery treat.

I made a couple of fast purchases and got Patricia home as quickly as possible. As soon as we got inside the house, I ordered her to raise her skirt above her waist.

"What on earth for?" Patricia asked.

"Don't be asking a lot of damn fool questions. Just do as I say!"

Patricia lifted her skirt. Sure enough, she was wearing no pants, and the black pubic panorama undoubtedly had given the boys at the shoe store a real eyeful.

"Young lady," I lectured, "no girl works for me unless she wears pants whenever she leaves this house. I won't have any bare-assed wenches parading around town."

"But I thought it would be a good come-on, to get the boys interested," Patricia protested.

"Toots," I said, "any time a customer wants a look at your snatch, he's got to pay. Never forget that!"

Following that lecture, I marched Patricia back to the shoe store and made her apologize to all the clerks. I never had any further trouble with the girl, although I did notice that all the clerks for whom she had put on a free show at the store did come to my house for dates with Patricia. I guess they wanted a closer look at her imposing "love machine."

My favorite Christmas girl, however, was a young auburn-haired woman named Sandra—a name which we changed to Terrific after a few weeks on the job at my Clay Street house.

It was mid-December when I received a telephone call from Sandra. She said she had heard I was looking for part-time girls to work in the house during the holidays, and she asked if she could stop by for an interview.

"Have you had any experience?" I asked.

"Well, I've had a couple of affairs, if that's what you mean."

"No, no," I said. "Have you ever worked as a prostitute?"

"Of course not," Sandra replied. "But I'm sure I could learn. I really do need the money."

Normally I wouldn't have considered an inexperienced young girl even for a part-time holiday job. But for some reason it was hard that year to line up girls who, in the past, had been eager to earn extra money. Times were too prosperous, and most of them had good-paying regular jobs. So in desperation I told Sandra to drop in for an interview.

Sandra was an attractive girl, a little over five feet tall with generous curves, a vivacious personality, lively brown eyes, and a merry smile. "I can't work full-time, Pauline," she said. "I have a job as a bookkeeper, but I do need extra work badly to make ends meet."

"Honey," I said, "usually I wouldn't consider using you. But I've got to have part-time girls this holiday season, for two or three weeks, if you're interested."

Sandra was delighted. "I have a two-week vacation during the holidays," she said. "It will work out perfectly because I really do need the extra money."

So with misgivings I hired Sandra even though I was convinced she was much too wholesome a type to be a successfully glamorous prostitute. She had her medical checkup, and then I turned her over to one of my experienced girls for "basic training" before her part-time boudoir chores began.

To my surprise Sandra turned out to be a natural. Her wholesome, good-natured personality really intrigued the tricks. I had five girls working over the holidays, and Sandra outdistanced them all. Several customers returned night after night for dates with her. It was the busiest Christmas season in my memory, and Sandra—beyond doubt—was our big attraction.

One evening as the holidays were drawing to a close, I had a talk with Sandra. "I don't know what you make as a bookkeeper, but it can't be very much," I said. "You'd really make a lot more, at least two to three hundred a week, here. The customers are nuts about you —they're already calling you 'Terrific.' "

Sandra was impressed by the money I cited, but she was still reluctant to make up her mind. "My dad's been sick, and I've been helping pay the doctor bills and the household expenses," she said. "I've also been paying the cost of educating my brothers. Sure I need the money, but I'm afraid someone I know will spot me working here and ruin my reputation."

After the holidays, however, Sandra—or Terrific, as most of us now called her—decided to work full-time for my house on Clay Street. "It's the only way I can pay up the bills and start saving some money," she said. "I'll just have to take my chances on not being recognized."

I spent that January vacationing in Florida with my husband. My assistant landlady, a former girl from one of my early-day stables, was in charge of the house during my absence, and when I returned she reported enthusiastically that Terrific had continued to be our big money earner. "The customers really flip over her," she said. "She's not exactly the sexpot type, but she's sure got something that keeps the boys coming back."

A couple of months later, Terrific called during her week off and reported she had married a "truly sensational man." Three months later she was back at my house again, tearfully reporting that her husband had turned out to be a "woman-chasing louse."

"I've moved out, bag and baggage," Terrific said. "Can I have my old job back again?"

I took Terrific back, and she had lost none of her old, magical appeal. When she was on the job she was a great moneymaker. But there was one drawback. Terrific was one of those females who live on a constant emotional roller-coaster. She'd be up in the heights one minute and down in the depths the next instant. She'd work reliably for months, then disappear without a word for weeks at a time. Once she returned to report that she'd finally divorced her heel of a husband and had promised herself that never again would she be lured up the aisle.

Again, after several months on the job, Terrific pulled another of her disappearing acts. This time, just as on her initial job-seeking visit, she returned to the house on Clay Street about ten days before Christmas.

"Pauline," she said, "I know you get terribly angry with me, but I just get itchy feet and I've got to get away for awhile. Please give me one more chance."

"Okay," I said. "I'll give you one more chance—but this is absolutely the last time."

So Terrific was back at work in the midst of the Christmas season. Four days later she was madly in love with a customer, a brawny big-spender from out west, a wealthy rancher in search of some good buys in Kentucky horseflesh.

"We're both deeply in love, Pauline. This is the real thing; I know it is," Terrific said.

"Nuts," I said disgustedly. "You're both plain loony."

"Don't say that, Pauline," Terrific said. "We want to be married here, right in this house, on Christmas Day, and we want you to give the bride away."

"Honey," I said, "now I know you're nuts! Whoever heard of a wedding in a whorehouse, especially on Christmas Day? And who ever heard of a madam giving away the bride? Hell, a madam never gives anything away!"

But Terrific and her boyfriend were insistent. They even had an answer for my argument that we could never get a Bowling Green preacher to perform a wedding ceremony in my brothel.

"Who in the hell said anything about a Bowling Green preacher?" the bridegroom-to-be snorted. "I'm flying in my own Bible-thumper from Oklahoma. I've just given him fifty thousand bucks for a new church, so he'll be here, don't worry."

Reluctantly I agreed to the Christmas Day wedding. I even agreed to give the bride away, provided I could select my own costume. The ceremony started at noon on Christmas Day. The Oklahoma minister was on hand. We even managed to get a recording of the wedding march for the jukebox. The bride was lovely in a two-piece blue silk gown with a huge orchid corsage, and the groom was resplendent in high-heeled boots and pearl-gray Stetson. As for me, I arrived on the scene in a rented Santa Claus costume, complete with a beard and a jolly, red false nose.

"As long as this is Christmas, I thought we might as well have Santa Claus give the bride away, to make it official," I explained.

With the Clay Street wedding completed, the groom piled the entire wedding party—including my husband and several of my girls—into his plane and we flew to Oklahoma for a rip-roaring four-day wedding party on his ranch. All in all, it was the screwiest romance and screwiest wedding I've ever encountered. Strangely enough, though, it's been one of the happiest marriages I've ever known. Terrific and her impetuous cowboy still live on a ranch out west. They've got four fine kids, a big herd of beef cattle, and a mediocre racing stable which loses enough money to provide them with a sizable tax break.

How did a screwball brothel marriage like this succeed? Well, I like to think that is was good old Santa, giving away the bride on Christmas Day, who guaranteed its success. After all, Santa's a pretty reliable guy when it comes to gift-giving, even in a whorehouse.

Not all Christmas stories centered around a brothel are happy, however. Despite the tinsel, the gifts, the party fun, it's a sad time for some girls—mainly the ones who have no family with whom to share the season's fleeting joys. Some of these girls have families, including children. But they've been turned away in disgrace to face a tough life alone and unloved. It was one of these unwanted, unloved girls who provided me with my only suicide scare in the four decades of my madamship.

It was on a Christmas morning when one of my girls rushed downstairs screaming that Meg had killed herself. I hurried up to the bedroom and found the girl sprawled on the bed. Two empty sleeping tablet vials were on the night stand, and the girl scarcely seemed to be breathing. I telephoned the doctor, ordered some coffee, and got one of the girls to help me walk—or drag would be a more accurate description—Meg around the room. The doctor arrived, applied a stomach pump, and shipped her off to the hospital. Meg luckily recovered, underwent psychiatric treatment, retired as a prostitute, and eventually was reunited with her family. She had thought she was tough enough to take the hurts of life as a prostitute, but the deeply entrenched sentimentalities of Christmas were more than she could stand. She was lucky to escape with her life.

Another nearly tragic event occurred during Christmas week. One of my girls became quite ill several days before leaving on her holiday vacation. We had her rushed to the hospital where it was decided she required major abdominal surgery. I contacted the girl's family, but they had little money. In fact, they had relied on her income and seemed a bit incensed that she could be so inconsiderate as to become ill and cut off their source of income.

I reported the situation to my girls, and we all dug down into our savings to help pay the girl's surgical and hospital costs. After several months of recuperation from surgery, which included a hysterectomy, she returned to work at my house. However, she didn't last long. She seemed depressed, discontented, and definitely not interested in sex. She quit and took a job clerking in a department store. It is quite common, I understand, for a hysterectomy to destroy a woman's emotional acceptance of life as a prostitute.

Through the years I've encountered a number of fine, dedicated doctors, but I've also met a few first-rate quacks who are far more interested in money than they are in healing. This fact was brought home to me various times when I operated the house on Clay Street. In this out-of-the-way location, the few neighbors we had were too poor to afford such luxuries as a telephone. As a result they often would come to borrow my telephone in times of emergency.

Almost every time when a call of this nature was made, the doctor would get me on the phone and ask if I would guarantee payment if he responded to the call. Each time I'd assure the money-hungry medic that I'd pay the bill. But finally on one Christmas Eve I lost my temper.

A Negro father came knocking at my door that night, asking to use our phone. One of his children was sick with a fever. He needed a doctor's help. The anxious father made the call, and, sure enough, the doctor asked to speak with me.

"Pauline," he said, "do you know if this family has the money to pay me for making the trip down there on a Christmas Eve?"

I'd heard that same question so many times I was sick to death of it. I lost my temper. "Hell, no, doctor, you know god damned good and well they don't have any money. But they've got a real sick kid, and I've got the money, so you can get your damned ass down here *right now.*"

I banged down the receiver without waiting for an answer, wondering if he would show up after the tongue-lashing I'd given him.

Actually, there was no need to wonder. About two hours later the doorbell rang. It was the doctor, icily reporting that he had made the house call and treated the boy. Nothing serious, just a case of measles.

"That will be twenty dollars," the doctor reported.

"Just a moment," I said. I fetched my purse and pulled out a crisp $20 bill. I rolled it up tightly and poked it into the startled doctor's mouth.

"Take your money, you hypocritical bastard," I yelled. "You take an oath as a doctor to help people, but you can't even do a little charity on Christmas Eve. So here's a whore's money to help the poor—and I hope you choke on it."

Getting that blast off my chest, I shoved the sputtering doctor out onto the porch and slammed the door on him. As far as I was concerned, it was a perfectly tawdry ending for a frustrating Christmas Eve in a whorehouse.

*A 'moonlighting' madam*

# A 'moonlighting' madam

It was a professor from Vanderbilt University, an expert on modern methods of agriculture, who first roused my long-dormant interest in farming and turned me into a "moonlighting" madam.

As a child during the period when my father was involved in real estate speculation, I had lived on several farms and developed a love for the land and plant and animal life. In later years this interest was manifested in the long hours of landscaping work I devoted to my houses. As I've noted earlier, even my property on Clay Street was a garden spot of considerable beauty, set down in the midst of a shabby railroad and stockyard environment.

I guess it was the careful landscaping of my farm that first interested the Vanderbilt professor when he began visiting my country home on his occasional trips from Tennessee to Bowling Green—trips during which he availed himself of the pleasures offered at 627 Clay Street. Before long he was spending more time talking with me and helping me putter around in my garden than he devoted to the more exotic charms of my girls in town.

It wasn't that the professor's interest in sex was waning. It was just that he was a fanatic on one subject—the "rape" of our precious land resources by generation after generation of stupid farming methods—and he found in me an interested, devoted listener. Occasionally he would take me on rides across the Kentucky countryside, angrily pointing out miserably rundown, eroded farm land and lecturing me on how this once rich soil had been despoiled by year after year of tobacco crops with no thought given to occasional resting and rejuvenation of the land through natural, organic farming methods.

"We're a nation of greedy, money-hungry despoilers who give no thought to the welfare of future generations," the professor fumed. "Just drive across our country. See the dust bowls, the eroded, weed-cluttered land, the abandoned farms too poor to support even the lowest type of sharecropper. And remember that this land was once rich and productive but was badly used and thrown away like so much garbage when it ceased being profitably productive."

I enjoyed the professor's indignant lectures on the shortsighted greed of American farming methods. But it was after he introduced me to two books, Louis Bromfield's *Pleasant Valley* and *Malabar Farm*, that I really began thinking seriously about trying my hand at organic farming.

Bromfield, in case you may not be familiar with his writings, was a well-known American author who, in the 1940s, returned to his native Ohio to try out some of his revolutionary ideas about farming and the restoration of burned-out land. The two books which the professor had me read were dramatic accounts of Bromfield's experiences during his return to the land.

Like the professor, Bromfield was outspokenly angry over our extravagant and heedless waste of land. I still recall one of his passages in *Malabar Farm* in which he compared agricultural methods with prostitution, claiming that both were the victims of whorish greed.

"Agriculture is the oldest of professions," Bromfield wrote. "Yes, it is older even than the one you are thinking of, for it began when Adam and Eve were expelled from the Garden, and prostitution did not begin until at least one more woman entered the world. It should be remembered that both professions spring from fundamental urges in man: (1) The necessity to eat; (2) The urge to propagate, legitimately, indiscriminately, or otherwise. . . . Indeed, the social and economic diseases spread by a poor agriculture have been and still are as bad as or worse than the diseases spread by the prostitute."

Anyhow, between the professor's lectures and reading and rereading Bromfield's books, I soon found myself eagerly planning to conduct my own experiments in organic farming. I began devoting my spare time to shopping for a farm. In 1951 I finally found what I was looking for, a 160-acre hunk of rundown land with several houses and a number of decrepit outbuildings. It was a beautiful location—hilltop land looking out over the rolling Kentucky countryside, sloping down to a stretch of timbered river bottom. Once it had been a lovely, productive farm. But when I bought it for $18,500, its main features were weeds and eroded desolation.

I quickly learned that operating a brothel and running a farm, especially a badly neglected section of land that has to be restored, are two full-time jobs. For years I had devoted all of my time, except for an occasional vacation when the Holy Joes forced a temporary closing, to the personal supervision of my brothel and its stable of girls. Even when the business prospered beyond my most optimistic dreams, I continued to operate as a full-time madam. It was the only way, I felt, that I could be sure of maintaining the high standards on which I insisted.

However, after I bought the farm I soon discovered how tough it is to try to serve two masters. I soon learned that "moonlighting"—the effort so many breadwinners make to hold down two jobs—is no joke. For nearly nine years I operated the house during the evenings and nights, caught a few hours of sleep, and then hurried out to the farm to help my hired hands with the seemingly hopeless task of getting the land back in shape. It was no easy job. I worked like a horse, driving trucks, shoveling manure and chemicals, riding tractors. In fact, one of my friends, after seeing me on a tractor with the edges of my broad butt flopping over the sides of the narrow seat, sent me a present. It was a custom-built, wide-gauge tractor seat, big enough to accommodate the king-sized dimensions of my monumental bottom. After that I rode the tractor in comfort.

After too many years of this kind of moonlighting, I decided that I had to slow down my pace. I hired an assistant housekeeper, a former girl in one of my early-day stables whom I trusted completely, to oversee the house full time. My husband and I moved out to the farm so I could devote more time to its development and still spend part of each afternoon and evening at the house on Clay Street, overseeing its operations, taking care of its financial complexities, and keeping my finger on its pulse.

Ruby, my newly acquired housekeeper, was indeed a great help in taking pressure off my hectic schedule. She was honest and reliable and, equally important, she was a veteran prostitute who was wise in the ways of bawdy house procedures.

However, I quickly discovered that Ruby had one of the less-desirable traits of many prostitutes. She was, at heart, an oversentimental jerk, a sucker for the hard-luck story of any sister in sin. For example, through Ruby's gullible generosity, her blind trust in fellow humans, and the amazing productivity of my farm, the house on Clay Street for several months supported an Indiana hippie commune in lavish style.

It all started when I suggested to Ruby that she hire two or three part-time girls to help us handle our booming sex traffic on Friday and Saturday nights. Ruby came up with three candidates, two brunettes and a blonde. They were young; claimed they were twenty-two and that they had fled Indiana to get away from a hippies' pad in artistic Brown County because they were tired of being "exploited" by their long-haired boyfriends.

They looked like hippies, all right. They were unwashed, with long, matted, ratty-looking hair, ragged jeans, love beads, sweatshirts and no shoes—the standard hippie uniform of that period.

"Good God, get rid of them," I told Ruby after one look at these models of modern youth.

Ruby, however, pleaded for a chance to get the girls in shape. "They're just trying to get back to a decent life," Ruby said, for she viewed the female hippie type as several social stratas below the raunchiest streetwalker.

I was too busy to argue, so I told Ruby to try her reformation. Within a week the three hippie girls were devastatingly lovely. They had been bathed and rebathed; their hair and fingernails were beautifully groomed; they had, to my surprise, even passed their medical checkups.

For two months these exhippies were the sex-sations of my weekend traffic. But before long strange things began to happen at the house on Clay Street. My former residents of the Brown County pad were making good money for their Friday and Saturday night labors, but things began to disappear. My other girls started to complain that someone was stealing their earnings; clothes and other valuables began to disappear; and meat and other foodstuffs which I shipped from the farm to a large frozen-food locker on Clay Street began to vanish with amazing rapidity.

I informed several of my younger customers of these mysterious raids. Early one Sunday they followed my three exhippies. The trail led directly back to the Hoosier hippie pad, which my three "reformed" girls had been supporting in royal style with whatever they could earn and steal at my house in Bowling Green. After that I took over the job of hiring once more, and—despite Ruby's shortcomings—the house on Clay Street continued to prosper.

If the development of my farm had been as simple and as profitable as the operation of my house, life would have been easy. Business on Bowling Green's sex market never faltered. In fact, as the years passed the fame of my Clay Street house spread, and our customers—the big-moneyed ones, that is—came from many states. My farm, however, was not such a simple, moneymaking proposition. Quite the contrary. There never seemed an end to the improvements it required, and most of them were costly. I guess if the farm had merely been a hobby, I would have abandoned it. But I had a deeply rooted love of the land, and being a stubborn female I was determined to restore this farm to its full potential.

During these years I got to know every foot of that farm. Working with a bulldozer I helped fill in eroded gullies and sinkholes, I tore down thorn trees and plowed under vast stretches of weeds. I hauled manure, rotted hay, sawdust, and all the other vital ingredients for compost heaps—some nearly two hundred feet long and twenty-five feet wide. I shipped in five train carloads of phosphate from Florida and four train carloads of granite dust, a natural potash, from Georgia to use in rebuilding the natural vitality of my soil. In addition I hauled in at least three hundred and fifty tons of chicken droppings from poultry farms all over the state to help build up the soil, and I used manure from my own cattle herds as well.

Slowly, with the help of compost, fertilizers, chemicals, and other vital organic materials, the soil's natural vigor returned. Then it was time to think of other phases of the farm's rejuvenation. I separated the farm into various fenced fields including four pastures for my herd of Black Angus beef cattle. I set up a system of portable irrigation pipes, with four- and six-inch pipes leading to huge sprayers capable of watering several acres at a time. I planted a large pecan grove and other fruit trees. I shipped in seven tractor-trailer loads of hand-split chestnut rails from Virginia to fence the entire farm. And I developed a large pond down below the site my husband and I had selected for our new ranch home.

The house was our pet project. For several years we came up with all sorts of plans and scrapped them for one reason or another. Finally about ten years ago we started building the one-story, fourteen-room ranch house in which we found a proper setting for the many beautiful things we had collected through the years.

Our farm, which produced practically all the food we used, was indeed a show place. We had geese, pheasants, and even a large flock of tame peacocks to add a special touch of glamour. However, the combination of life on a country estate and running two such illegal businesses as a brothel and a bookmaking operation had its perils.

Once we had moved full time to the farm, holdups became an increasing menace at the house on Clay Street. And in many of these stickups attempts were made to learn the location of our farm, which we had kept a closely guarded secret known to only a few friends and relatives.

On one occasion three gunmen forced their way into the Clay Street house late one afternoon before the start of the evening's business. At the time I had a full-time watchman as well as a housekeeper, and he raced from the house when he realized what was happening. One of the gunmen fired a couple of shots, but missed, and the watchman ran up the street to a telephone at the stockyard.

He was nearly incoherent when he got me on the phone at the farm, but I managed to understand that my house was being robbed. I telephoned the police and the Sheriff's Department, grabbed my shotgun, and headed for town, inching my car cautiously through a heavy snowstorm.

By the time I arrived in town the house on Clay Street was packed with law-enforcement officers and hysterical girls. The thugs had tied the girls up with stockings, systematically looted their rooms, and beaten several of them in an effort to learn where my farm was located. Evidently they figured that I had my "big" money stashed away at the farm. But they had no success, for none of the girls had ever been out to the farm.

Anyhow, to be on the safe side, the Sheriff followed me back out to the farm that night to make sure the hoods hadn't discovered where I lived. While he was at the farm, he received a call from his office. The three gunmen had been caught in a road block, and all the loot was recovered. So we were lucky that time.

Another time two armed hoodlums forced their way into the house while I was at the farm. They robbed the girls and then discovered a small safe in my room. They finally opened it and found out it was empty. Cursing with frustration, they looted the jukeboxes, coke machines, and cigarette venders, and fled. Behind them they left several cardboard boxes I'd carelessly left on top of a bookcase. These boxes contained nearly $1,000 in receipts. What these thieves didn't know is that I never used the safe because I couldn't remember the combination. Instead, I'd put cash in boxes and other silly places until I could get to the bank. During the years when my mother was alive I'd usually send the night's receipts to her by a trusted cab driver, and she would make the deposits for me. Later, after my marriage, my husband handled many of my financial transactions, as well as his own, until his health began to fail badly.

The house on Clay Street was even the scene of a kidnaping. One of my girls for more than a year had been seeking to evade her former pimp, an evil, brutal thug who had threatened to kill her if she ever ran away.

The girl, Wilma, frankly told me of her fear when she came to work in my house.

"Maybe he'll forget all about it," I suggested. "It doesn't seem logical that he'd hunt you down here, all the way from St. Louis."

"You don't know that man," Wilma said. "He's a devil. He figures that once a girl works for him, he owns her for life."

"Well," I said, "we'll try to protect you, but you'd better let your folks know everything, including his name and address, in case something should happen."

Fortunately the girl took my advice. She wrote all the details to her parents, including her fears. "If you don't hear from me at least once a week, get in touch with the FBI," she told her folks.

A couple of months later I was at the farm when I received a frantic phone call from a long-time customer. He had shown up at the Clay Street house that evening and was met at the door by a large, gun-toting character who told him to get lost.

"I rushed back to a phone and called you, Pauline," the frightened trick said. "I don't know what's going on, but there sure is something wrong!"

I telephoned the police. By the time they arrived the gunman was gone, and so was Wilma. Her fears had been well founded. Her ex-pimp had somehow tracked her down and, marching her out of my house at gunpoint, had driven away. I telephoned the girl's parents and they notified the FBI, supplying them with the information provided by their daughter. Three days later the demented pimp was arrested as he drove up to his house in St. Louis with Wilma still a prisoner in his car. He's still serving a prison term for kidnaping, and Wilma has long since retired to the more placid life of a housewife, mother, and leader of a Brownie troop.

However, it wasn't only criminals invading the house on Clay Street that I had to worry about. We also had problems with criminal elements out at the farm, especially from burglars and rustlers.

Although we kept tenant farmers on the place to help with the more arduous tasks of farm life, they were not much help as "watchdogs." Once we made the mistake of telling a few persons in town that we were taking a month's vacation in Florida. When we returned our house had been burglarized. Drawers had been emptied, furniture moved, pictures taken from the walls. The burglars even went through everything in our fallout shelter. Obviously they were looking for a safe, something we always relied on banks to provide rather than hoard large sums of money around the house. As a result, all the burglars got was a truck, about $1,800 worth of silver, and a watch my grandfather had given me when I was a teen-ager. Luckily, they seemed to have no awareness of the value of antiques, for they didn't touch a single one of the precious things I had collected through the years, items valued at several hundred thousand dollars. After that we always made sure we had an armed guard in our home whenever we were away on vacation.

As for rustlers, we've had several cases of a couple of steers or hogs turning up missing. We just chalked this up to one of the hazards of farming. But one day when twenty-five head of my prime Angus steers vanished, I figured things had gone too damned far. I found the fence cut down in one of the lower pastures and tracks where the cattle had been run across the creek into the woods.

Through the Cattlemen's Association, I hired a detective. He worked hard, but a Sherlock Holmes he wasn't. He chased all over the countryside asking questions and getting nowhere. Finally one of my neighboring farmers dropped in one day, a fellow who had been a good customer of my house on Clay Street for years.

"How's that detective feller of yours making out?" my friend asked.

"Hell's bells, he's still trying to find out on what side of the hills the sun rises in the morning," I said disgustedly. "I'm not even sure he knows the difference between a cow and a goat!"

My farmer friend chuckled and lighted his pipe with a big wooden kitchen match. "Pauline," he said, "there sure as hell is no mystery about who took your cattle. It's that damned white-trash family that rented the place down in the bottom land."

"How can you be so sure of that?" I asked.

"The old man just got out of jail last year after serving three years for rustling," the farmer said. "And a few days ago they bought themselves a car that must have cost at least fifteen hundred. So you might as well figure they got your cattle."

"By God, I'm going down and have a talk with that old bastard," I fumed.

"You just mind your own business, Pauline," the farmer warned. "Those folks are bad actors, and you don't have a chance to prove anything. If you start bad-talking them, they'll really start giving you a hard time—burning your barns, ripping down fences, and things like that."

"What do I do, just let them get away with it?" I asked.

"Miss Pauline," the farmer said. "Suppose you just let some of us menfolk around these parts see what we can do about it."

During the next few months the rustler family seemed to encounter all sorts of strange mishaps. Fires started in their pasture land. Fences broke. A ladder collapsed and the Old Boy fell and broke a leg. At last they seemed to take a hint. They moved on to greener, and no doubt friendlier, pastures. After that we had no more problems with rustlers.

I suppose the most nerve-wracking moments came at night when I drove from the house on Clay Street out to the farm, a long fifteen-mile stretch over lonely, dark country roads. By this time all sorts of ridiculous rumors were circulating around the Bowling Green area, stories that I had a vast fortune hidden on my farm. As a result, I soon began to have company on my homeward trips. Cars began to tail me. Several times they tried to overtake me and force me off the road. I zigged and zagged and took various routes, shaking my followers off my trail. However, it was too terrifying. I finally reported the situation to my friends in the Sheriff's Department, and after that I was convoyed safely home by an armed officer every night.

As the years passed the job of overseeing the farm and operating a brothel became tougher and tougher. Suddenly I found myself with still another moonlighting chore. My husband's health had become increasingly frail. At last the doctors advised that he no longer should attempt to run his "book." So in addition to my chores as a madam and a farmer, I became Bowling Green's first lady bookmaker. It was a new business for me, but my husband advised me on its intricacies so I managed to get by without any serious blunders. In fact, we continued to make a profit.

One day, after I'd operated his book for more than a year on a modest, careful scale, he received a phone call from a friend in the rackets up in Louisville. When he hung up, he summoned me for a conference.

"Pauline," he said, "my friend just tipped me that a few of the big boys have decided to give you the business. They're planning to gang up on you and break the book."

"What in the hell do I do in a case like this?" I asked.

"You can't fight them," he said. "Just beat them to the punch. Get on the phone and call all our customers. Tell them we're closing down immediately. As of now, we're taking no more bets. They're going to have to find a new bookie if they want to play the ponies."

That was the best news I'd had in a long time. I never had really understood bookmaking. To me it was just another tough job in my already hectic schedule.

"Honey," I said, "don't worry about losing the bookie business. With all that prime pussy we've got down on Clay Street, who in the hell needs horses?"

However, despite the rigors of moonlighting, I never regretted my venture into farming. God knows how much money I poured into the place, revitalizing the land, investing in the many building projects, and developing broad green lawns, landscaped terraces, and lovely flower gardens, and raising prize crops and herds of livestock. One thing's sure: the farm never made enough money to begin to make up for the investment. But for my husband and me it was a lovely, private little world in which we could retreat from the grimy, rough-and-tough, illicit businesses in which so much of our lives had been involved. We found pleasures in so many simple things: watching herds of deer venture up to the house for handouts in the winter, making friends with squirrels and birds, fishing down along the river, watching crops and animals grow and mature, marveling at the change of seasons, and reveling in the beauty of our world. Somehow the peace and tranquillity we found gave us a deeper understanding of each other and ourselves.

I recall one occasion when a black limousine pulled into the parking lot of the house on Clay Street. A uniformed chauffeur got out and helped an elderly lady out of the car. With his assistance and the help of a cane, the old lady made her way up to the door. I answered the bell and found myself staring at a wrinkled, white-haired old lady with bright, twinkling blue eyes.

I squealed with delight. "Miss May," I said, "what a wonderful surprise to have you come calling after all these years!"

Miss May, who must have been well up in her eighties, grinned impishly. "I didn't think you'd recognize an ancient battle-ax like me, Pauline."

"Remember you?" I said. "How could I ever forget you? Come on in. We've got a lot to talk about."

Miss May slowly toured my house. Then over coffee and cookies she told me she had been retired for more than ten years, living in comfort in Florida.

"I've never been much for writing letters," she said. "But I decided I'd take one last trip, seeing folks like you whom I've always meant to look up."

We gossiped for several hours. Miss May complimented me on my good taste and took special delight in my collection of antiques. She met my girls, joked with them, and told them a few hair-raising stories of her early days as a prostitute and a madam.

"I recall one time out west when I was working in a house in a small town. The folks appointed a woman as a sheriff's deputy, and the first thing she did was raid our house. I jumped out a window without a stitch of clothes on and hid in a clump of sagebrush." Miss May chuckled at the remembrance. "Well, that lady deputy came out looking for me. I clouted her over the head with a hunk of wood, stripped her down to the buff, tied her up, and put on her clothes. I also took her money, went back in the house and got the few bucks I'd earned, and I caught the night train out of town, heading east. That was the last time I ever went out west. Tennessee was wild and woolly enough for me."

The girls and I enjoyed Miss May's company and conversation. She was one of those born storytellers who can delight an audience, and despite her years her humor was as lively and bawdy as it had been years before.

After a time, I told her about the farm and how much I loved living in the country.

"A farm?" she asked. "Who in the world ever heard of a madam doubling up as a farmer?"

Miss May's skepticism vanished when she saw the farm. "It's positively beautiful," she said. "I just don't see how you've had the time or energy to handle both jobs."

"Well," I said, "I told you a long time ago in Clarksville that I wasn't afraid of hard work."

Miss May chuckled. "As I recall, I told you then that maybe you were innocent, but that you had the gall and guts to make a good madam. But I sure didn't expect you to turn out as good at raising crops as you were at running a whorehouse!"

*A madam looks at sex in our society*

## *A madam looks at sex in our society*

As far as book learning is concerned, I guess I'm as out of date as an old tin lizzie. It's not that I've neglected my reading because I have a library of a thousand or more books and I've plowed my way through most of them. It's just that I've never had any of these smart college professor types, like the ones who have done such notable jobs at places like Berkeley, Kent State, and Columbia, to steer my thinking in the right direction. So perhaps I'm out of step with the "mod" generation.

Nevertheless, during nearly forty years of sitting in my old rocking chair in a whorehouse parlor, I've seen a lot of life that isn't mentioned in textbooks. I've seen a lot of human beings from all walks of life in a basic setting where their true emotional torments break through the camouflage behind which most of us hide. And I've had a lot of time to do some plain, old-fashioned thinking about the hangups which seem to plague so much of our so-called civilization today.

Take this bra-burning women's lib nonsense, for example. One of the biggest human problems I've encountered as a madam has been the breakdown in communications between men and women. I know of no other single factor that drives so many married men into the arms of prostitutes. In the lonely void of their own marriages in which even the most simple of everyday communications seem hopelessly stalled, they reach out desperately to "boughten" love for at least a temporary gratification of warmth and understanding.

I'm not saying that this breakdown of communication is solely the fault of women. It takes two to tango, and men, I'm sure, are equally to blame for many of the woes which beset modern marriage. However, I do say that these women's lib females are complicating an already serious situation, a situation in which women are becoming more malelike in their attitudes and men are becoming more submissively feminine. And in the process the guts of our American society are vanishing.

The women's lib adherents scream that for centuries women have been abused and forced to play a secondary role. They shout for equal rights, they cry for equal pay, they yell for equal treatment. In fact, they demand just about everything except a pair of balls and a penis. Maybe they'll be screaming for those accessories one of these days because their female equipment sure seems to be drying up.

What these female crusaders seem to overlook in their determined push for full equality is that they're upsetting the balance of nature. Men were created with strength, imagination, ambition, and a sense of adventure—an inherent desire to create, invent, build. However, they also were created with a weakness, a need to be loved and praised and stirred to action by the warmth of a woman's embrace. Thus, women, from the beginning of time, have possessed in their capacity for love, tenderness, and family devotion the power to inspire men to great deeds. Now they seem to scorn these qualities and want to take over the job of running the world.

I'm not saying that women should get back into the kitchens, nurseries, and bedrooms and stay there. I believe women should be privileged to use whatever God-given talents they have and to be properly rewarded for these abilities on the same basis as a man. But what I am saying—as a female who has worked and operated a profitable business most of my life—is that we mustn't forget that above all we are women. If we practice what so many of the lib looneys preach —get full equality with men and the hell with being women—then the world is going to be in a hell of a lot sorrier shape than it is now. Frankly I can't see what the libs are griping about anyhow. It seems to me that in most respects American women already have a mighty damned cozy deal for themselves. Maybe it's that old female weakness: give a woman an inch and pretty soon she'll want the whole damned yardstick.

More and more during my lifetime the male-female role has changed. More and more the male has become the low man on the totem pole in American family life. It's Good Old Dad who pays and pays and pays and too often gets nothing but ulcers or a coronary as a reward. Perhaps he should stand up and clout the Old Lady a couple times just to let her know he's still the boss.

I suppose a lot of women's lib leaders will argue that I'm a betrayer of my sex, a woman who is trying to cover up her tracks as a sex exploiter of hundreds of girls. Here, again, I say baloney. No girl was ever forced against her will to work in my house. Their health was guarded zealously. They were protected against brutality. They made good money and were encouraged to save it and get out of the business while they still possessed their youth. In fact, many ended up making better wives than so-called respectable women because they had a deeper, more compassionate understanding of basic male needs as a result of their brothel experience.

I could fill a book with pitiful case histories of men who ended up in my house in an effort to repair the emotional devastation resulting from their marriages to unfeminine, frigid females. Of course, a number of my married tricks were philanderers—men whose childish egos needed a constant supply of female conquests—and other males who sought to satisfy their particular odd hangups in the privacy of a brothel. But a number of my married customers were lonely men, desperately in search of at least a few moments of warmth and understanding. Some of these men often didn't even indulge in sex at my house; they just sought companionship, a chance to talk out their problems.

For example, I recall one Bowling Green businessman who used to drop by my house several times a week. Occasionally he'd date a girl, but most of the time he preferred to talk, to seek to analyze the reasons for the failure of his marriage. He had been a successful businessman when he married an attractive young divorcee, but he soon learned he had picked a lemon in the garden of love.

"She seemed like everything a man could want," the businessman said, "but in bed she was an iceberg. Oh, she would submit to sex, but every time she made it plain that she hated every minute of it. She made a nightmare out of what should have been a pleasure. Then, to make matters worse, I was impotent with her after awhile—and she just laughed at me."

By the time the businessman started patronizing my house he was hitting the bottle hard and his business was going downhill fast. I explained his problem to a couple of my better girls. After a few dates they convinced him that he wasn't impotent, that, in fact, he was quite a capable stud. With his confidence in his manhood restored there was an amazing change in this man. He stopped the heavy boozing. He worked hard to get his business back in shape. And he divorced his hopelessly frigid wife. A couple of years later he remarried, a warm-hearted, plain Jane sort of a woman this time. They had two children and seemed to enjoy an ideally happy marriage. At least he never returned to my house. I guess his sexual ego no longer needed bolstering outside his own home.

This businessman's case, and it was one of several similar ones, always seemed proof to me of one of my pet theories. I believe that self-confidence is the basic ingredient in the makeup of any successful man. And self-confidence is largely a product of a man's relationship with a woman. If a woman is capable of making a man feel like he's a *real man*, he feels that he can lick the world, do anything he sets his mind to. Maybe it's childish, but that's how the male animal is made. That's why a smart wife can make him think he's something special and in the process turn him into a real winner.

It seems to me that today's sick mix-up of the man-woman role in life is leading to some increasingly weird hangups among couples. A few years ago, to cite just one case, a Mr. and his Mrs. showed up together one evening at my Clay Street house. To my amazement, they casually explained that they were looking for a new "kick." They wanted two of my girls and two customers to join them in a real "ball-banging" party. What's more, they were willing to give me $125 for the "gang bang."

"I'm sorry, folks," I said. "A lot of stuff goes on here, but I don't set up parties for married couples. If you folks are this hard up for kicks, you'll have to find them somewhere else."

The discontented Mr. and Mrs. left and never returned. I learned later, however, that they set up a couples-swapping club that was one of the "in" spots among the town's bored young and not-so-young married set. A fun-loving adventure in sex? Hell, clubs like this are animalistic, worse than the lowest type of brothel.

In another, funnier case a married couple I had known for years came to my house one night with just about the strangest request I ever received.

I saw their car pull into the parking lot, but they didn't come to the door. Curious, I stepped outside and found my friends, Jason and Edna, sitting in chairs on the patio.

"What the hell are you two doing here?" I asked. "This is no time to come visiting."

"We're not visiting, Pauline," the husband explained. "We're here on business."

"Business!" I exclaimed. "And just what in the hell do you have in mind?"

Nervously the husband explained that, although he had adequate sexual powers, medical tests had revealed that he was unfertile, that he could not give his wife the child she wanted so badly.

"Edna and I discussed the problem like *sane* adults," Jason said. "We finally decided that she should come to your house, go to bed with a couple of high-type customers, and get pregnant."

"Are you folks drunk, or just plain crazy?" I asked.

"Neither," Edna said in a matter-of-fact tone of voice. "We're very serious about this, and we need your help!"

"Listen to me, the two of you," I said. "I run a sex business. But I sure as hell don't run a maternity service. If you folks want a baby, adopt one, or talk to your doctor about a test-tube baby, but don't come around my place looking to get knocked up."

Another married couple visited me one time and asked for a private consultation. The husband, some years older than his wife, admitted that he was impotent. He no longer could satisfy his wife.

"I want her to be satisfied, but I don't want her having affairs behind my back," he said. "Finally we decided that if a man can come to a whorehouse, there's no reason why a woman can't get the same kind of service."

"In other words," I told the wife, "you want to get screwed here at my house."

The woman was embarrassed. She nodded. "We decided it was the best way to handle our problem, though I know it sounds kind of strange."

"Strange?" I snorted. "It's ridiculous. No man is going to bring his wife to my house to be screwed. You'd better take your problem to a head shrinker, or buy a rubber penis, or get one of your friends to take over the job. But, for God's sake, don't try to get me involved in your family affairs!"

A brothel gets quite a bit of its trade from philandering husbands, but occasionally a two-timing wife drives her mate into the arms of prostitutes. Tim, for example, was a successful tobacco merchant, a well-to-do, handsome man in his late thirties. But despite his success Tim was a miserable man. He was deeply in love with his wife, but she seemed frigid. She resisted his advances, refused to go out on dates with him or accompany him on business trips.

"Honey," I told Tim one night after listening to his woes, "I don't think your wife's frigid. I think she's got a boyfriend on the side and just can't be bothered with you."

"I can't believe that, Pauline," the frustrated husband replied. "I give her everything possible. I just can't believe she'd cheat on me."

A few weeks later, however, Tim came rushing into my Clay Street house. "You were right," he said. "That goddam woman was playing footsie with one of my best friends."

"What in the hell happened?"

It was a slight variation of an old, old story. Tim had to go out of town on business. Outside Bowling Green on the road to Louisville, he remembered that he had left some important papers at home, and he headed back. When he pulled into the driveway he noticed that all the lights except in his bedroom were out, even though it was fairly early in the evening.

"I went back to the bedroom and found my wife, stark naked, frantically trying to close the window," Tim said. "I went over to help her, and I heard someone outside groaning with pain."

Tim rushed outside and found his best friend, naked, writhing in pain, and begging for help. "I think I broke my hip, falling out of the window," the two-timing friend moaned.

"What did you do—help him?" I asked.

Tim grinned with malicious satisfaction. "I sure did," he said. "But first I changed his looks a bit. I smashed his face in, busted his nose and jaw, and knocked out a few teeth. Then I dragged my wife, bare-assed, out of the house and made her take a good look at her boyfriend. I told her that if I ever caught her cheating again, she'd end up looking a lot worse. After that I called an ambulance to haul her lover-boy's ass out of my yard."

Tim's revenge may have been a bit drastic, but it seemed to be effective. For years he'd drop in at my house about once a month for a date. "I tell my wife I'm coming here just to make sure she's performing as good as your girls do in bed," he'd say with a grin.

"And your wife doesn't object?" I asked.

"Hell," he said, "since that night I caught her cheating, she's never given me a bit of trouble. I guess I put the fear of God in her. Ever since then, we've had an ideal marriage. I'm the boss—no questions asked."

Tim's heavy-handed solution to his marital problems, I'm sure, wouldn't work with all women. His wife was apparently one of those females who can respect only a domineering husband who'll not hesitate to slap her around if she gets out of line. However, she was one of many wives I've encountered who willingly accepted their husbands' patronizing of a brothel.

Tim's wife, of course, was willing to accept his sexual straying because she was afraid to cross him. Other wives, however, agree to their husbands' tomcatting habits for far different reasons. A lot of biddies who are bored with sex are delighted to have prostitutes handle the "nasty old job of sex" for them. And some women who have known that their husbands' sex drives were much stronger than they could cope with have thanked me for having a good house with clean girls where their mates could find satisfaction without getting involved in messy outside romances.

In fact, I believe this difference in sex drive is another cause of much marital unhappiness. Too often there is an imbalance in sex urges that sends either husbands or wives in search of outside romancing. Perhaps the idea of trial marriages of six months to a year isn't too farfetched. It at least would give a couple an opportunity to discover if they are not only sexually compatible but also suited to each other temperamentally and intellectually. Too many couples, after the fires of early passion subside, discover that they have nothing in common except a wedding certificate.

Personally I've always felt that our society has attached too much significance to the act of intercourse. We've made it practically a holy ritual designed primarily for the purpose of procreation. Now, I certainly won't argue the fact that copulation is a human process vital to the continuing of our species, but I do not believe that is its only legitimate purpose. The coupling of a man and woman shouldn't be taken so damned seriously. It can be an act of beautiful and abiding love, but it also can be a manifestation of friendship, the easing of tensions, or merely an effort by two lonely people to find a momentary lessening of their inner torments. In all these forms the sex act should be something warm and beautiful, not a sinful, ugly act. So many of our hangups as humans are due to our inability to accept sex as a normal urge, the same as hunger or thirst is.

I've never been one to downgrade the importance of sex. Indeed, I've made a mighty good living catering to the sex urge in its many forms. But insofar as marriage is concerned, I believe that sex is vastly overpublicized as a decisive factor in holding a couple together. As Philip Wylie noted, the key question of modern-day American marriage seems to be: "Madam, are you a good lay?"

So much of our culture is spuriously concentrated on false concepts about sex and youth. Advertising is the biggest offender. If one is to believe the incredible amount of bullshit produced by Madison Avenue, one has to be convinced that (1) life isn't worth living if you're in the shadowlands of senility at twenty-five; (2) you don't have a chance of a tumble in the hay unless you use the right soap, deodorant, mouthwash, toothpaste, after-shave lotion, or special female douche; (3) unless you eat the right kind of diet, fortified by all manner of vitamins, your sex equipment is going to wither away and fall off; and (4) unless you stay slender, prevent the onset of gray hair, and wipe out those creepy old wrinkles with the proper brand of magical skin lotions you'll be a total loss as a sex machine.

This incessant barrage of sex-oriented garbage emerging from our nation's advertising agencies certainly helps complicate our society's increasingly freakish hangups.

Contrary to the phony concepts of life which emerge from the boob tubes of the nation hour after hour, sex and youth, a faultless breath, a slender belly, and sweet-smelling armpits are not necessarily the most vital ingredients of living and loving, although an awful lot of fools seem to think so.

Sex can be one of the fine parts of a good marriage. But, believe me, it isn't the whole ball game. A lasting, reasonably happy marriage depends on a variety of other factors. As I noted earlier, communication is a vital link to human understanding. Unless a couple can communicate, can find many things in common to share in addition to bedroom frolicking, their marriage is doomed. And, as far as a slender, sirenlike wench with flawless skin, lovely hair, pearly teeth, and a youthful "Pepsi generation" zest being essential to a happy marriage, that also is a lot of crap.

Sex is a funny business. I've known a number of men who have had beautiful, sexy wives, yet went wandering in search of other female companionship. Many times these husbands would divorce their sexpot wives and marry women who, on the surface, seemed completely devoid of sex appeal.

The answer to this puzzling mixup of male sexual preferences is not difficult to figure out. Too many beautiful women falsely believe that they have all the accessories needed to win and hold a man. True enough, they have the natural endowments to attract a man, but once they get down to the nitty-gritty of life together, the woman discovers that it takes more than beauty to hold a marriage together. On the other hand, the ugly-duckling female often attracts and holds a man because, to compensate for her lack of beauty, she develops a sweet, lively personality, a wide awareness of things beyond her own selfish interests, and an astounding capability in sexual activities.

Somehow, so many of these ugly ducklings instinctively learn the lesson so many of their more richly endowed sisters ignore. They learn to be honest with themselves, to face up to the facts involved in the winning and holding of a man. They seem to realize that a man wants a wife to take care of his house and be a good mother for his children. But, beyond this, he wants a companion to share his interests, and—even more important—he wants a mistress, a warm-blooded, sexually exciting woman who not only welcomes his embrace but adds a few fun and games of her own. A tough job? Certainly it's no easy task to be a real-life, responsive woman. But as a lot of our women's lib enthusiasts are going to discover when they finally get the male equality they've been squawking about, the job of being a man is no cinch either. What we need today is a lot less of this lib bilge, and a helluva lot more women who are women and more men who are men.

Now there's a lot more I could say about this sorry state of affairs in today's male-female relationships. But there are a few other things I'd like to get off my chest while I'm percolating ideas here in my old rocking chair.

One of my main peeves is the pornography that's been flooding our country in recent years, thanks to some of the senile nitwits with which our Supreme Court has been infested. I've dealt in sex—the merchandising of women's sexual favors—for many years. But this aspect of sex is as old as history itself, a catering to one of mankind's basic, natural urges. Assuredly it has its bad points, but none so evil as the peddling of pornography.

Pornography is a far different matter than sex. I'm not a prude, and I see nothing wrong with the reasonable portrayal of sex in litera-ture, in films, or on the stage if it is an integral part of a legitimate story. However, the out-and-out crude pornography that's flooding our nation today from all parts of the world is perversion in its worst form. In movies, in books, in magazines sex is portrayed in its most depraved forms, adding new sickness to the already sick minds who delight in this sort of garbage. Certainly there is no element of art to this pornographic material; it's purely a moneymaking bonanza for racketeering elements, sanctioned by the high courts of our land. And it feeds new fires to our nation's already serious sex-crime problems, creating constant headaches for our police, whose hands are tied by the insanities of our court system.

I find it ironic and rather frightening to consider the fact that our public officials will support the circulation of this perverted material, which can do so much damage in undermining the moral fiber of our nation, and still refuse to consider the long-standing question of legalized prostitution—a factor which I believe could provide a healthy outlet for our society's sex urges. We have restaurants for our hunger, drinking fountains for our thirst, but when it comes to that other basic appetite we have no legal source of appeasement outside of marriage. It just doesn't make sense.

I realize that the Holy Joes raise their voices in alarm whenever legalized prostitution is mentioned. How terrible, they say, it would be to sanctify sin by legalizing prostitution. It would be, they claim, a one-way ticket to hell for our young people, and just another evil temptation like old demon booze for the older menfolk. Furthermore, the Holy Joes proclaim, legalized prostitution would help spread the terrible blight of venereal disease.

I would be a fool to claim that legalized prostitution, even with closely enforced weekly medical checkups of all girls, would completely eliminate the venereal disease problem. But it certainly would go a long way toward keeping the spread of V.D. under control.

If you doubt this, look at the present dismal venereal disease record in the United States, Italy, France, and other countries where there have been continuing drives to close houses of prostitution during the last decade. Governments and police agencies may have succeeded in shutting down the brothels, but they haven't been able to put an end to vice. They've only succeeded in turning the girls out from closely supervised houses, producing an ever-growing legion of unsupervised, medically unchecked streetwalkers, B-girls, and free-lancing call girls. The result has been a steady spiraling of the venereal disease rate in the United States and other countries, despite the effective V.D. cures provided by modern medicine. And accompanying this frightening gain in V.D. has been a steady increase in crimes committed by girls and their pimps who set out to victimize unsuspecting tricks. The Holy Joes have really reaped an unholy harvest in this crusade.

Yes, I'm in favor of legalized prostitution, set up, operated, licensed, and supervised by federal, state, county, or city governments. With legal houses operating with licensed girls and a uniform schedule of fees, I realize there'd no longer be opportunities for madams to make huge fortunes in the merchandising of sex. However, racketeering elements could be eliminated, payoffs would be ended, and a new source of badly needed tax revenue would be established. I don't believe there's a chance in hell of ending prostitution in one form or another. So it seems only logical to make it legal and keep it under tight control. Under such a system the public, and *not* racketeers and crooked cops and politicians, would reap the benefits.

There's one other point I'd like to touch on as long as I'm waxing philosophical, and that's sex education. I'm all for it as long as the instructors know what they're talking about. Most parents are hopeless when it comes to this task, and the average teacher isn't much better. Personally, I suspect that madams and their girls could do a far better sex-education job.

Seriously, I do believe that we need a new approach to sex education among our young people. It's necessary, I know, to teach the clinical aspects, the physical differences, the dangers of venereal disease, and the perils of pregnancy a girl faces in any casual romancing. But beyond this I think we should teach youngsters that sex can be a beautiful, inspiring experience that is as natural as food and drink. We should also teach birth-control methods at the high-school level, for it is utter idiocy to expect all sexually mature teen-agers to abstain from sex for six, eight, or ten years until the time comes for marriage. Furthermore, I believe all church or parental influence on sex education methods should be carefully screened to make sure that the old-fashioned bogeyman of sex as a nasty, dirty, sinful business is eliminated. This attitude, above all others, has twisted beyond repair the sex lives of a tragically large number of people.

I recall one young trick who came to my house several years ago. The first few times he balked at dating girls. Finally one evening he confessed to me that he had never had relations with a girl; that his parents had told him repeatedly that intercourse was dirty and sinful. While in college, he had suffered an emotional breakdown and spent several years in a psychiatric institution.

"I've just been out a few months, and I'm still trying to get up enough nerve to have normal sex relations," he said. "But so far I'm not having much luck. I can't get over the fear of sex my parents planted in my mind."

I asked one of my more compassionate girls, Vera, to take over the young man and patiently teach him the facts of life. It was not an easy job. I guess Vera took the young fellow under her wing every time he came to the house for several months.

At last he came downstairs one night and excitedly told me that he finally had overcome his sex-fear hangups. "It's finally worked," he said. "Vera has taught me to enjoy sex. I can experience a normal life now, with no more fear or shame."

That young man was lucky that he had a girl as understanding and patient as Vera to lead him to sexual normalcy, a job which none of the experts at the mental institution were able to accomplish with all their scientific mumbo jumbo. Not only did he gain a normal sexual attitude, but he married, became the father of a fine brood of youngsters, and developed a successful business.

Several professors and administrators at Kentucky Western University also seemed to look upon my house on Clay Street as a worthwhile sex-training ground for their students as well as an excellent frolicking place for their own amorous adventuring. With a rare understanding of human nature, these school officials would keep a close eye on the youngsters and seek to put an end to campus romances that seemed to promise to end tragically.

Often they would send the young romantics down to my house for a lecture on the facts of life. I'd tell them the dangers of getting V.D. from promiscuous girls and warn them that marriage and parenthood before completing their education could ruin their future lives. I told them that sex was a beautiful experience, but that there were a lot more things vital to a permanent, satisfying marriage. Also, I lectured them on the fact that sex was a two-way street; that a young man should learn to give a girl as much enjoyment as he expected to get from her.

I guess, in a way, I was sort of an unofficial sex-education teacher. And lots of times the professors would help out by bankrolling one of their lovelorn students to the price of a party with one of my girls, to help him forget his campus romance and gain some skills from an experienced "teacher" in the process. In fact, a few times a month on slow nights we'd feature special "cut rates" for Western Kentucky students as part of their off-campus sex education.

On one point, however, I never strayed from my original policy. I never permitted a coed from Western Kentucky to work in my house even on a part-time basis. From time to time I would hire a girl who had dropped out of other, out-of-town colleges because of money problems. Most of these girls, I might add, worked long enough to save up sufficient tuition money, and then "retired" and completed their education. But even though I got applications from several hundred Western Kentucky coeds through the years, I turned all of them down. It was too close to home, too much of a potential dynamite keg that could have blown me and my house right out of existence. Quite a few of the boys at Western Kentucky learned the ABCs of sex at the house on Clay Street, but the coeds had to look elsewhere for their birds-and-bees education even though I often suspected that some of them could have taught my girls a few tricks.

I guess my reputation as a "sex educator" extended beyond the campus because, from time to time, fathers would come to my house with their teen-aged sons in tow.

I recall one father saying: "Pauline, I remember my teen-aged years when I was sex crazy half the time and didn't even suspect what the score was. My boy is at that age now, and I don't want him to go through what I did."

"What do you want me to do about it?" I asked.

"My boy is sixteen," he said, "and I don't want him getting messed up with young girls around town or getting dirty ideas about sex. I want your girls to teach him the right kind of sex and how to make it a beautiful experience so he'll be a good husband some day."

"Aren't you afraid of disease or your boy getting a lot of sinful ideas?" I asked jokingly.

"Pauline," he said, "I don't think there's a cleaner place, with nicer girls, in the whole state of Kentucky. And as far as sex being sinful, I'm a good churchman, but that idea is a lot of hogwash."

"Okay," I said, "I'll take your boy as a student, and I hope we can meet your expectations."

Needless to say the boy was a willing and eager learner. His father gave me $20 a month to finance his lessons. One day after a couple of months of instruction, the boy showed up for another "lesson in the arts of sex."

"Sorry, Butch, but you've already used up your twenty bucks for the month," I said.

"That's okay," he replied breezily. "Just charge it to my dad."

I telephoned his father. He snorted indignantly. "That boy has learned his lessons real fast," he said. "Tell him that my twenty a month for lessons is finished. From now on, if he wants a piece of ass, tell him he can go out and earn the money for it himself. Tell him that's lesson number two about sex—that there's no such thing as free pussy. In one way or another, a man's going to pay, and my son might as well get that through his head right now!"

Butch was just one of several dozen boys who were brought by their fathers to my house for sexual indoctrination. All of them, I'm proud to report, turned out to be first-rate "students" and later became husbands who apparently enjoyed the blessings of happy marriages. At least, once they were married their patronage of my establishment ceased.

My handling of these young sex "students" never varied. They were always frightened out of their wits in one respect and always curious as hell in another. I'd spend about an hour talking to the boy, telling him what to expect and how to act. I'd lecture him on the need for cleanliness and the importance of looking upon sex as a normal human urge rather than something nasty to be ashamed of.

With the lecture completed, I'd turn him over to one of my better girls, and his lessons would begin. I'm happy to say that never once did these youngsters give me or my girls a bad time.

My favorite sex student, however, wasn't brought to my house by his father. He came to my house after an eloquent telephone plea by his mother, a well-to-do widow from Nashville, Tennessee. She told me that her son had gotten sexually involved with a girl while attending college in Tennessee—a coed who apparently had been accommodating half the male student body.

"Pauline," the rich widow said, "I don't want my boy to get involved with any more coeds. I know he needs sex, so I want him to patronize your house whenever he feels the urge. Just send me his bill the end of each month and I'll mail you a check."

"Well," I said, "I've got to admit that you're the first mother who ever called and asked me to provide girls for her boy. Most mothers take a pretty dim view of my kind of business."

The broad-minded mother laughed derisively. "Hell," she said, "most women don't have enough brains to know up from down. That's why the world's so full of sexual misfits. They're the product of dear old mom's dim-witted concepts of morality."

"And what are your views?" I asked. "I don't mean to pry, but you do seem to be a mighty unusual mother."

The wealthy widow chuckled. "I'm a mother who has enough sense to realize that her young son is sexually mature," she said. "And I'd rather have him enjoy sex properly in your house on Clay Street than get involved with cheap, diseased tramps around town."

Her son used his charge-account sex privileges for several months. Then one evening he drove up from college in Tennessee with six of his buddies packed in his car. They, too, were to enjoy his credit-card sex-privileges, he said.

Again, I got on the telephone. I explained to his mother that her son had showed up with six of his campus pals for a full-scale sex party on credit.

The mother sighed wearily. "Okay, tell him he can get away with it this one time. Tell him I'll pick up the entire tab. But warn him this is the last time. After this I just pay for him. Tell him I'm damned if I'm going to keep the whole college supplied with free ass!"

*The closing of the house on Clay Street*

## The closing of the house on Clay Street

The notorious house on Clay Street is now just a memory. The police couldn't close it, and the county attorney couldn't close it, and the Holy Joes couldn't close it. But progress in the form of urban renewal moved in and the walls came tumbling down.

There's nothing left but a pile of worthless rubble, waiting for more than two years now for the urban renewal brain-trusters to decide just why in the hell they wanted the property in the first place. Even the bricks from my two-story house have vanished, sold by a couple of entrepreneurs at $4 each to collectors around the country who wanted a memento of my Bowling Green brothel.

Well, the bricks from the house on Clay Street may make interesting keepsakes, stirring memories of long-past indiscretions, but as I've noted before, the walls of a whorehouse can't talk. That's one advantage a madam has—and one of the main reasons I've written my memoirs. If a couple of shrewdies figure to make a killing on the bricks of my house, by God I'll not be upstaged. I'll tell the stories that the bricks can't voice. Names may be altered or eliminated and dates and places changed occasionally to protect reputations and the sensibilities of families, but the actual incidents and characters recounted in this book are as authentic as the walls that housed the secrets of my madamship for so many years.

Actually, my Clay Street house lived on borrowed time for several years. Although it had been designated as a part of a large, overall renewal project back in the mid-sixties, it was one of the last of the properties to be condemned and closed for razing.

This delay led to all manner of unpleasantness within the city. Church and club groups demanded to know why federal renewal officials continued to delay the closing of a scandalous bordello while condemning and razing other properties within the renewal area. Adding to these indignant outcries, unfriendly elements in City Hall and police headquarters stepped up their harassment tactics. At times it seemed as if I were on a constant round trip between my house and police court. Even the out-of-town newspapers began joking about the raids. As columnist Jay Searcy wrote in the *Chattanooga Times:*

"Every few months three or four squad cars from the police department wheeled into the driveway at Pauline's. Sometimes they would drive away with Pauline's friends, and sometimes they would drive away with Pauline. But Pauline always came back in an hour's time, scoffing all the way down the sidewalk until she disappeared into the sanctity of her home. . . ."

The closing of the Clay Street house was, in itself, quite a production. It is not easy to close the door on more than twenty-five years of your life. And adding to this melancholy task was the question of disposing of the furnishings of the large house. The antiques and other favored possessions, of course, I moved out to my farm. But still I had a considerable amount of furniture and housewares to get rid of. At first I planned to hold a sale, but I learned that a large group of clubwomen were planning to buy my possessions as curiosities. A friend phoned me and tipped me off to the fact that a number of the clubwomen who had always wanted to see the inside of a whorehouse were planning to "invade" my establishment for the sale. I decided I'd never give them that satisfaction. When I learned of their plans, I canceled the sale and gave away everything to needy families in Bowling Green. And the town dowagers never did get the chance to tour the infamous house on Clay Street, an establishment with which most of their husbands were quite familiar.

In retirement I've had time to look back over my life as objectively as possible. Financially I've been a success. In my last marriage I was happy beyond my fondest dreams. My children and grandchildren have turned out well. To my knowledge I've never harmed anyone but myself. I realize there are people who are ashamed of me, people who despise me, and people who are jealous or envious of me. But I've stopped worrying about these folks a long time ago because I can buy and sell most of them.

Also, I'll frankly admit that I'm tired, that I should have gotten out of the business a long time ago. For one thing, I found it increasingly difficult to understand just what motivated a lot of the younger girls who worked in my stable during my last few years in business. Far fewer of them seemed to be working as prostitutes because they needed money badly or had a specific ambition in life. More of them seemed to be in the business strictly for kicks.

I recall one girl in particular because of her strange kick. She drove up to my house in an expensive convertible. Her clothes and accessories were obviously from costly, exclusive shops. She told me she had been working as a call girl in Chicago but had left town to get rid of an obnoxious boyfriend. Anyhow, she worked for me for about two months, then announced that she had decided to move on to Florida.

A few weeks later a well-dressed, middle-aged gentleman stopped at my house and inquired about this girl. He was, he told me, the girl's father, and for more than a year had been trying to track her down and get her to return home. When I told him that she had moved on, presumably to Florida, several weeks before, he sighed dejectedly.

"We don't know what's wrong," he admitted. "We have plenty of money and a fine home, and we've tried to give our daughter everything she's ever wanted. But she seems to take special delight in torturing us by working as a prostitute. It seems like she's trying to destroy us and debase herself in the process. There's just no logical reason for her actions."

What can you say to a father with that kind of a problem? You can only wish him luck and wonder what weird kind of thinking motivates a girl like his prostitute daughter.

When I think of spoiled, selfish kids like this one, who seem to get their kicks by hurting people close to them, I remember special friends of mine of years long past. I especially remember a friend of mine named Lola, the owner of a concession in a carnival that visited Bowling Green once or twice a year.

It was Lola who came to my rescue on the first night I opened my new house at 627 Clay Street for business. Everything was in great shape. A big turnout was assured. There was only one problem. Two of my girls telephoned from Nashville, saying they'd be delayed forty-eight hours because of personal problems.

Lola's carnival was in town at that time, putting on a benefit show for one of the local civic clubs. In fact, all my friends at the carnival had assured me they'd drop in during the night to help break in the new house.

I hurried to the carnival grounds late that afternoon to tell Lola of my problem.

"I'm two girls short on opening night," I said. "I don't know how I'm going to handle all the business."

"Hell," Lola said, "I'll fill in for you until your other two girls get in town."

"Don't be ridiculous," I said. "Why should you turn prostitute just to help me out?"

Lola laughed. "Honey," she said, "how do you think I got my start? How do you think I got enough money to own a carnival concession? I may be in my thirties, but I can still show your tricks a good time."

Lola convinced me. She took time out from her carnival concession for two nights to help make a big success of the grand opening of the house on Clay Street. At the end of her emergency stint I tried to give her the money she had earned. She refused to take it.

"Use it to buy something nice for your house," she said. "I quit taking money for screwing a long time ago. Let's just say that the pleasure was all mine!"

During my last ten years on Clay Street I had several opportunities to sell the business for a big profit. The syndicate, of course, was one of the potential buyers, but with the help of influential friends I managed to put an end to that deal. Another time a couple from Ohio came to Bowling Green with an offer to buy me out. They were friends of one of my girls, a blond, veteran prostitute named Annie. She claimed that they had operated a house outside Lima, Ohio, and would be an ideal couple to take over my Clay Street operation. She seemed mighty anxious for me to do business with them—maybe too anxious.

I don't know if the Ohioans were legitimate buyers or merely acting as a front for some underworld operator. In any event I didn't like the sound of their proposition. I sent them on their way, much to Annie's disgust. She, too, moved on a few weeks later, perhaps to join her Ohio friends in attempting to set up another deal.

I had another potential customer about a year later. This one was, beyond doubt, a legitimate buyer. One of my girls inherited a considerable sum of money. She wanted to buy my house, offering a large down payment and sizable monthly installments. It was a tempting offer, but finally I turned it down.

"It's not that I don't trust you," I said. "It's just that, by and large, Bowling Green's been good to me. I try to operate in the way I think is best for the town. I think I'll just keep operating that way until I retire, and then I'll close the doors and throw the key away. That way, nobody can ever blame me for selling out to bad elements harmful to the town."

I've been retired now for nearly two years, and I've found a lot of things to do besides sitting in my rocking chair dreaming about the good old days. I recall several years ago I was up at Louisville for the races. I discovered that the State Junior Chamber of Commerce was holding its convention in the hotel where I was staying. Before long I got a phone call from a couple of my Jaycee friends from Bowling Green. They asked to come up to my room for a conference.

A few minutes later they arrived with a full-fledged brainstorm. "Pauline," one of the visitors said excitedly, "we're running a fellow from Bowling Green for state president, and we think you're a natural to speak on his behalf to the rest of the delegates."

"Fellows," I said, "you've lost your marbles. How in the hell do you expect the madam of a cathouse to impress this bunch of young businessmen?"

"Well," one of the delegates explained, "this is sort of a strange convention. The other candidate for state president has flown in a couple of prostitutes from his home town to add glamour to his campaign. But we figure you can really outshadow those gals. With your reputation, you'll pack the convention hall."

I finally agreed to address the Jaycee convention. When I reached the hall the next morning the place was packed, and I discovered that a lot of the delegates were past or present customers of my establishment. Quite a few of them greeted me, and some pretended they didn't see me when I waved in greeting. Nevertheless, I made a speech in support of the Bowling Green candidate, and it must have been pretty good. (The candidate wasn't elected, but my business sure as hell profited by my speech!) After the talk, given at a closed session, one of the Louisville reporters asked me what topic I'd managed to pick for a speech to a Jaycee convention.

"Hell, that wasn't difficult," I said. "I talked about the only kind of business I know anything about. Sex."

It was an unexpected honor, being asked to speak before a Jaycee convention. But I was even more honored later when the Jaycees introduced me to their wives, and one of the women asked me to address a Jaycette meeting in Bowling Green.

"Honey," I said, "I'm sure honored, but I just couldn't do that."

"How come?" one of the husbands asked.

"Well, in the first place, I want to see the races. And in the second place, if I talked plain old sex facts to the ladies, I'd put madams like myself out of business."

"What in the world do you mean by that?" one of the wives asked.

I chuckled as I considered her question, then decided to shock her. "Honey," I said, "if I talked to you ladies, I'd have to tell you how to handle your men. And judging by the number of husbands who turn up at my house regularly, that's a subject you girls need some lessons in real bad."

I guess the Jaycee wives weren't amused by my answer because they didn't repeat their invitation. Nevertheless, they might well have given some heed to my reply, for so many of my memories are of frustrated husbands whose wives, through ignorance or indifference, turn them into bordello customers.

Actually there are so many memories that flood upon me in my idle hours. I remember my good customers and wonder what they're doing for a decent sex outlet now that my place is closed. I worry especially about the older fellows, the ones who would be reluctant to chase around bars in search of young stuff. And I worry about my girls, wondering how they're making out, wondering if they've got enough sense to get out of the business before it's too late. Sometimes I even fret about my old foes, wondering just what they've got to crusade about now that my sinful sex emporium is closed for all of time.

There's no use worrying about such things, though. All good things eventually come to an end, even the house on Clay Street. And, really, it's better to remember some of the more humorous things. For example, I recall the evening of the great Nervine crisis.

I had hired a new girl and sent her to town for her medical checkup so she could work during a busy weekend. As dinner time approached, I found Molly, the new girl, stretched out on a parlor sofa, dead to the world.

"She really must be tired," I told the other girls. "We'll let her sleep through dinner, and then wake her up."

After dinner, however, Molly was still out cold. "What happened to her?" I asked the housekeeper. "Did she get boozed up in town?"

"Oh, no, Pauline," the housekeeper replied. "She came back from the doctor's office with two bottles of Nervine. She drank both of them. She's just completely doped up!"

I grabbed Molly and shook her until her teeth rattled. I poured coffee down her, and walked her up and down the room. Finally I got her back on her feet, packed her bags, called a cab, and told her to get the hell lost.

"I don't have time to fool with saps like you," I said angrily.

After Molly, still woozy, had departed, I relaxed wearily in my rocking chair. As I sat there sipping a coke, a customer arrived. He took one look at me and foolishly offered his advice.

"Pauline," he said, "you look like hell. You don't need a coke. You need something to relax your nerves. Something like Nervine."

"Nervine!" I yelled insanely, tossing the coke bottle and narrowly missing the customer. "If any son-of-a-bitch mentions Nervine in this house again, I'm personally going to cut his throat."

At last they calmed me down and explained the situation to the bewildered customer. From that time on, though, Nervine was never mentioned in my house. *My* nerves couldn't stand the strain.

I also have many fond memories of the soldier boys, the G.I.s who added so much zest to my house during the time they were stationed at Camp Campbell and Fort Knox. A lot of these young men didn't make it back, but at least they got a brief touch of life at my place— and I'm not just talking about sex.

On weekends we used to give the men in uniform special attention. Lots of times, for those who stayed overnight, we'd have special mid-morning Sunday brunches—fried chicken with all the trimmings prepared by my talented colored cook, followed by good, old-fashioned bull sessions before they returned to camp.

During the war years and after the fighting was over, we received hundreds of letters from soldiers far and near, thanking us for our brand of "Kentucky hospitality." Actually, it should have been the other way around. We should have thanked them for having the privilege of their friendship. They were a fine, fun-loving, loyal collection of men, lusty and eager to get the nasty job of war finished. They may have been a headache from time to time, but one thing's sure—they never were a bore.

Since my retirement many folks have asked me what happened to the famous Clay Street milk can, a long-standing tradition of my house. It all began when I opened the Clay Street establishment. We had a wide driveway with a tall, white wooden gate which we'd leave open when the coast was clear and lock across the entrance when the house was closed.

There was only one problem. A lot of our impatient customers never noticed the closed gate. They'd ram their cars through it with annoying regularity. Finally I replaced the gate with a thick logging chain. It produced the same disastrous results. Then a farmer friend suggested that a large, old-fashioned milk can, weighted down with rocks and anchored securely by heavy-duty chains, might be a more eye-catching type of warning system.

We painted the milk can a bright silver that glowed in the dark. We soldered one end of the chain to a handle and attached the other end to a large tree at the edge of the driveway. When the house was open, the milk can reposed along the edge of the drive. But when we were closed, the bright silver milk can stood like a sentinel in the middle of the driveway. For years that milk can was the "open-and-shut" tipoff for my Clay Street house. When the house was closed by urban renewal, one of the first questions asked was: what happened to the famous milk can?

The answer: it was one of the first things I shipped out to my farm. It's safely stored with other mementos—a retired sentinel that has seen some busy, frantic times alerting the studs of Bowling Green to the "lay of the land" on Clay Street.

Life, I guess, has been just like one of Miss May's girls revealed it to me during my long-ago visit to the Tennessee bordello. This prostitute's name was Bunny, but everybody called her "Sweet and Sour."

The reason for this odd nickname was apparent when Bunny was stripped for action. Tattooed above her left nipple was the word "Sweet" and over her right nipple, the word "Sour."

It seems that Bunny at one time had acquired a moodily philosophical sort of boyfriend, one of those melancholy mortals who ponder the futility of life. One night, while deep in their cups, he hired a tattoo artist to adorn his girl's firm young breasts with the sweet and sour designations.

"I was furious when I sobered up and discovered my breasts were tattooed," Bunny told me. "I asked my boyfriend whatever possessed him to do such a thing to disfigure me."

"What was his explanation?" I asked.

Bunny laughed without much trace of mirth. "That fellow was some kind of philosophy freak," she said. "He told me that, because my breasts were so lovely, he wanted to engrave on them a reminder that nothing in life is permanent—that youth and beauty must fade; that with the sweet, one must also taste the sour."

Bunny was not impressed by the philosophical significance of her "sweet" and "sour" nipples. At the time, however, it seemed to me the tattoos—like words carved on great monuments—gave Bunny's breasts a special mark of distinction. After all, how many women go through life with such inescapable truths carved on their tits?

If Bunny still is alive, I'm sure the tattoos no longer stand out with distinction. Like my house on Clay Street, they are things of the past. But the ironic philosophy etched on Bunny's breasts somehow reminds me of the sweet-and-sour memories of my life as a brothel-keeper.

I suppose there will be people who will say that I'm writing my memoirs to apologize for the life I've led, or that I'm seeking to glamorize a shoddy, illicit business. I assure you that this has not been my intention. I'm a lot of things, but I'm not hypocritical. I've had my laughs and tears, my ups and downs, my surprises and my disappointments. But I've never lost faith in myself.

I firmly believe that even though I operated a whorehouse for almost forty years, it has not lowered me or soiled me as a human being. I believe that for the most part I'm the same woman I would have been if I had remained a respectable matron all my life. There's one difference, however. I believe that by working in a rough-and-tough business outside the law I've developed a compassion for people and a deeper understanding of the problems which twist and torment their lives. At the same time, I have developed an intense contempt for the phonies, the hypocrites, the corrupt, and the perverted with whom I have dealt. I've been mercenary, but I've run a square business, never a clip joint. And because I've never forgotten the despair of my own years of poverty, I've tried to quietly share my success with folks who needed help.

I know that the business I've run has done nothing to improve this sorry old world, but in that respect it's no different than a lot of so-called legitimate businesses. After all, the peddling of panty hose, perfume, ice cream sundaes, wigs, cigarettes, and other such merchandise scarcely shapes the destiny of nations.

At least, as a peddler of sex I can say that I've provided moments of pleasure, passion, and human warmth to a lot of lonely lives. In the process I have deeply sampled Bunny's tattooed philosophy. Youth has fled, and the once-sweet cup of life is no doubt souring with age. But as I said at the beginning of this book, I have no regrets, no apologies, no complaints.

*Pauline's*

April 14, 1975